A Small but Spartan Band

A Small but Spartan Band

The Florida Brigade in Lee's Army of Northern Virginia

ZACK C. WATERS AND JAMES C. EDMONDS

THE UNIVERSITY OF ALABAMA PRESS
Tuscaloosa

Copyright © 2010
The University of Alabama Press
Tuscaloosa, Alabama 35487-0380
All rights reserved
Manufactured in the United States of America

Typeface: Caslon

∞

The paper on which this book is printed meets the minimum requirements of American
National Standard for Information Sciences-Permanence of Paper for Printed Library
Materials, ANSI Z39.48-1984.

Library of Congress Cataloging-in-Publication Data

Waters, Zack C., 1946–
A small but spartan band : the Florida brigade in Lee's Army of Northern Virginia /
Zack C. Waters and James C. Edmonds.
p.   cm.
Includes bibliographical references and index.
ISBN 978-0-8173-1679-2 (cloth : alk. paper) 1. Florida—History—Civil War, 1861–
1865—Regimental histories. 2. Confederate States of America. Army of Northern
Virginia. 3. United States—History—Civil War, 1861–1865—Regimental histories.
4. Lee, Robert E. (Robert Edward), 1807–1870—Military leadership. 5. Confederate
States of America. Army of Northern Virginia—Military life. 6. Soldiers—Florida—
Social conditions—19th century. 7. Soldiers—Confederate States of America—Social
conditions. 8. United States—History—Civil War, 1861–1865—Campaigns. I. Edmonds,
James C., 1984– II. Title.
E558.4.W38 2010
973.7'459—dc22
2009022878

To our fathers

I will blow against you with the fire of My wrath,
And deliver you into the hands of brutal men who are skillful to destroy
You shall be fuel for the fire—
Your blood shall be in the midst of the land,
And you will not be remembered.
—Ezekiel 21:31–32

Contents

Illustrations

Foreword

Soldiers who were recruited from states at the outer fringes of the short-lived Confederacy suffered disconnection from their homefolk to an extent far more wrenching than that faced by their counterparts from central regions of the South. Virginians and South Carolinians in the Confederate armies faced plenty of daunting ordeals—indeed, even death in a painful percentage of cases—but at least they were able to maintain a degree of contact with their homes and families.

Several Confederate regiments raised in Kentucky became famous on the basis of their campaigns far from their geographical roots, as the "Orphan Brigade." Troops from the Trans-Mississippi theater fighting in the east were cut off from their origins, especially after the fall of Vicksburg. Similarly, soldiers in the small detachment of Florida men who fought with the Army of Northern Virginia enjoyed virtually no prospect of a visit to (or from) their families during the long war. Even letters to and from home dwindled as a result of Unionist occupation of Florida and the intervening territory.

The Florida brigade's isolation from home resulted in an archival vacuum still evident today, long after the soldiers' discomfort with their fate has evaporated. The letters that usually serve modern historians as raw material do not survive for the Florida men in much volume—in fact, they never wrote them in many cases, knowing they probably would not reach home. Contemporary newspapers, which printed reports from the front, suffered from the same gap.

Over many years and across many miles, Zack Waters and Jimmy Edmonds have diligently mined every conceivable source in repositories around the country in quest of traces of the Florida Confederates. Their zealous quest uncovered letters, diaries, and memoirs in Atlanta, Boston, Durham, Jackson, Richmond, Ocala, Carlisle, and points between. The bibliography at the end of this book cites twenty-seven manuscript collections and twenty-four contemporary newspapers, as well as published sources both familiar and arcane.

Primary material harvested in that fashion provided the grist for production of this book. Waters and Edmonds inject substance into the profiles of the officers and men of the brigade, chronicling their campaigns in their own words and in accounts by their contemporaries.

The Florida brigade stood near the epicenter of many a musketry maelstrom during four long years of fighting. From Virginia's peninsula in 1862 through the famous incursions into Maryland and Pennsylvania in 1862 and 1863 to the dreary days at Petersburg and the bitter end at Appomattox, the Floridians carved out a solid military record.

In a long succession of combat experiences, the brigade's two most famous moments came at Fredericksburg and Gettysburg. As part of the Confederate force defending Fredericksburg's waterfront in December 1862, the Florida men came under criticism for their performance. Split into widely separated detachments, and led by junior officers when seasoned commanders went down, some of them surrendered to enemies who attacked across the Rappahannock River. Historians Waters and Edmonds conclude that at Fredericksburg their subjects "certainly set no standard for steadfast heroism."

When fighting under good leadership, and in a unified line, the brigade made a fine record on numerous other fields—including at Gettysburg. On July 2, the Florida regiments attacked with élan enemy units emplaced along the Emmitsburg Pike. A Pennsylvania major in their path wrote that he had never "seen such desperation on the part of the rebels, who hurled their columns upon us."

Civil War books continue to leap from the presses in astonishing numbers. Most of them endlessly belabor familiar topics. Yet another new title that finally, breathlessly, reveals "the real truth" about the battle of Gettysburg, or some supposedly pivotal fragment of that conflict, seems to appear every fortnight or so. Meanwhile, in the 140 years since Appomattox, fewer than a dozen books have focused on Florida's soldiers. Much more attention has been given to the state as a Confederate commissary locker than as the source of military personnel.

On the verge of the Civil War sesquicentennial, Zack Waters and Jimmy Edmonds have resurrected the Florida brigade of Lee's army from relative oblivion. Nearly a century and a half after their campaigns, the Florida men who fought under Perry, Lang, and Finegan on the battlefields of Virginia and Maryland and Pennsylvania emerge from the shadows in the pages of this book.

Robert K. Krick
Fredericksburg, Virginia

A Small but Spartan Band

Introduction

This book is designed to fill a void.

In a recent volume Dr. Irvin D. S. Winsboro posed the question "What do Florida and national audiences actually know about the state's involvement in that conflict [the Civil War] and how accurate is that knowledge?"[1] The answer to the first query, unfortunately, seems to be "Almost nothing." In fact, many intelligent Americans know so little about Florida's role in the War between the States that geographic location would be their only clue regarding whether the soldiers from the southernmost state fought for the Union or the Confederacy. In over twenty years of researching Florida's Rebel soldiers, the authors have lost count of the times we've been asked: "Oh, did they actually fight?"

The second question is harder to answer, but we suspect that much of the "knowledge" about the southernmost state during the Civil War is similarly flawed. Even some serious students of the war still believe that Florida's only real contribution to the Confederacy was as a supplier of cattle and salt. Others believe that all the "Flowers" ("Land of Flowers" being the state's nickname in the 1860s) had deserted the army by the end of 1864. Confederate heritage groups, on the other hand, seem to believe that their ancestors were mighty warriors, so devoted to the cause of Southern independence they could do no wrong on the battlefield or in camp. All of these positions are incorrect, to one degree or another.

Part of the reason for these misconceptions is likely due to trends in scholarship. Florida historians of the Civil War era have, for almost a century, turned their gaze inward. They have examined many aspects of Florida's Civil War experience—as long as it happened within state lines. Some valuable, even exceptional, books have been the result of this scholarship.[2] It seems to the authors, however, that studying World War II (for example) by looking only at industrial war production, civilian rationing, the changing role of women in society, and U.S. internment camps for Japanese Americans tells only a part of the story. Many might consider the soldier's experiences at D-Day, the Battle of the Bulge, Iwo Jima, or Okinawa and the strategies that led to victory or defeat as topics worth exploring.

Admittedly, some military history topics have been "done to death." Such is not the case with the Florida brigade. A few unpublished master's theses have dealt with the military experiences of troops from the southernmost state in the Army of Northern Virginia and the Army of Tennessee,[3] but fewer than ten titles still comprise the entire published library dealing with the Florida regiments that served in the Confederacy's major armies. Few are written to appeal to scholars and none of these tell the complete history of the Flowers in the Army of Northern Virginia.

Two of the most widely known books were written during the heyday of the "Lost Cause" era and reflect the philosophy of that period.[4] In them, Confederates were hard-hitting fighters who would never consider retreating without orders, and mention of desertion, scavenging, and other indiscretions are studiously avoided. Two recent books—Don Hillhouse's *Heavy Artillery and Light Infantry: A History of the 1st Florida Special Battalion and 10th Infantry Regiment, CSA* and Gary Loderhose's *Far, Far from Home: The Ninth Florida Regiment in the Confederate Army*—are more evenhanded, dealing extensively with desertion, conscription, and the final days of the war.[5] Unfortunately for students of Florida history, the Ninth and Tenth Florida served only one year in Virginia. The six-volume set *Biographical Roster of Florida's Confederate and Union Soldiers, 1861–1865* by David W. Hartman and David J. Coles has also been a noteworthy recent addition to the study of the troops from the Land of Flowers.[6] It is not intended, however, as a chronological account of battles and the political maneuvering that impacted the decisions of officers and the lives of ordinary soldiers.

Part of the lack of attention paid to the Florida Rebels is understandable. The authors have spent more than twenty years researching this volume and can attest that material for Lee's Floridians is scattered, difficult to locate, and, in some cases, virtually nonexistent. There is no vast repository of contemporary source material for the Flowers. The *Official Records* usually offer little help, as battle reports by Col. David Lang, Brig. Gen. E. A. Perry, or Brig. Gen. Joseph Finegan are few and far between.[7]

Truth be told, the units from the southernmost state never equaled the combat record fashioned by Lee's Texans or earned the reputation (whether deserved or not) of the fabled "Stonewall Brigade." In fact, the Floridians quickly gained the distinction of being harbingers of bad fortune. Still, Perry's brigade fought well in some battles and poorly in others. Its members are best known today for an embarrassing spate of desertions that plagued the unit during the siege of Petersburg. Determining the factors that motivated the Florida graycoats to enlist, fight, desert, persevere, and lose hope seems to us as important as how many head of Florida scrub cows were sent to Atlanta or Charleston.

The Florida troops also developed a healthy streak of paranoia during the war, and events later proved their suspicions were partially justified. Shortly after Gettysburg, a Florida officer wrote to his wife: "When the Secret history of the war is Known—then we will get justice I hope."[8] The authors have tried to tell "the Secret history" with honesty and accuracy. If we have succeeded, then the Florida soldiers will have the "justice" they requested and deserve.

1 "Our Gallant Little Florida Brigade"
Organization of the Second Florida
Infantry Regiment

A soft, stuttering breeze began to rise in the early afternoon, rippling the long grass and ripening grain in the fields bordering the Emmitsburg Road. Three elderly men, sweat-soaked in the July heat, shivered a little but pressed on toward the base of Cemetery Ridge, stopping occasionally to point with their canes or simply to gaze with dimmed eyes into the horrors of the past.

The three old Rebels—David Lang, William Duncan Ballantine, and Walter Raleigh Moore—had spent the morning at the Gettysburg battlefield, marking the field with stakes to pinpoint the positions and movements of Perry's Florida brigade during the three days of battle. When they had completed their assigned task, the three compatriots were reluctant to leave so the park employee had dropped them off near Seminary Ridge before returning to town.

Memories of long-dead friends and comrades drew Lang, Ballantine, and Moore irresistibly to take one last look at the scene of their brigade's unrecognized sacrifice and near destruction. Thirty-two years earlier they had all been young and confident of victory. Lang commanded three small regiments, the Second, Fifth, and Eighth Florida Infantry, during the battle and agonizing retreat to Virginia. Ballantine and Moore, both of the Second Florida, had been wounded and captured. Now, on July 6, 1895, each step brought a flood of flashbacks. They recalled with anguish and pride that they had purchased each foot of ground with their blood and devotion to the Southern cause. The faces of the dead, forever young, returned to their memories, as did the nagging questions of just how close they had come to victory.

In a news article describing the postwar visit, Ballantine (writing in the third person) reported: "We found the spot where Colonel Moore had fallen and asked Ballantine to assume command. We found the spot where J. D. Perkins [captain of Company M, Second Florida] was wounded, and Ed Hampton [of the same unit] was killed. We pointed out where we had broken the enemy's front line and driven them before us pell-mell into their second line and staked off the spot where we were on when the order came to fall back."[1]

Reaching the base of Cemetery Ridge, the three friends halted in the shadow of the newly erected Federal monuments bristling along the spine of the plateau, wondering if their gallantry and sacrifice would ever be so commemorated. "We found upon examination of the field," Ballantine proudly noted, "that our gallant little Florida band had advanced as far as any Confederate troops." Such claims were generally ignored. Accusations of cowardice had been widely circulated, and little they would do on the field that day would change the historical record.[2]

Lang had long suspected what would happen. Immediately following the engagement he pleaded: "The men I have the honor to command are staid, sober men, most of them having families, who, knowing the perilous condition of their country, entered the service to do all in their power to avert the impending danger; they fight not for vain dreams of glory, nor yet for newspaper fame or notoriety. . . . All we ask of those who record history, whilst we make it, is simply justice. Give us this, and we ask no more."[3]

Modern Florida bears little resemblance to the antebellum state that joined the fledgling Confederate States of America in 1861. After the state entered the Union in 1845 its population began to slowly increase. The 1860 census revealed approximately 140,000 residents (almost half of them black slaves). These numbers placed Florida as "last of the eleven Confederate States, with only thirty percent of the population of Arkansas, [which] ranked tenth." Of Florida's total population only about 15,000 were white males deemed eligible for military service.[4]

Before statehood, "renegades and runaways," fleeing the law, financial or personal disappointment, and encroaching civilization, were among the territory's first settlers, but during the period between 1845 and 1860, the new arrivals were pioneers coming primarily from Georgia and South Carolina. The newcomers braved the state's reputation as a breeding ground for alligators, mosquitoes, and malaria (or in the quaint Cracker phraseology, "Gators, skeeters, and malary") and the lack of good roads and other transportation facilities. The lure of cheap land, virgin loam for cotton plantations, seemingly endless forests, and an opportunity for social advancement proved irresistible to these settlers. They brought with them the beliefs and traditions of their native states. "Most of them were Democrats and remained loyal to the party and concepts of their patron saint, John C. Calhoun."[5]

Much of the population growth occurred in the interior of the state's peninsula region, but the area south of Marion County remained only sparsely inhabited. Big cities simply did not exist in prewar Florida. "Pensacola and Key West vied for honors as the largest cities," writes historian Canter Brown, "but each had fewer than 2,900 residents. Jacksonville, Tallahassee, St. Augustine, Apalachicola, Milton, Monticello, and Fernandina followed in size. Tiny Lake City, with about 650 inhabitants, came tenth."[6]

The backbone of the state's economy was agriculture. As was the case with much of the Deep South, Florida's wealth rested firmly on the shoulders of King Cotton, and a wide band of plantations spread from west of Tallahassee to Marion and Alachua counties. These plantations depended on black slavery to provide the workforce for their day-to-day operations, and "two of every three black slaves [in Florida] lived in five cotton growing counties— Jackson, Gadsden, Leon, Jefferson, and Madison." The planter aristocracy, with its wealth and influence, exercised great political power and generally provided the state's leaders. Assessing Florida's prewar economy, one of the state's early historians concluded: "Cotton fields were many and large and factories few and small. . . . The output of cotton fields, turpentine orchards, and lumber camps constituted the exportable wealth of the state. Almost everything consumed except vegetables, forage, and cornmeal was imported."[7]

By 1860 the long-standing political, economic, and cultural differences between the North and South had reached the breaking point. Abolitionist martyr John Brown's unsuccessful attempt to spark slave uprisings in Virginia sent shock waves throughout the South. Many Floridians, including Gov. Madison Starke Perry, were convinced that the Republican Party had instigated Brown's scheme. The fact that some in the North applauded Brown's actions further incensed many in the slave states. A St. Augustine newspaper spoke for many Southerners when it claimed that "Black Republicans" planned to "loose four millions of slaves upon us unrestrained, who will at once, embark in the work of murder and rapine." A Cedar Key journal mirrored that opinion, asserting that secession was the only way to protect "our domestic institutions and sacred Constitutional Rights." In November of 1860 the citizens of Marion County began clamoring for secession, even defiantly raising a banner bearing a "white ground . . . and one blue star, and beneath it the words, 'Let Us Alone'" as a warning to Northerners.[8]

The election of Abraham Lincoln provided all of the impetus most Deep

South states needed for leaving the Union. In the 1860 presidential election Florida's popular vote went to States' Rights candidate John C. Breckinridge, and the state's citizens also narrowly elected ardent secessionist John Milton as governor. Lincoln and the Republicans were not on the state ballot and did not receive a single vote. In fact, Lincoln "won the presidency without receiving a single Electoral College vote from Southern States." Shortly thereafter, South Carolina adopted an ordinance of secession, followed almost immediately by Mississippi.[9]

Florida's experiment in rebellion officially began on January 10, 1861. Shortly after noon on that date, the state's county representatives voted to adopt the ordinance of secession by a final tally of 62 to 7. Wild celebrations erupted throughout the state. Citizens of Tallahassee, for example, greeted the news with fireworks and a "mammoth torch-light parade." The common wisdom seemed to be that if war came, it would last less than sixty days, and the conflict would be essentially bloodless. Newspaper editors and politicians even offered to "drink all of the blood which will be spilt."[10]

Not all Floridians greeted secession with optimism and jubilation. The Constitutional Union Party, formed in Chicago in order to "allay sectional animosities and in an attempt to save the Union," had made a strong showing in the state's 1860 gubernatorial vote, and enclaves of antisecession sentiment were scattered throughout the state, particularly in the Panhandle. Like Jeremiah, or some biblical prophet of doom, former territorial governor Richard Keith Call railed against the decision to leave the Union. He called secession treason and predicted the action would ruin the state. As had been the case with Jeremiah, few heeded Call's warning. Even some Southern Unionists eventually became reluctant Rebels. Those who "initially opposed or hesitated to support it [secession] came around to the cause, simply because their children, relatives, and neighbors were suddenly in harm's way."[11]

Slavery and maintaining white supremacy may have been the root cause for the War between the States, but the reasons that individuals actually enlisted in the Confederate army were as varied as the men themselves. Many obviously concluded that the election of Abraham Lincoln fundamentally threatened their way of life. A few suspected that their agrarian lifestyle was under attack by a North controlled by banks and corporations. Others believed that they owed the state more allegiance than a government in Washington, while another segment succumbed to social pressures from females, family, and friends. Protecting their homes from Federal invaders motivated many, while some considered war a lark and a chance to bring some excitement into their lives or a way to escape their parents' strict discipline. A constant theme in the letters of Rebel soldiers was a belief that they were fighting a second war of independence, drawing courage and resolve from stories of their grandfathers' defeat of the British Redcoats.[12]

Forming an army proved less of a problem than Gov. Perry (who, due to a fluke in the state's voting laws, would remain the lame duck chief executive for almost a year after the election) likely anticipated. Despite Florida having the nation's oldest militia tradition, its state army had virtually disintegrated at the end of the Third Seminole War (locally known as "the Billy Bowlegs War") in 1858. Volunteer companies began forming again as tensions between the North and South increased. By 1860 larger cities, like Pensacola, Jacksonville, St. Augustine, and Tallahassee, had two or more units, while smaller towns and rural areas usually had a single company. Many of these poorly armed companies served a purely social function—allowing the young bucks in a community to parade around impressing the area's ladies with their often outlandish uniforms and devotion to the cause. "Secession produced a martial air and numerous military units were formed, mostly without official sanction and without the necessary equipment. . . . In spite of the repeated discussion about secession causing no bloodshed the State of Florida decided the formal organization of militia was necessary."[13]

A significant minority of the volunteers had seen service with the militia during the Third Seminole War. Unfortunately, that experience did little to instill military discipline in the men. If anything, their service gave a false impression of army life. Most of the state units consisted of cavalry troops commanded by local politicians or men with political aspirations. Those officers could hardly be expected to demand strict constraint and good order from their present or future constituents. As a result, complaints reached state and Federal officials from South Florida citizens that "the volunteers . . . were dreaded more than the Indians."[14]

Despite the recruits' shortcomings, Perry moved quickly to take advantage of the fruits of this patriotic fervor. On February 12, 1861, the legislature approved a bill allowing the chief executive to integrate existing units, if they numbered at least thirty-two men, into state service. This permitted the governor to form regiments by simply cobbling together companies as soon as the call for troops came from the Confederate War Deparment.[15]

The initial state unit, designated the First Florida Infantry Regiment, received orders to join troops from Georgia, Alabama, Mississippi, and Louisiana near Pensacola in the vain attempt to oust the Federals from Fort Pickens. The unit eventually became a part of the Army of Tennessee, fighting in every campaign in the West from Shiloh to Bentonville. Perry and later Gov. John Milton seemingly favored sending Florida troops to the "Army of the Heartland," and only reluctantly sent Florida troops to Virginia.[16]

The Second Florida Infantry Regiment was the first state unit dispatched to the Old Dominion. It exhibited a spirit of elitism missing from other units sent from the southernmost state during the War between the States. The unit called itself the state's "representative regiment," and further claimed its personnel comprised "the bravest, most gallant and gifted of Florida's patriotic sons." Surprisingly, there was a measure of truth in their hyperbole.[17]

Capt. John W. Starke's company, for example, boasted on its roll a former governor's son, an associate justice of the state supreme court, and a state senator, the latter serving as a lowly private. The wealthiest man in Florida commanded the unit, and its lieutenant colonel had achieved hero status by leading the state militia to victory in the Billy Bowlegs War. As other units joined the Second in Virginia, they viewed the regiment, which had been tried in the fires at Seven Pines and the Seven Days, as the brigade's Old Guard.[18]

Ten of the eleven original companies of the Second Florida mustered into Confederate service at the Old Brick Church on the outskirts of Jacksonville on July 13, 1861. These ten had the following nicknames, counties of origin, and commanders: Co. B (Alachua Guards), Alachua County, Capt. Lewis Williams; Co. C (Columbia Rifles), Columbia County, Capt. Walter R. Moore; Co. D (Leon Rifles), Leon County, Capt. T. W. Brevard; Co. E (Hammock Guards), Marion County, Capt. John D. Hopkins; Co. F (Gulf State Guards), Jackson County, Capt. James F. McClellan; Co. G (St. Johns Grays), Duval County, Capt. J. J. Daniel; Co. H (St. Augustine Rifles), St. Johns and Putnam counties, Capt. John W. Starke; Co. I (Jasper Guards), Hamilton County, Capt. Henry J. Stewart; Co. K (Davis Guards), Nassau County, Capt. George W. Call; and Co. L (Madison Rangers), Madison County, Capt. William P. Pillans. The Second Florida numbered 927 men. It was easier for Company A, from distant Escambia County, to meet the unit in Virginia than travel across the state to Jacksonville.[19]

The first duty of the regiment required the new soldiers to elect their officers. The men selected George T. Ward, a sixty-year-old native of Kentucky, as colonel. Samuel St. George Rogers, a Marion County attorney, planter, and Indian fighter, became the unit's lieutenant colonel, and Louis G. Pyles, of Alachua County, won the vote for major.[20]

The election of Ward, a banker, planter, and slaveholder from Leon County, must have raised some eyebrows. He had vehemently opposed disunion and declared as he reluctantly signed the state's ordinance of secession: "When I die I want it inscribed upon my tombstone that I was the last man to give up the ship." With the die cast, however, he began actively lobbying Confederate secretary of war Leroy Walker to send a regiment to Virginia to represent the "Land of Flowers." Within days the order reached Tallahassee, and Gov. Perry designated the Second Florida Infantry Regiment for duty in the Old Dominion.[21]

The composition of the Second Florida mirrored fairly accurately the data recently compiled for "the volunteers of 1861" in Dr. Joseph Glatthaar's book *General Lee's Army.* Available information indicates that Col. Ward's troops had an average age of twenty-three. Henry M. Mercer, who was born in 1848, appears to have been the unit's youngest member. Henry, and three other men named Mercer, joined Company K at Fredericksburg in December of 1862, but the diminutive youngster served only two months before receiving a medical discharge. Sixty-two-year-old Elijah Carver, of Company L, may have been the regiment's oldest soldier. He enlisted in May 1861 and remarkably endured more than a year of campaigning. Carver received a medical release shortly after the battle of Antietam.[22]

Complete information is not available on all enlistees, but from extant records it appears that Northern-born soldiers totaled only 3 percent of Ward's command, but they included future unit leaders E. A. Perry, W. D. Ballantine, and Capt. James F. Tucker. Foreign-born soldiers comprised about 7 percent of the regiment. Fourteen of these men hailed from Ireland, seven from Germany or Prussia, and three from England, with Canada, Cuba, Italy, Norway, and Russia each supplying a single representative. Somewhat surprisingly, considering the large Spanish and Minorcan communities in northeast Florida, only about 3 percent of the Second Florida members bore Hispanic surnames.[23]

Native Floridians comprised approximately one-third of the unit, while 57 percent hailed from other Southern states (including Kentucky). Georgia and South Carolina, in that order, supplied by far the largest number of Southern-born recruits in Ward's command. Glatthaar reported: "Rich and poor shouldered arms in equal proportion in 1861," and that seems to be the case with the representative regiment. Slave owners, or those with a "direct connection to slavery" also likely mirrored percentages of troops from the other Confederate states.[24]

Two days after being sworn into the Southern army, the Second Florida Regiment began the six-day trip by rail to Virginia. Arriving at Richmond on

Fig. 1. Col. George T. Ward, Second Florida Regiment

July 21, 1861, the Floridians spent the next few weeks learning the rudiments of drill and guarding Union prisoners captured at the first battle of Manassas. Lt. C. Seton Fleming, a recent graduate of the King's Mountain Military School in South Carolina, had whipped Starke's raw company into the pride of the regiment. He assumed the duties of drilling the Second Florida, "notwithstanding the Adjutant [supplied by the Confederate War Department] was a graduate of West Point." When not busy with the rank and file, Fleming tutored the officers on proper commands.[25]

Like the rest of the unit, Fleming chafed at not having an opportunity to immediately face the Federals. The men wrote home of being disappointed at not being sent into battle quickly, perhaps thinking that the war would be over before they received their baptism of fire. Being detailed to guard Union prisoners—not exactly an exciting task or one that provided opportunities for glory—further displeased members of the Second Florida.[26]

2 "Lavish of Blood"
The Battles of Seven Pines and Seven Days

After a month of monotony near Richmond, the Second Florida received orders to report to the Southern forces at Yorktown. The Floridians arrived at their new post on September 17, 1861, joining Maj. Gen. John B. Magruder's small Army of the Peninsula. The Confederate War Department assigned Ward's unit as an independent regiment in Brig. Gen. Gabriel Rains's brigade. The dreary season of inactivity continued, and the Flowers spent the bitterly cold Virginia winter camping near the site where Lord Cornwallis's redcoats surrendered to George Washington's rebels. Looking at a monument commemorating the event, a Floridian observed that "fanatical intolerance" had brought a "war of coercion" upon the true sons of American liberty, wryly noting: "Patriotism in 1781 became treason in 1861."[1]

Shortly after the Second Florida had settled in its new quarters, the Pensacola Rifle Rangers of Escambia County joined it as its eleventh company. The new unit had participated in the early stages of the siege at Fort Pickens before boarding the trains for Richmond. The trip through Georgia had been a "regular ovation," but in East Tennessee the sight of Unionist mountaineers hanging from the bridges they had attempted to burn shocked and horrified the West Florida troops. After their arrival at Yorktown, the Rifle Rangers were designated as Company A of the Second Florida.[2]

Two Northern-born members of the new company would make significant contributions to the Florida regiment. Massachusetts-born Capt. Edward A. Perry soon became the unit's first brigadier general, and Florida troops would thereafter be known in the Army of Northern Virginia as Perry's brigade. The other Yankee Confederate was Lt. William D. Ballantine. Born in 1837 in New York, Ballantine had been a merchant in Fernandina before enlisting at

Pensacola in May of 1861. He was wounded four times during the war, gained fame as one of the "Immortal 600," and boasted that he "frequently commanded" the Second Florida. The men of Company A elected Ballantine captain in May 1862, and he later claimed to have served the regiment as both major and lieutenant colonel. (No official record exists of Ballantine's promotion beyond the rank of captain.)[3]

The return of spring in 1862 brought the beauty of nature's rebirth and the ugliness of war to the Old Dominion. In mid-April, Maj. Gen. George B. McClellan landed a Union army, totaling more than 120,000 soldiers, near Fortress Monroe on the southern tip of the Peninsula. "Prince John" Magruder had only his 13,000-man Peninsula Army to oppose this huge force. Fortunately for the Confederates, McClellan, who had been dubbed the "Young Napoleon" by the fawning Northern press, was a brilliant organizer but tentative in battle. It did not take long for the Union commander to convince himself that Magruder's Rebels outnumbered his own army. As a result, he began a snail-like advance toward Richmond, all the while bombarding Washington with requests for reinforcements. Prince John established a defensive line south of Yorktown, and for almost a month used bluff, theatrics, and McClellan's timidity to block the Union offensive.[4]

The Second Florida finally received its baptism of fire in a skirmish near Yorktown. The 530-man unit had recently been reassigned to Brig. Gen. Jubal A. Early's brigade in Maj. Gen. D. H. Hill's division. It was perhaps a sign of confidence in Col. Ward that he had also been given command of Lt. Col. John G. Taylor's Second Mississippi Battalion.[5]

On May 3, with Federal skirmishers "closely pressing" the Confederate defenses near Yorktown, Early dispatched Ward's demi-brigade to "dislodge him [the enemy] from Palmentary's peach orchard." A letter by one of Ward's soldiers, published in a Tallahassee newspaper, reported the battle as "exciting and somewhat amusing, for such scrambling out of rifle-pits and foot races of [Yankee] troops—our men in hot pursuit—has rarely been witnessed." The writer believed that Col. Ward escaping harm was "a miracle," because the elderly officer "was mounted on his fine sorrel charger and [in] full uniform and thus afforded a conspicuous mark for the enemy."[6]

After driving off the bluecoats, the Deep South troops cut down the peach trees, burned several buildings used by the Yankee snipers, and returned to camp to receive the accolades of their comrades. In his after-action report Magruder enthused: "The quick and reckless charge of our [Ward's] men by throwing the enemy into a hasty flight, enabled us to effect, with little loss, an enterprise of great hazard against a superior force, supported by artillery, when the least wavering or hesitation on our part would have been attended with great loss." The Florida regiment and Mississippi battalion suffered combined casualties of two killed and twelve wounded.[7]

That night Magruder's graycoats began evacuating Yorktown, marching north through Williamsburg toward the Confederate capital. Though disappointed by the retreat, Prince John's Rebels had bought enough time for Gen. Joseph E. Johnston, commanding the army in Virginia, to begin consolidating his widely scattered troops before Richmond. With Maj. Gen. James Longstreet's division covering the withdrawal, the Floridians slogged through the old colonial seat of government toward the Confederate capital.[8]

The Federals finally caught Longstreet's division just south of Williamsburg. D. H. Hill's division, including Ward's two units, hastily countermarched to reinforce Longstreet near Fort Magruder. (This earthen bastion sat astride the main route to Williamsburg, and a series of redoubts guarded the fort.) As Ward's troops reentered the town, "a girl young & fair, waved before them a blood-stained cloth, calling out 'go and avenge this blood.' With a yell they passed at a double quick, and they did avenge it." The Floridians reached the battlefield during the early afternoon of May 5. Hill recalled: "On reaching the ground the Second Florida and Mississippi Battalion were sent to the support of the troops [of Brig. Gen. Cadmus Wilcox's brigade] on the right."[9]

By late afternoon, two of Wilcox's three regiments had managed to push the Federals back, but his troops immediately became "engaged in a sharp musketry fight" with Brig Gen. Joe Hooker and Brig. Gen. Phillip Kearney's bluecoats, hidden nearby in heavy woods. Long before Ward's reinforcements began to arrive, Wilcox's Ninth Alabama and Nineteenth Mississippi had expended their ammunition and lay prone, waiting to be relieved. As soon as the Second Florida and Second Mississippi Battalion began to arrive, the Alabama graycoats arose and rushed toward the rear. This threw the green troops into confusion. Supposing that an order had been given for a general retreat, Ward's soldiers started to join the Ninth Alabama in a disorderly retreat. Dismayed by the Second Florida's hasty movement to the rear, Ward rode forward, calling: "Floridians, Oh Floridians, is this the way you meet the enemies of your country?"[10]

The Florida and Magnolia State soldiers responded instantly to their colonel's plea, and roared toward the enemy with the rash courage of green troops. Their impetuosity cost them dearly. Francis P. Fleming, a future Florida governor and regimental historian, recalled: "The Second Florida . . . was . . . thrown

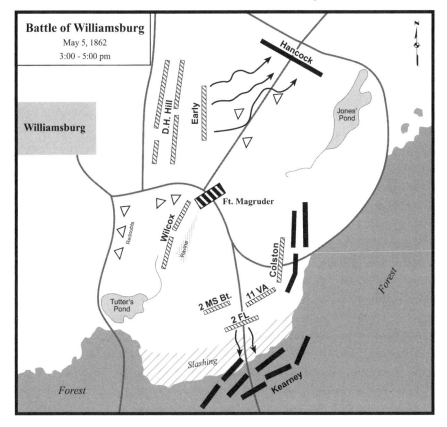

Fig. 2. Battle of Williamsburg, May 5, 1862

into line of battle . . . and advanced with the steadiness of veterans across an open field, under a heavy fire from the enemy, who were posted in a fallen woods. . . . On reaching the fallen timber, the advancing lines of the Second Florida were halted and opened fire." The Yankees returned the volley, killing Col. Ward, Florida's reluctant Rebel. Fleming reported: "A ball struck him under the right shoulder and came out the right breast." Ward died as he fell.[11]

All of this occurred within minutes of engaging the Federals, and Lt. Col. Rogers, the Marion County lawyer and Third Seminole War hero, assumed command of the Second Florida. The old Indian fighter immediately ordered his men to press forward, despite receiving an increasingly heavy fire from the front and both flanks. Longstreet, from his position near Fort Magruder, realized that the Flowers were in danger of being encircled, and ordered Rogers's units to withdraw immediately. They fell back and re-formed in a shallow ravine near Williamsburg. In addition to Ward, the Florida Rebels lost forty men, killed and wounded, reducing the unit's size to about 500 effectives.[12]

In the confusion of the withdrawal, the Second Florida left Col. Ward's body on the field. When the men discovered their mistake, they were mortified. In the fading light, Capt. E. A. Perry led a small group of volunteers back across the open field, under a heavy fire, to retrieve the corpse of their beloved commander. The group included Perry, Capt. George Call, Capt. Theodore W. Brevard, Lt. Seton Fleming, Cpl. Eben Burroughs, and Cpl. David Maxwell. Remarkably, the group returned with Ward's remains with only one soldier, Seton Fleming, seriously wounded. By chance, Perry left Ward's body at "the house of an Episcopal minister, who had been a classmate and warm personal friend of Col. Ward, who performed for him, at Williamsburg, the last sad rites of Christian burial."[13]

Due to the battle, the reelection of officers, originally scheduled for May 3, had been postponed. On May 10, during a hiatus in the retreat, the Second Florida held its second election of officers. The men selected E. A. Perry as colonel to replace Ward and Louis Pyles as the unit's lieutenant colonel. George W. Call, one of the state's ablest attorneys and son of a former governor, won the post of major. Additionally, all of the companies in the regiment, except Companies B and C, voted themselves new captains.[14]

The election of Perry as regimental commander proved a wise, if slightly unusual, choice. Born in Berkshire County, Massachusetts, in 1833, Perry attended Yale University for a year before moving to Alabama to teach school. He married a local belle and received admittance to the Alabama bar in 1857 after completing the requisite course of study. Shortly thereafter he moved to Pensacola, Florida, to begin building his legal practice. Though he conceded that he was "almost a stranger [who] knew nothing of military tactics," in the fall of 1860, the Pensacola Rifle Rangers chose Perry captain of the volunteer company. Despite his Northern birth, Perry "fully shared the sentiments of his adopted state," and proved his devotion to the Southern cause upon many hard-fought fields of battle.[15]

Perry's first combat as a regimental commander came on May 31, 1862, at the Battle of Seven Pines. Following the Williamsburg fight McClellan's army had continued its creeping pace toward Richmond, the Young Napoleon intent upon laying siege to the Confederate capital. McClellan still believed that the Rebels outnumbered his massive force, and he had badgered Pres. Lincoln into sending Maj. Gen. Irvin McDowell's corps from Fredericksburg to reinforce the Army of the Potomac. In preparation for McDowell's arrival, McClellan

Fig. 3. Brig. Gen. Edward A. Perry,
commanding, Florida brigade

split his army—with three corps north of the Chickahominy River and two corps south of the stream. Johnston resolved to attack this tempting target, and his decision seemed to receive aid from the heavens—recent heavy rains had swollen the Chickahominy, making it difficult to cross.[16]

The Second Florida fought at Seven Pines as part of Brig. Gen. Samuel Garland's brigade in Maj. Gen. D. H. Hill's division. On the afternoon of May 31, Hill's troops pushed east along the Williamsburg Road, with Garland's units spearheading the assault. The Second Mississippi Battalion served as skirmishers, followed by E. A. Perry's unit "on the left and in advance" of Garland's brigade. The conditions in which they fought were atrocious. Garland reported: "The recent rains had formed ponds of water throughout the woods with mud at the bottom, through which the men waded forward knee-deep, and occasionally sinking to the hips in boggy places." As if this were not enough of a challenge, the forest was "thick" and the undergrowth extremely "tangled."[17]

The Florida troops struggled and stumbled through the thickets and bogs, driving the Yankee pickets before them. Emerging into a clearing, panting and completely disorganized by the rush through the woods, they found Battery A, First New York Artillery posted atop a long slope, and supported by troops from Brig. Gen. Silas Casey's Union division. *Abatis* (an obstacle of felled trees with the sharpened ends pointing toward the enemy) further strengthened the position.[18]

Garland ordered the brigade to charge and take the Federal position. The Second Florida and Thirty-eighth Virginia loped forward together under heavy fire from the enemy troops and artillery. This frontal charge brought Perry's troops directly into the deadly fire of Battery A's guns, resulting in appalling casualties. A member of the Federal cannon crew recalled: "Our shot tore their ranks wide open, and shattered them asunder in a manner that was frightful to witness; but they closed up again at once, and came on as steady as English veterans. When they got within 400 yards, we closed our case-shot and opened on them with canister; and such destruction I never elsewhere witnessed."[19]

During this part of the engagement one of Casey's infantrymen wounded Cpl. Eben Burroughs, who had helped to retrieved Col. Ward's body at Williamsburg. A postwar account notes: "In the terrible battle at Seven Pines, he [Burroughs] was desperately wounded while standing in water waist deep. He was in the act of aiming his rifle when a minie ball struck him on the extended arm glancing then to the left side of his face, shattering the jawbone, passing through the throat & windpipe & making its exit at the point of the right shoulder. He was taken up for dead but recovered."[20]

The Floridians and Virginians refused to retreat or take cover. The Federal gunner's account of the fight for the artillery notes: "At each discharge [of canister], great gaps were made in their ranks—indeed, whole companies went down before that murderous fire; but they closed up, with an order and discipline that was awe-inspiring. They seemed to be animated with the courage of despair, blended with the hope of a speedy victory." The graycoats overran the battery and drove the Yankees before them until they had exhausted their ammunition and Garland ordered them to the rear. Col. Perry's troops captured the cannons and fifty prisoners. Lt. John T. Parker of Company D received credit for capturing the flag of the Eighth New York Battery.[21]

In the fight for the battery, the Second Florida apparently lost its own flag. Col. William "Extra Billy" Smith, a former Virginia governor, found a Confederate flag while "pressing through the abatis." Smith called for one of his Forty-ninth Virginia Regiment to take the banner, but his troops failed to respond to the appeal. "At the time," Col. Smith averred, "a youthful stranger was hard by, probably not twenty years old and heard the message I delivered. He stepped promptly up, stated that he belonged to the 2d Florida, had lost his regiment, and would like to join mine for the fight, and with my permission would gladly bear the flag, and if need be, plant it in the cannon's mouth.

Without a word I handed it to him and nobly did he bear it, and curiously enough it turned out to be the flag of his own regiment."[22]

The Second Florida's onslaught at Seven Pines crippled the unit. The regiment suffered 198 casualties of the 435 men carried into the battle, a loss of 45 percent. Losses to the officer corps were even more dreadful. Ten of the eleven company commanders were either killed or wounded. Lt. Col. Pyles received a serious wound, and Maj. Call was killed. "We were lavish of blood in those days," D. H. Hill later lamented.[23]

Southerners claimed victory at Seven Pines, but they could ill afford many such successes. They had lost almost 2,000 more men—killed, wounded, and missing—than the Federals, and failed to destroy, or even cripple, the exposed Union corps—and McClellan's huge army still camped before the gates of Richmond.[24]

The Virginia army also lost its commander at Seven Pines—which turned out to be a blessing in disguise. While conducting a twilight reconnaissance, Joe Johnston had been struck in the chest by a large shell fragment, and Pres. Jefferson Davis quickly named Gen. Robert E. Lee as Johnston's successor. Lee had a reputation as an able administrator, but he immediately brought a new attitude to the battered Rebel army. A modern historian summed up the change in seven words: "Vigor replaced turpitude, aggression supplanted terminal caution."[25]

After the battle, the Florida soldiers went into camp southeast of Richmond, enjoying a well-deserved rest. At least a portion of the manpower lost at Seven Pines could still be replaced during the early days of the war. Two weeks later, Capt. George Washington Parkhill's "Howell Guards" became Company M, the Second Florida's twelfth company. Raised in Leon County, Parkhill's unit had been serving in Virginia since the fall of 1861, first as an independent company and then as part of the Fifth Alabama Battalion.[26]

Lee quickly devised a plan to relieve the threat to the Confederate capital. His scheme called for leaving a small force in the trenches around Richmond, then attacking the Union left flank and supply line north of the Chickahominy, forcing McClellan to retreat back down the Peninsula. Using Lee's strategy, the Rebels drove the Yankees from the outskirts of Richmond, but it took a solid week of bloody carnage to dislodge the Federals. The new commander's succession of assaults and counterattacks became known as the Seven Days battles.[27]

The Floridians fought during the Seven Days in the brigade of Brig. Gen. Roger A. Pryor. Pryor, a thirty-four-year-old lawyer, politician, and newspaper editor, proved on several fields to be one of the Confederacy's most incompetent generals. Pryor's brigade included the Second Florida, Fourteenth Alabama, Fourteenth Louisiana, Third Virginia, and First Louisiana Battalion. The Second Florida likely numbered only about 300 men at the beginning of the Seven Days.[28]

The fighting began on June 26 with a futile attack by Maj. Gen. A. P. Hill, one of Lee's "more impetuous subordinates," on Brig. Gen. Fitz John Porter's V Corps, strongly entrenched along Beaver Dam Creek. Porter's Federals easily repulsed the graycoats, inflicting 1,500 Confederate casualties, compared to about 300 for the Yankees. With Maj. Gen. Thomas J. "Stonewall" Jackson's Shenandoah Valley army closing in on Porter and his supply line threatened, the Young Napoleon ordered Porter to retreat to the Chickahominy River.[29]

The next afternoon the Confederates found Porter's corps partially entrenched atop a plateau on the north bank of the Chickahominy near Gaines's Mill. A series of piecemeal assaults throughout the afternoon accomplished little except to inflate the Confederate casualty list. Late in the evening, with Jackson's army finally united with Lee's forces, Marse Robert combined all of his troops in an enormous attack in an attempt to "fracture the Union line." The brigades of Pryor, Cadmus Wilcox, and Winfield S. Featherston joined the attack on the western end of the Northern defenses. The Confederate assault broke the bluecoats' line, but many of the Yankees escaped in the gathering darkness. Lee's army incurred almost 9,000 casualties, while the Federals lost about 6,000.[30]

Pryor provided a fair description of his brigade's twilight assault in his after-action report.

> I moved from my position at Gaines' house straightforward to the wood in which the enemy was concealed. Ascending the hill in front of his [the enemy's] position, my men were staggered by a terrific volley at the same time that they suffered severely from the battery across the Chickahominy. I was compelled to retire them to the cover of a ravine in my rear. After a lapse of a few moments I again moved them forward, and again they encountered a fire which it was impossible to endure. This time, however, they were not arrested before they had rushed down to the edge of the wood where the enemy lay.[31]

Brig. Gen. John Bell Hood's Texas brigade received the lion's share of the credit for the breakthrough, but Francis Fleming reported that the Second Florida "bore a distinguished part [at Gaines's Mill], and added to the laurels it had already won." Even the Yankees displayed a grudging admiration for the Florida troops. One of E. A. Perry's staff officers heard a captured Federal bemoan: "God save our poor fellows, if there's more than one Florida regiment. . . . It is no use killing them for they won't run; and they seem to have only two commands—'Fire at will' and 'Charge.'"[32]

A Union bullet took the life of the unfortunate Capt. Parkhill while he led his company in its first engagement. His cousin, Lt. Richard Parkhill, witnessed his uncle's death. He later wrote: "When he fell it almost killed me. I was so much excited I scarcely knew what I was doing. The men over all wanted to lay down and they did so, when I walked down the line & told them to avenge their noble captain's death. Then the balls began to fall like rain, but they all gave a yell and started towards the enemy, & they [the Federals] ran in confusion." After the battle, Lt. Parkhill and a party of officers recovered the captain's body from the field, and forwarded the corpse to his widow, Lizzie, in Richmond.[33]

E. A. Perry again received high marks from his men. One declared: "We have as brave a Col[onel] as ever walked the earth." Lt. Parkhill, though wounded, vowed to exact revenge for the death of his uncle. In his first engagement, the young officer seemed at a loss for words to describe his experience. "We *fought* nearly all day yesterday and drove the enemy back about eight miles. I can't describe to you the sight we saw, the moors are perfectly covered with dead & wounded."[34]

There was no rest for the weary, and combat continued the following day. Neither the fighting on June 28 at Garnett's and Golding's Farms nor that on the 29th at Savage Station proved decisive for Lee's army, but it accomplished its main objective: the fear of an imminent attack by the Virginia army hastened McClellan's retreat toward the James River. Despite McClellan's tremulous leadership, however, the Army of the Potomac remained intact and a dangerous foe.[35]

The battle fought on June 30 is known by various names, including Glendale, Frazier's (or Frayser's) Farm, Nelson's Farm, and Riddell's Shop. Southern artillery officer E. P. Alexander, with his infallible gift of twenty-twenty hindsight, adamantly declared this engagement as the Confederacy's best opportunity to win the war.[36]

Four roads converged at Glendale, and seven Union divisions had halted their retrograde movement, forming the familiar semicircular defensive they had used at Gaines's Mill. This created a bottleneck, slowed the bluecoats' retreat, and seemed to present an excellent opportunity to capture or destroy the Federals. Gen. Lee had four columns converging upon the Yankees, but as nightfall neared only James Longstreet's and A. P. Hill's divisions were in position to assault the Union line. The Confederate commander felt that he could wait no longer and ordered the attack.[37]

Longstreet's and A. P. Hill's brigades advanced along the Long Bridge Road, while the Yankee artillery and infantry hammered the approaching Rebels. Pryor reported that due to thick woods "and other obstructions," he sent his men forward one regiment at a time. The Fourteenth Alabama apparently led the way. According to Pryor, that unit bore "the brunt of the struggle, [and] was nearly annihilated." The Fourteenth Louisiana also suffered severely, thereafter referring to Glendale simply as "the Slaughterhouse." Pryor reported that the retreat of the brigade to his right (possibly Wilcox's Alabamians) exposed his units to "a destructive fire in the flank as well as in the front. Nevertheless, they stood their ground and sustained the unequal combat until reinforced." Both sides claimed victory, but the Confederates captured eighteen cannons, and the Army of the Potomac continued its retreat. As usual, Rebel losses exceeded Union casualties.[38]

No record has been found detailing the actions or losses of the Florida troops at Glendale. Col. E. A. Perry received a severe wound leading his regiment, and Longstreet praised him as being "distinguished . . . for gallantry and skill." Total losses for the Florida troops at Gaines's Mill and Glendale numbered 137, though how many were killed is unknown. Confederate secretary of the navy Stephen Mallory, a Floridian, summed up the condition of the unit in a report to Gov. John Milton: "Since the 1st of May, its [the Second Florida] killed and wounded amount to four hundred and seventy-one (471) and is now commanded by the gallant young Captain [Alexander] Mosely." Their trials had so weakened the members of the Second Florida that they were held as reserves at the climactic battle of Malvern Hill.[39]

On the evening of July 1–2, following the fight at Malvern Hill, the Young Napoleon continued the retreat, assuming a strong defensive position at Harrison's Landing. Thus the Seven Days battles ended. The Confederate army prevented McClellan from taking Richmond but failed to crush the Union army on the Peninsula. It was becoming obvious to all thinking men that the war would last longer than anyone had imagined. For the bloodied and battered Floridians the war had already proven very costly; yet the hardest and most trying days still lay ahead.[40]

A new contingent of men arrived in Virginia from Florida in August 1862.

The Fifth and Eighth Florida regiments were united with the Second Regiment, forming a partnership that would last until Appomattox. Initially they joined E. A. Perry's regiment in Pryor's brigade in Longstreet's wing.[41]

The Fifth Florida had been organized at Camp Leon in early April 1862 and mustered into Confederate service the following month. Raised primarily in the state's rich cotton-producing panhandle region, the unit had originally been earmarked by Gov. Milton as reinforcements for the Florida contingent in the Army of Tennessee. An appeal by Confederate secretary of war George W. Randolph, coupled with Mallory's report on the condition of the Second, apparently convinced Milton to assign them to the Army of Northern Virginia instead.[42]

The following nicknames, counties of origin, and commanders indicate the original composition of the Fifth Florida Infantry: Company A (Milton Light Infantry), Jefferson County, Capt. Abram Z. Bailey; Company B (Baker Guards), Columbia County, Capt. Garrett Vanzant; Company C (Trapier Guards), Leon County, Capt. William D. Bloxham; Company D (Bartow Rebels), Madison County, Capt. A. J. Lea; Company E (Madison Guerillas), Madison County, Capt. John W. Holleyman; Company F (Frink Guards), Hamilton County, Capt. John Frink; Company G (Anderson Infantry—formerly a militia unit known as the Aucilla Guards), Jefferson County, Capt. William Bailey Jr.; Company H (Liberty Guards), Liberty and Calhoun counties, Capt. William T. Gregory; Company I (Wakulla Tigers), Wakulla and Leon counties, Capt. Samuel A. Spencer; and Company K (Dixie Yeomen), Leon County, Capt. Richmond N. Gardner. Companies D and E apparently contained a sizable minority of men from neighboring Taylor and Lafayette counties. The Fifth Florida originally mustered 1,080 men.[43]

The men of the Fifth elected John C. Hately as colonel, Thompson B. Lamar as lieutenant colonel, and Benjamin F. Davis as major. Hately, before the war an attorney in Jasper, had served as a lieutenant in the Mexican War. Lamar had listed his only occupation as that of "Gentleman" in the 1860 census, but he would prove a hardy warrior on several fields of battle before being killed in action during the Petersburg campaign. Little is known of Benjamin Davis, though he may have been an overseer in Marion County before the war.[44]

Several other members of Hately's unit were men of distinction in the Panhandle. Council A. Bryan, Leon County's clerk of the circuit court, gave up his promising political position to serve his state. With Capt. William Bloxham's resignation in early 1863, Bryan became captain of Company C. (Bryan's letter collection remains an invaluable resource for Florida historians.) Richmond Gardner, a twenty-nine-year-old doctor, had been educated at the University of Virginia in Charlottesville, and the three Blake brothers, Joel, Isham, and Walter, were affluent planters from Miccosukee. Joel, who owned 118 slaves, would be killed at Gettysburg.[45]

The units comprising the Eighth Florida came from all parts of the state and south Georgia. The unit's nicknames, counties of origin, and commanders were as follows: Co. A (nickname unknown), Madison, Taylor, Lafayette, and Columbia counties, Capt. B. A. Bobo; Company B (Young Guards), Gadsden County, Capt. Robert A. Waller; Company C (nickname unknown), Suwannee County, Capt. David Lang; Company D (Grayson Artillery), St. Johns County, Capt. William Baya; Company E (nickname unknown), Jackson County, Capt. Thomas E. Clarke; Company F (nickname unknown), Nassau, Baker, and Columbia counties, Capt. Felix Simmons; Company G (Ward Avengers), Orange County, Capt. Jonathon Stewart; Company H (nickname unknown), Madison, Suwannee, and Hamilton counties, Capt. James M. Tucker; Company I (Milton Artillery), Duval and Baker counties, Capt. John Pons; and, Company K (nickname unknown), Hillsborough County, Capt. Frederick Worth. Two oddities marked the second and last companies of the Eighth Florida. The majority of men in Company B, including Capt. Waller, hailed from Decatur County, Georgia, while Company K represented the only unit in the Army of Northern Virginia from southwest Florida.[46]

Over fifty of the members of the unit had Hispanic or Minorcan family names, including two of the regiment's highest officers—Baya and Pons. Thirty-four Hispanics enlisted in the St. Augustine company (D), and Company I (from Jacksonville) had several, but most of the companies had at least one. (The Fifth Florida seemed to be much more homogeneous group, containing primarily English, Scots, Irish, and Huguenot surnames, with a few typically Jewish last names sprinkled through the unit.)[47]

The men elected Richard F. Floyd as colonel, John M. Pons as lieutenant colonel, and William I. Turner as major. Floyd, a fifty-two-year-old St. Johns County farmer, had been a brigadier general of the state militia before entering the Confederate army. Pons remains obscure but was apparently thirty-one years younger than Floyd and a resident of Pensacola in 1860. Turner had come to Florida as a member of the U.S. Army during the Second Seminole War, fell in love with the state, and eventually settled in Hillsborough County as a farmer (and one of the area's largest slave owners). Sending Turner's company

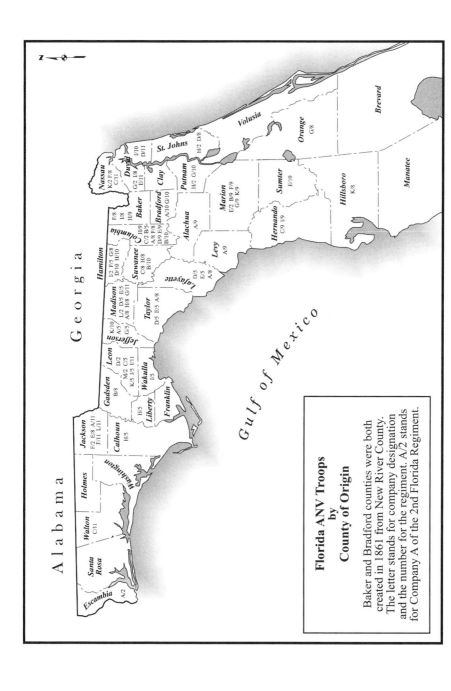

Fig. 4. Florida ANV troops by county of origin

to the Virginia killing fields seems to have been Gov. Milton's revenge for an earlier piece of slick dealing that Turner had put over on the chief executive. As Turner learned, it was not in Milton's nature to forgive or forget a real or perceived slight.[48]

Two of the captains of the Eighth played an important role in the history of the Florida brigade. By war's end, Capt. David Lang would become the heart and soul of the Second, Fifth, and Eighth Florida regiments. Born on May 9, 1838, in Camden County, Georgia, he graduated from the Georgia Military Institute near Marietta. Before the war, Lang worked as a surveyor in Suwannee County, Florida. When the first call for troops sounded, Lang enlisted in Company H of the First Florida Regiment and spent a year at Pensacola as part of Gen. Braxton Bragg's army. At the expiration of his term Lang returned to Suwannee County and raised the unit that became Company C from the "farms and villages of Spring Grove, Little River, and Houston." Rising from captain to colonel, Lang led the unit at Gettysburg, Cold Harbor, and Appomattox—the Florida brigade's moments of greatest tragedy, triumph, and sorrow. Defeat did little to moderate his devotion to Dixie—he remained throughout his life "an unremitting Rebel with a continuing dislike of 'the [Northern] invaders of a Heaven gifted people.'"[49]

Capt. William Baya was born in St. Augustine in 1834, and worked as a molder before the war. In 1861 he led a band of C.S. Marines that served on the Southern privateer *Jefferson Davis,* which raided Yankee shipping. When the *Jefferson Davis* sank, Baya joined the infantry and would later command the Eighth Florida at Gettysburg, Bristoe Station, and during the Petersburg campaign.[50]

Initially, the veteran Floridians dubbed the Eighth the "Bloody Eighth" when they observed the newcomers cracking body lice, which left tiny traces of blood.[51]

While the Florida troops fought to save Richmond and reinforcements rushed north from the southernmost state, Jefferson Davis and his advisors reached two decisions that would have a significant impact on both the Southern nation and the Land of Flowers. Most important, the Confederate Congress approved, in April 1862, "the first draft law in American history." Conscription went into effect just as the enlistments of the volunteers of 1861 were set to expire. It increased the one-year term of the soldiers to three years and called for the draft of all white males between the ages of eighteen and thirty-five, subject to various exemptions. (A few months later the upper age would be extended to forty-five, and by mid-1864 the conscription age included all white males between the ages of seventeen and fifty.) A historian from the southern-most state concluded, the "majority of Floridians loathed conscription."[52]

That assessment may be accurate for those still within the state, but it certainly does not indicate the disposition of Florida troops. They did not desert en masse nor fight with diminished dedication. Noted historian Gary Gallagher suggests: "Historians should avoid portraying Confederate desertion as a linear problem of constantly increasing gravity. A recent study . . . described a bulge of desertions in 1862 that probably represented anger at implementation of the conscription Act, the terms of which extended the service of thousands of men who originally had signed on for one year. After this initial wave, rates dropped off until the final months of the war."[53]

This seems to be the case with the state's representative regiment. A review of their records reveals almost fifty men of the Second Florida taking French leave during mid-1862, though a few of those later joined cavalry companies assigned to the southernmost state. The rest of the unit reenlisted for two additional years, figuring that two years were better than three, and so they could remain with their old companies and regiments.[54]

The second decision exacerbated the in-state problems created by the Conscription Act. By the spring of 1862, the government in Richmond decided to abandon Florida. A small force was left to guard the Apalachicola River, but only because it provided a natural springboard for invading lower Alabama and southwestern Georgia. From a military viewpoint the decision made perfect sense. The war would be won or lost by the Virginia or Tennessee armies. From a human perspective the citizens of the southernmost state began to feel like the Confederacy's redheaded stepchild. "The worst fears of the Floridians were now realized. Most of the state's military men were fighting for the life of the Confederacy in faraway places, and those at home must be prepared to defend themselves as best they could."[55]

In every part of Florida the families of the soldiers were now vulnerable to attacks by Federal raiders, outlaws, and, in some areas, revolts by slaves. Pleas from wives, children, and aged parents put the Florida Rebels on the horns of a dilemma—stay true to their comrades and cause or leave, by whatever means necessary, to protect their families. For men not already in the military, evading the draft became more attractive, especially to those with no great attachment to the cause. Historian John M. Sacher concluded from his research: "Southerners' impression of the measure [conscription] varied based on where they lived, particularly on their family's proximity to the Union army. An area safely within Confederate lines might accept conscription, but if later that home front faced Union occupation or simply lost the protection of the Confederate army, men might be less willing to leave their families to fight." After April 1862, no place in Florida was safe from Federal incursions. The difficulties with conscription and desertion would only increase as the home folks lost faith, and it became apparent to even the most hardcore Southern fanatic that the Confederacy was going up the spout.[56]

3 "Five Times Our Colors Fell"

Second Bull Run and Antietam

The Union's manpower advantage virtually guaranteed that the Army of Northern Virginia would have no time to rest on its laurels. Three armies still confronted Lee's forces. McClellan's Army of the Potomac, totaling more than 100,000 men; Maj. Gen. Ambrose Burnside's small 10,000-man unit, which had just returned from a successful expedition along the coasts of North Carolina; and Maj. Gen. John Pope's Army of Virginia, 40,000-strong, all posed a serious threat to the Confederates in the Old Dominion.[1]

The Southern commander decided to move first against Pope's Army of Virginia. He did this to maintain the strategic initiative, to prevent Lincoln from consolidating his three armies, and to counter a threat to the Confederate supply lines. This decision proved popular with the Rebel soldiers, who were incensed at Pope's reported mistreatment of Southern civilians. In fact, a lot of people, in both armies, despised the Union commander. Pope "was a difficult man to like," according to historian John S. Salmon. "If possible, Pope was even more full of himself than McClellan—pompous, impetuous, abrasive, loud-mouthed, and a braggart. Given to windy proclamations, he allegedly datelined his pronouncements 'headquarters in the saddle.' Both Union and Confederate wags quickly joked that his headquarters were where his hindquarters ought to be, and he didn't know one from the other."[2]

Lee divided his army, sending Stonewall Jackson's wing to damage the Federal supply line and draw the enemy into battle. Jackson accomplished both goals, in spades. After a bloody engagement at Cedar Mountain, Jackson's troops pillaged, then burned, the major Union supply depot at Manassas Junction, before taking cover in an abandoned railroad cut near the old Bull Run battlefield.[3]

Pope's obsession to "bag" Jackson resulted in a case of tunnel vision that blinded him to all else. While the Yankee general threw division after division against Jackson's entrenched line on August 29, Lee and Longstreet fought their way through Thoroughfare Gap, taking a position on Pope's exposed left flank. On the afternoon of August 30, Longstreet's wing of Lee's army crashed into Pope's Army of Virginia, sending the bluecoats into headlong flight before the gray battle line. "Pope, facing disaster, patched together a makeshift defense, trying to get his army safely off the field." The Federal defenders held long enough to allow the rest of Pope's troops to escape, but the Union commander had been tried in battle and found wanting.[4]

In the first battle of the combined Florida brigade, the three units received extravagant praise from Roger Pryor, but they failed to earn the tributes. The Floridians took a few casualties from artillery fire, but otherwise they were not actively engaged. Apparently, Pryor and Brig. Gen. W. S. Featherston held their units in the safety of Groveton Woods throughout the fight. In his after-action report, Pryor enthused: "The Fifth and Eighth Florida regiments, though never under fire before, exhibited the cool and collected courage of veterans." Seton Fleming of the Second Florida watched as the battle played out across the fields near Bull Run, later confiding to his mother: "Our brigade was not fought, but was held in reserve during the fight. Though several times we were under a heavy fire of grape and shell, a few of our men being killed and some wounded. I was not hurt."[5]

Pryor's men may have missed the fighting, but they engaged wholeheartedly in scavenging the battlefield the following morning. Fleming recounted, with obvious glee: "Several hours next morning, after the fight, were spent examining knapsacks that we had captured, and appropriating what we wished of their contents. I have a Yankee sword, canteen, and several other things; the paper, pen, ink, and portfolio that I use in writing this letter, were all taken in battle."[6]

Gen. Lee sent Jackson after the fleeing Federals, but a vicious fight at Chantilly, during a pouring rain, ended the Confederate pursuit. Current estimates put total casualties for Lee's and Pope's armies at more than 22,000 men, but few were from the southernmost state.[7]

Fresh from the triumph at Second Manassas, Lee convinced Pres. Davis that the time was ripe to take the war into enemy territory. The rapidity of the Confederate commander's new campaign forced Pres. Lincoln to make a difficult decision. With Pope disgraced by his poor showing at Second Bull Run, Lincoln reluctantly appointed McClellan to drive away the invaders. The president was obviously making the best of a bad situation, but rapidly changing events left Lincoln few other realistic options.[8]

By September 4, the Army of Northern Virginia began crossing the Potomac River. The Floridians entered Maryland near Leesburg on either the 5th or 6th, passing through Frederick, Maryland, on the morning of September 7. The brigade, still commanded by Roger Pryor, had been assigned to Maj. Gen. R. H. Anderson's division in Longstreet's wing.[9]

As the Army of Northern Virginia began reuniting around Frederick, Lee also faced a major problem. The fly in the ointment was the Federal garrison at Harpers Ferry. The Southern leader likely assumed that the 14,000-man force stationed there would be withdrawn to join the Army of the Potomac, but instead the U.S. War Department ordered Col. Dixon Miles, commanding at Harpers Ferry, to hold the post at all hazards. This placed a large Union army in position to cut the Confederates' vulnerable lines of supply and communication, but Lee knew the "capture of Harpers Ferry would yield large numbers of prisoners and huge amounts of ordinance that his [Lee's] army badly needed, and it would clear almost all remaining Union pockets of resistance on Virginia soil."[10]

Gen. Lee boldly divided his army into four parts. Three sections he put under the command of Stonewall Jackson, his most reliable lieutenant. Jackson had orders to capture the town at the confluence of the Potomac and Shenandoah rivers and to rejoin Lee by the 15th of September.[11]

Col. Miles did his best, but he must have realized the hopelessness of his situation. Most of the bluecoats he commanded had been in uniform less than three weeks, and high ground surrounded Harpers Ferry. Miles posted troops atop Maryland Heights, Loudoun Heights, and School House Ridge, but the raw recruits proved no match for the veterans of the Army of Northern Virginia. Jackson soon had artillery emplaced along the heights. On the night of September 14, Maj. Gen. A. P. Hill closed the net on the southwestern side of Harpers Ferry, sealing the fate of Col. Miles's garrison. An early morning bombardment by the Confederate cannon soon convinced Miles to surrender. It was one of the most lopsided victories of the war, with a total of nearly 13,000 Union casualties, almost all captured, compared to fewer than 300 Confederate losses.[12]

While Jackson's troops gobbled up the entire Federal force, the Florida regiments guarded the back door to Harpers Ferry. As they had at Second Bull Run, the Floridians, stationed at Weverton Gap (the modern spelling appears to be Weaverton Gap), missed the action. Weverton, an opening between the southern edge of South Mountain and the Potomac, would have been an ideal route for reinforcements, but McClellan and the War Department in Washington abandoned Miles and his men. Sgt. Isaac M. Auld of Co. C of the Fifth Florida informed his mother: "We were there [at Harpers Ferry], but were not engaged. We were placed to guard a gap in the mountains expecting the enemy every minute, but well for them they did not come."[13]

Stonewall Jackson left A. P. Hill to oversee the surrender of the Harpers Ferry garrison—paroling prisoners and collecting stores, military and edible. Jackson, meanwhile, immediately set a punishing pace as he marched almost nonstop to reach Lee's army at Sharpsburg. Jackson pushed his troops unmercifully because he was privy to information that the common soldier—bone-weary, dusty, and grumbling—did not know. Lee's plans had, by an extraordinary fluke of bad fortune, fallen into a McClellan's hands, and the Young Napoleon had shown unusual vigor in closing upon Lee's command.[14]

The gait of Jackson's northward march took a particularly heavy toll on the new regiments from Florida. Many fell out along the way. Isaac Auld reported: "The night before [the battle of Antietam] they traveled very fast and . . . about half of the regiment broke down that night." (A recent historian estimated that Lee lost "a third to a half" of his army due to sickness and straggling.) Anderson's division, minus those who dropped out along the way, arrived at Sharpsburg on the morning of September 17, but Lee held them in reserve near his headquarters.[15]

The battle of Antietam began at first light on the morning of September 17, and the initial blow fell on the Confederate left. Maj. Gen. Joseph Hooker's I Corps assailed Jackson's troops stationed around a Dunker church north of Sharpsburg. Back and forth the fighting raged through the East Woods, West Woods, and local farmer David Miller's cornfield—charge and counterattack, as the Yankees and Rebels fought to break or hold the lines. Four hours later, battered and bloody, the graycoats still held the left, but all around them several thousand Americans lay dead and wounded upon the field.[16]

Almost by mistake the fighting shifted south to the Confederate center, anchored in a sunken road. The thoroughfare was a rural shortcut that allowed area farmers to move back and forth between the Hagerstown Pike and the Keedysville Road, while bypassing Sharpsburg. Years of wear by the wheels of heavily laden farm wagons and erosion had turned the byway into a natural entrenchment. Maj. Gen. Daniel Harvey Hill had recognized the strength of the position and stationed the Alabama brigade of Brig. Gen. Robert E. Rodes and the North Carolina units of Brig. Gen. George B. Anderson in the sunken road. A conglomeration of regiments, traditionally attributed to the brigades of Col. Alfred H. Colquitt, Col. Duncan K. McRae, and Brig. Gen. Howell Cobb, filled "the 150-yard gap between Rode's left and the Hagerstown Pike." Gen. Lee had come by to inspect the position, and likely promised to send R. H. Anderson's division if things got too hot for the 2,200 graycoats in the sunken road.[17]

Union brigadier general William French, commanding the Third Division of the II Corps, had apparently gotten lost as he moved toward the fighting in the East Woods, and a little after 9:00 a.m. blundered into D. H. Hill's position in the sunken road. The graycoats held their fire until French's Federals were silhouetted along the hilltop fronting their position, and the first volley "brought down the enemy as grain falls before the reaper." The survivors retreated in considerable disorder over the crest of the hill and opened fire on D. H. Hill's Confederates. At least three times French's troops charged the sunken road, only to be bloodily repulsed.[18]

McClellan had held Maj. Gen. Israel Richardson's division as a reserve, but it soon joined French's assault on the Rebel center. Richardson's veterans, including Brig. Gen. Thomas F. Meagher's celebrated "Irish Brigade," smashed into D. H. Hill's hardened fighters, but Richardson's men fared no better than French's. Leaving over 500 dead or wounded littering the field, Richardson finally sent the sons of Eire, their ammunition exhausted, to the rear. Still more Yankees filled the gap, repeatedly hammering Hill's line, and Southern casualties continued to mount.[19]

At around 10:00 a.m., R. H. Anderson's division received orders to move to the support of D. H. Hill's beleaguered troops, entering the Sharpsburg fight without "rest or food." Anderson likely planned a flank attack on "French's exposed right," but whatever they accomplished, they would be the only help Hill's veterans could expect. Lee had no other reserves to send to any threatened point on his line.[20]

Unfortunately for Confederate hopes, R. H. Anderson was shot through the thigh early in the engagement. His replacement, "the incomparably incompetent Roger Pryor," apparently neither knew Anderson's plan nor what to do in the emergency. As a result, Pryor's units filtered into the sunken road by regiments and companies. With Pryor in command, and the loss of officers within the Bloody Lane, "there was no one in overall control of events on the Confederate right."[21]

Lamentable as the command situation was at the division level, it was multiplied tenfold by the leadership woes of the three Florida regiments. Writing after the war to Union veteran and historian E. A. Carman, David Lang explained the situation the Flowers encountered as they struggled toward the sunken road.

> I have to say that the [Eighth Florida] regiment went into the battle in command of Lt. Col. [George A. C.] Coppen, formerly of the [unreadable] Louisiana Zouaves, by assignment of Gen. Roger A. Pryor, just preceding the battle, because of the absence and sickness of Col. Richard Floyd and Lt. Col. Jon M. Pons. Major W. I. Turner having resigned. . . . Col. Coppen was killed almost immediately after getting under fire in the cornfield below the stone barn near bloody lane! Capt. Richard [actually Robert A.] Waller then assumed command as senior Capt. and was also killed with the colors of the regiment draped over his shoulders, almost immediately afterward. . . . The next in line, the writer [Lang], had been previously wounded between the time of the killings of Col. Coppen and Capt. Waller. Capt. Wm. Baya, next in rank, commanded the regiment until the end of the engagement. . . . Col. John C. Hately, of the 5th Fla Regt., succeeded to the command of Pryor's Brigade immediately upon coming on the field and becoming engaged. . . . Col. Hately was shot through both thighs at the Bloody Lane, and carried from the field.[22]

Col. E. A. Perry, still recovering from the severe wound he had received at Frayser's Farm, missed the fight at Sharpsburg, as did Maj. Walter Moore. As a result Capt. William Duncan Ballantine, the next ranking officer, led the 240-man Second Florida into battle. At least one source states that "Lt." (actually Sgt. Henry E.) Geiger directed the unit after Ballantine fell to enemy fire.[23]

Virtually leaderless, the three Florida regiments approached the vicinity of the sunken road in fragments. The initial approach of the Second Florida provides a good example of the brigade's situation. The state's "representative regiment" crossed the Hagerstown Pike, passed the Piper farmstead, and took a position near Piper's apple orchard. Ballantine ordered his men to lay prone to avoiding unnecessarily exposing themselves to enemy fire. Gen. Rodes noticed the unit halted "in the hollow immediately in my rear and near the orchard." Rodes galloped to Ballantine, gruffly demanding to know the commander, who the troops were, and why they were not engaged. Ballantine explained that they belonged to Pryor's brigade and further informed Rodes that Pryor had given his outfit no orders to advance or where to deploy. Rodes quickly located Pryor

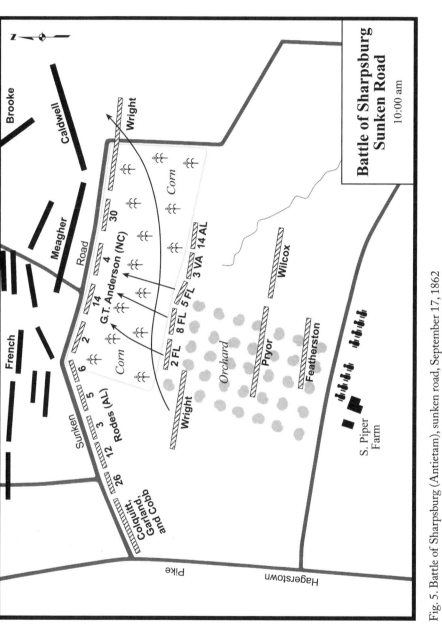

Fig. 5. Battle of Sharpsburg (Antietam), sunken road, September 17, 1862

and informed "him as to their [the Second Florida's] conduct, and he [Pryor] immediately ordered them forward."[24]

Between the fruit trees and the sunken road lay a cornfield, now just shattered stalks after an hour of battle. The alignment of the brigade as it advanced through the blasted cornfield had the Second Florida on the left, followed by the Eighth Florida, Fifth Florida, Third Virginia, and Fourteenth Alabama. They took a position to the rear of the Fourteenth and Fourth North Carolina regiments, though other elements of Pryor's unit apparently rushed through the sunken road and up the hill toward the bluecoats, only to be repelled with severe losses.[25]

Losses to the Florida officers' corps continued unabated. Capt. Ballantine fell and was carried to the rear, and "Col. Hately was shot through both thighs at the bloody lane." The soldiers also suffered appalling casualties. Capt. Council Bryan noted that the Florida boys "double quicked a mile and a half into the fight Wednesday morning about 9 o'clock, fought three Yankee brigades all day and came out at night with 63 men for duty . . . the whole Regiment was cut to pieces—[My company] went in with 17 men and came out with 3 unhurt." Another Flower reported: "we rushed into the thickest of the fight, and were badly cut up in one hour's time, though we held our ground and pressed the enemy back a little."[26]

Col. T. R. Bennett's Fourteenth North Carolina particularly needed help, but the aid he received apparently failed to meet his rather demanding standards. He bitterly claimed in his after-action report that "portions of the Sixteenth Mississippi and 2nd Florida, coming to our succor, broke beyond the power of rallying after five minute's stay." This has been the accepted dogma of historians since 1862, and most have concluded that Sharpsburg constituted "a blemish on their [the Florida brigade's] . . . record."[27]

Contemporary letters and reports tell a different story. Chaplain J. W. Mills of the Fifth Florida recorded:

Many of our regiment fell in the terrible battle of Sharpsburg. We occupied the centre [of the Confederate line], where the enemy made his fiercest attack, hoping to break our lines in that vital part of the field, and so win the day. The enemy were formed in a semicircle on the side of a hill. Our brave men marched up to the attack until they could see the heads and shoulders of their adversaries over the summit of the hill, when firing commenced. From two wings and the centre of this semicircle they poured upon us a murderous fire for about one hour. Five times our colors fell, but as often our men rushed to the spot and raised them to the breeze. Finally, a retreat was ordered—at that moment the colors fell and were left. The enemy had suffered too much, and notwithstanding his advantages, to pursue, and our gallant Lieutenant-Colonel [Lamar], already wounded in the arm, went back and brought them away under a shower of bullets.[28]

Peter W. Alexander, a respected battlefield reporter for numerous Southern newspapers, noted that "the 5th Florida behaved with distinguished courage and intrepidity." He wrote that Pvt. Ben Flowers "was wounded five different times in as many places; yet he continued to shoot away as fearlessly as ever until he received the fifth wound, which disabled one of his hands, so he could not load his piece."[29]

The battle at the sunken road had begun by accident, and a mistake by a harried Southern officer began the evacuation of the position. One of Rode's regimental officers on the left tried to shift his companies to meet a Federal threat, but blundered and gave an order that led his unit to withdraw to the rear. This caused the left of the line to collapse, allowing the Yankees to flank and enfilade the Confederate defenses. The Rebels could stand only so much, and the defenders of the Bloody Lane gave way to rout and headlong flight. Pryor's men, along with the rest of R. H. Anderson's reinforcements (and W. S. Featherston's brigade) were caught up in the confusion and retreated rapidly through the cornfield and orchard.[30]

Col. Floyd of the Eighth Florida had been left sick in a Virginia hospital, but he struggled valiantly to rejoin his unit in time for the battle. He arrived on the field just as D. H. Hill's line collapsed, and left a vivid account of the confusion he encountered during the retreat. Reporting to Gov. John Milton on September 22, he recalled:

The battle was raging for nearly 5 miles. I reached the centre, dismounted and started walking toward the fight but every inquiry for the Florida 8th made by me from officers riding to & from the field was answered by "I know not—no man can unless by accident find his Brigade in the field[.]" Of course I was in no condition to take command for I had to stop, panting from weakness, and sit down every hundred yards. Still I went on to see all of the battlefield; I saw enough to make my heart ache for our poor fellows, for every instant of time they were passing me supported, even [carried on] litters, all covered with wounds—Finally, I met several of our poor fellows [members of the Eighth Florida] coming off wounded, some mortally, and asking them for our Regt they piteously replied "they are all killed, wounded, or dispersed." The 8th Florida Regiment went that morning into the action with but 120 men and was commanded by Capt Waller (who was killed)[.] All the rest of this fine Regt. was scattered among the Hospitals sick, for 150 miles. There was no field officer present, nor the adjutant [Benjamin F.] Simmons. He and Lieut. Col. Pons had been left sick on the road—There were only three Captains on the Field. One Company (Bobo's) [Capt. Burwell A. Bobo's Co. A] was not represented at all—all sick; one other company (Simmons; he having resigned) [Capt. Felix Simmons's Co. F] only mustered three men on the field—[unreadable name] (1st Sgt) commanded the other two and [same name above] was killed—This remnant of the 8th Regt (120 men who went into battle) was in the thickest of the fight and were almost annihilated—The 5th Regt. also suffered terribly. I saw Col. Hately as he came out with his thigh broken. I expected any moment to be shot without having a post to command. By this time both Regts & also the gallant 2d [Florida] and other contiguous Regiments had been cut up and scattered here and there in small squads. The next day it was difficult to find any men at all of these Regts, except the wounded who were brought off. All our dead remain there unburied.

Col. Floyd resigned his commission a few days later, citing ill health as the cause for his decision.[31]

With a gaping opening in Lee's center, the Confederate line was in danger of being broken asunder. The repulse of D. H. Hill's and R. H. Anderson's units, scattered and dispersed, left the Confederates with no infantry capable of resisting a concentrated Federal attack. In yet another example of battlefield timidity, the Young Napoleon declined to exploit the advantage gained by his troops, even though he had Maj. Gen. William B. Franklin's entire VI Corps massed to attack. When the smoked cleared, more than 5,000 Confederates and Federals lay dead near the wretched little shortcut.[32]

The battle of Antietam shifted once more, this time to the southern part of the Rebel line. Fortunately for the graycoats, Maj. Gen. Ambrose Burnside spent three hours trying to get his 11,000 men across a bridge over shallow Antietam Creek while confronted by Brig. Gen. Robert Toombs with only 550 Georgians. Late in the afternoon, as Burnside's men were pushing the Rebels through Sharpsburg, A. P. Hill's brigades arrived from Harpers Ferry. They struck the bluecoats in the flank and drove them back across Antietam Creek. Night finally came to the Maryland countryside with Lee still in control of the area around Sharpsburg.[33]

The next day, Lee stayed north of the Potomac, inviting McClellan to renew the attack. The Union leader declined, and the following evening the Confederates crossed back into Virginia. Pres. Lincoln immediately declared the battle of Antietam a victory, and soon thereafter issued the Emancipation Proclamation. This document virtually ensured that no European nation would dare recognize, or give monetary or military support, to the Southern Confederacy.[34]

The performance of the Florida brigade at Sharpsburg is difficult to judge. The assault of R. H Anderson's division certainly accomplished far less than Lee or D. H. Hill envisioned. The most obvious difficulty with the Florida brigade at the Bloody Lane was the lack of effective leadership due to an unprecedented spate of casualties to the unit's officer corps and the command failures of Roger Pryor. For a while a lieutenant directed the Second Florida Regiment and noncoms commanded several companies. Still, the casualties suffered by the Florida units seem to indicate that want of courage had not been the reason for the failure to hold the sunken road. Of the approximately 570 Floridians who entered the battle, 282 became casualties, a loss of approximately 50 percent. Antietam was the first real engagement for the Fifth and Eighth Florida, and considering their rookie status, it seems remarkable that they fought as well as they did.[35]

Whatever the truth of the Floridians' fight at Sharpsburg, several changes resulted that had a significant impact upon the three regiments. First, Pryor's luck finally ran out. He was stripped of his command in the Army of Northern Virginia, and after a brief stint commanding a small force in a military backwater, Pryor resigned his commission and ended the war as a volunteer cavalryman.[36]

During November 1862, the War Department in Richmond also combined the three Florida regiments into a single brigade. Col. E. A. Perry, who had received his brigadier's star the previous month, assumed command of the new brigade. Perry's appointment may have been a political move to blunt demands by Gov. John Milton to have the units returned to the southernmost state, but the decision had a positive effect on the brigade's morale. Perry's boys remained in Anderson's division of Longstreet's First Corps.[37]

Finally, the casualties and rigors of campaigning brought significant changes to regimental leadership. Maj. Davis assumed temporary command of the Fifth Florida as a result of the wounding of Col. Hately and Lt. Col. Lamar at Sharpsburg. Col. Floyd of the Eighth Florida resigned five days after the battle due to poor health. Lt. Col. Pons also left the army shortly after the bloodletting in Maryland, and Maj. Turner had already permanently returned to Florida. Capt. David Lang, who had already shown a flair for leadership, soon replaced Floyd as colonel of the Eighth Florida.[38]

4   "A Courage as Intrepid as That of Any Other"

Fredericksburg and Chancellorsville

After recrossing the Potomac, Gen. Lee divided his army. Stonewall Jackson's Second Corps encamped at Winchester, Virginia, only twenty-nine miles south of Sharpsburg, while James Longstreet's First Corps rested at Culpepper. The Confederate commander apparently had little apprehension that George B. McClellan would mount a vigorous pursuit or an aggressive offensive campaign in the near future. Lee's reports to Pres. Jefferson Davis dealt with mundane military matters. Stragglers were being brought in daily, he noted, and the conscript agents had collected a number of draftees from the Old Dominion's northern counties. For once, supplies were plentiful. Lee did express some concern with the "temper and condition" of his army, which precluded, for the time being at least, a second advance into the North. The Army of Northern Virginia needed a rest, and the Rebel leader seemed quite content to go into winter quarters.[1]

Lee's army had little cause to be discouraged and ample reasons for pride. From May through September of 1862 the army had fashioned a record virtually unequaled in the annals of American military history. The graycoats had fought major battles at Seven Pines, Gaines's Mill, Malvern Hill, Second Manassas, and Sharpsburg, and countless bloody engagements such as Williamsburg, Beaver Dam Creek, Glendale, and Cedar Mountain. Stonewall Jackson's brilliant Shenandoah Valley campaign had also added luster to the army's growing reputation. All told, the Southern forces in Virginia had defeated five Union armies, including McClellan's huge 120,000-man force during the Seven Days. There had been a few setbacks along the way, but by late fall its fighting forces had provided the Confederacy with reason for optimism.[2]

Conditions were not quite as rosy in Washington. Pres. Abraham Lincoln desperately wanted to capitalize on the victory at Antietam, but Gen. McClellan continued to display a frustratingly insubordinate attitude. The commander in chief ordered the Young Napoleon "to cross the Potomac and either fight Lee or drive him south." McClellan ignored the directive, treating it as a mere suggestion. He finally moved the Army of the Potomac a few miles south, but soon halted and began hounding Washington with demands for additional troops and supplies.[3]

By November 5 Lincoln had had enough. He relieved McClellan and appointed Maj. Gen. Ambrose Burnside as the new commander of the Army of the Potomac. Burnside, an affable and intelligent man, felt unequal to his new position, but he did not believe he could refuse Lincoln's mandate.[4]

Under intense pressure from Washington, Burnside began a winter campaign designed to capture Richmond and hopefully end the war. With the Army of the Potomac stationed at Warrenton, midway between Winchester and Culpepper, the Federal commander proposed swinging east of Longstreet's corps, and beating Lee's troops in a race to the Confederate capital. The key to the success of Burnside's plan required getting across the Rappahannock River before Lee could consolidate his forces on the west bank of the river. To accomplish this, the Federal commander ordered engineers to have pontoons and materials to construct bridges ready when the Army of the Potomac reached Fredericksburg.[5]

Burnside's flanking move caught Lee completely by surprise, and the graycoats responded slowly to the new threat. The Federals reached Fredericksburg on November 17, but due to a bureaucratic mix-up, the pontoons did not arrive until November 25. By the time the materials to construct the floating bridges arrived, Longstreet's First Corps had assumed defensive positions along Marye's Heights, and Jackson's Second Corps was hastening toward Fredericksburg.[6]

The morning of December 11 found Burnside ready to attempt the crossing. He tried spanning the stream above and below Fredericksburg, but the Confederates easily blocked his efforts. In desperation Burnside concluded, "I think now that the enemy will be more surprised by a crossing immediately in our front than in any other part of the river." Federal engineers proposed bridging the Rappahannock in three places, and Burnside quickly approved the plan. They would construct two spans into the northern end of Fredericksburg (between Hawke and Fauquier streets); a single bridge across the Rappahannock near the destroyed railroad bridge; and two more spans a couple of miles below town just south of the confluence of Deep Run and the Rappahannock.[7]

Lee had already guessed the Federal commander's plan, and he dispatched Brig. Gen. William Barksdale's Mississippians, of Maj. Gen. Lafayette McLaws's division, to the old city to impede the bridge construction and contest the crossing of the Rappahannock. The Confederates recognized that "an eventual Federal bridgehead could not be prevented," but "McLaws intended to make it as costly as possible." Barksdale was a fiery, pugnacious warrior whose "stubborn aggressiveness" made him an ideal leader for this task. To support the Seventeenth, Eighteenth, Thirteenth, and Twenty-first Magnolia State regiments, Longstreet also sent the Eighth Florida to Barksdale. Capt. David Lang, the unit's senior officer, directed the Florida regiment at Fredericksburg.[8]

Lang received orders, at about 5 a.m., to take his unit "to a point on the river forming the site of the old ferry" to support Lt. Col. John C. Fiser's Seventeenth Mississippi at Hawke Street. Barksdale intercepted the Eighth Florida, dividing the regiment into two sections. Barksdale ordered Companies A, D, and F, commanded by Capt. William Baya, to reinforce his troops in opposing the crossing near the destroyed railroad bridge.[9]

Baya's contingent hurried to support Capt. Andrew R. Govan's section of the Seventeenth Mississippi guarding the center of town. The Mississippian kept his troops under cover, at least partially protected by Fredericksburg's cellars and buildings, but Govan dispatched Baya to an open area on the west bank of the river. Baya's apprehension about opening fire on the bluecoats from this exposed position grew throughout the day. Govan carped that the Floridians "failed repeatedly to obey my commands when ordered to fire on the bridge-builders." A modern historian assessed the situation thusly: "Baya repeatedly disobeyed orders and refused to fire on the pontoniers for fear of attracting attention from the Federal artillery. But who could blame these men for wanting to escape the firestorm?" By 2:00 p.m., the St. Augustine native notified Govan that his Florida troops could no longer hold the riverbank, and Baya had decided to abandon the exposed position.[10]

Probably afraid of being branded a coward, Baya changed his mind and clung to his untenable position. At 3:00 p.m., the Yankees opened a furious artillery barrage on the Southern troops guarding Fredericksburg. Fifteen minutes later the Eighty-ninth New York crossed the Rappahannock in unused pontoons, landed near the city docks, and rapidly advanced through the city. Govan quickly moved his Mississippians back to Caroline Street, but neglected to inform Baya of his retreat. It did not take the New Yorkers long to silence Baya's Floridians, now completely alone. After a sharp skirmish the heavily outnumbered Flowers had little choice but to surrender. All told, the Federals captured twenty-two Floridians, including Capt. Baya.[11]

In his after-action report, Govan concluded "that if any [of Baya's troops] were captured it was from inefficiency and from fear of being killed in the retreat." Twice Lang tried to salvage the reputation of Baya and his men. In his post-battle account, the Eighth Florida's commander mentioned that companies A, D, and F were missing, noting sharply: "It is proper to remark that Captain Baya regarded the position entrusted to him as so exposed and admitting of so little means of support that he objected to occupying the same until the order was repeated." Forty years later Lang informed former governor Francis Fleming that Baya had been treated as a sacrificial lamb at Fredericksburg. The St. Augustinian had protested that his position "under the bluff of the river [was] entirely exposed to the fire of the enemy from a double line of rifle pits on the other bank of the river. He [also] protested, as there were no possibilities of escape in case the enemy carried any portion of the line, but General Barksdale made his order peremptory."[12]

Whatever the truth of the situation, Baya's contingent certainly set no standard for steadfast heroism, and it seems an accurate assessment that "[Baya's] Floridians . . . added no luster to their record" at Fredericksburg. Capt. Govan, however, appears to deserve at least a measure of responsibility for the failure of the Florida troops. The Mississippian kept his men sheltered in Fredericksburg but essentially pinned a bull's-eye on Baya's unit, stationing it in an open, unprotected area where it would be the focus of enemy fire.[13]

Lang's 150-man demi-regiment fared a little better in the Mississippi post-battle reports. Barksdale personally led the Florida graycoats to the north end of the city, assigning them to a position north of Pitt Street. Col. John C. Fiser, commanding the other half of the Seventeenth Mississippi, was stationed to their right while Lang's troops "anchored the left wing of the 17th Mississippi." Fiser apparently assumed direction of the Eighth Florida. The Floridians advanced until they were "in point blank range of the enemy above the [upper] bridge."[14]

David Lang wrote that the engagement began "about 5:30 a.m., the [Union] pontoniers having advanced the bridge about two-thirds across the river, the Seventeenth Mississippi opened fire, and my command at once did the same with good effect, the enemy being compelled to abandon his work and flee to points of security. The force of the enemy supporting the pontoniers immediately opened a heavy fire with artillery and musketry, which was kept up almost continuously the whole day. Each attempt of the pontoniers to continue their work was met by a well-directed fire from my command."[15]

With Burnside's troops occupying the east bank of the Rappahannock and Lee's army entrenched along Marye's Heights, west of the river, the beautiful old city of Fredericksburg sat between the warring forces. Lee hesitated to use his artillery on the town he'd known so well in his youth, but the Union leaders did not share that sentiment. The presence of the Florida and Mississippi troops ensured that Fredericksburg would suffer severely during this bloody December. Each time the Federal artillery began its bombardment, the Confederates would hunker down behind walls and in basements, but as soon as the Union engineers began work on the bridges, the men from the Seventeenth, Eighteenth, and Twenty-first Mississippi and the Eighth Florida emerged and drove them back. Fiser later recounted: "Such dispositions being made, we easily swept the enemy from their bridge from above, below, and in front." Fiser also praised Lang's actions. The Mississippian noted: "The [Florida] battalion did good service and acted gallantly while commanded by Captain Lang. He obeyed my suggestions with alacrity, and proved himself a worthy, gallant, and efficient officer." All through the long morning and early afternoon Barksdale's Rebels prevented the crossing of the Rappahannock.[16]

About 2:30 p.m., two significant events occurred that broke the stalemate. "Burnside was nearly beside himself" at the delay, insisting that the work must be completed before nightfall. With the bridges only two-thirds completed, Brig. Gen. Henry J. Hunt, the Army of the Potomac's artillery chief, proposed utilizing the unused pontoons (or bateaux) to ferry Yankee troops to the south bank while his artillery kept the pesky Rebels under cover. Frustrated by Barksdale and Lang's stout defense, Burnside approved the plan. The 7th Michigan and 19th and 20th Massachusetts regiments spearheaded the upper crossing, followed by the 42nd and 59th New York and the 127th Pennsylvania. Despite the Southern resistance, the Yankees managed to establish a beachhead, and began pushing into the old city. Further compounding the graycoats' problems, the artillery barrage set the downtown area afire.[17]

Around noon, Capt. Lang received a severe wound when an artillery shell struck a chimney and a large piece of masonry fell, striking him on the head. His men dug him out of the rubble and carried him from the field, and in his absence, Capt. Thomas R. Love of Company B assumed command of the

Fig. 6. Col. David Lang,
Eighth Florida Regiment

Eighth Florida. Love "maintained the position, though exposed to a galling fire of shot, shell, canister, and musketry, until about 4 p.m., when, in accordance [with orders], he withdrew his force."[18]

The Eighth held its position, but without Lang's strong leadership the regiment's performance suffered. Fiser noted the change, writing he received "little aid" from the Floridians after the loss of Capt. Lang, and adding that they "seemed troubled and in want of a commander." The Mississippian even felt compelled to move a small squad from the Thirteenth Mississippi Regiment to bolster the faltering Floridians. Equally embarrassing for the Eighth Regiment, Fiser complained "that a certain lieutenant (his name I do not recollect) so far forgot himself as to draw his pistol and threaten to kill some of my sharpshooters if they fired again, as it would draw the enemy's fire on his position." The Eighth remained in position until Barksdale ordered a withdrawal, but December 11 was not the unit's finest hour.[19]

The Union troops gradually took control of the Fredericksburg waterfront, and the Confederate forces fell back to Marye's Heights. The Floridians and Mississippians delayed the Federal crossing of the Rappahannock for almost twelve hours, inflicting numerous casualties on the enemy and allowing Gen. Lee time to strengthen his defensive line. The Eighth Florida reported a loss of seven killed, thirty-seven wounded, and forty-four missing or captured, the latter primarily from Baya's contingent.[20]

The Florida brigade saw no further action at Fredericksburg, but the Second Florida had a proud moment during the main battle on December 13. Maj. Walter R. Moore described the event to his wife, writing: "For two days we remained in line of battle where the shells were bursting over our heads nearly all the time. . . . None of us got hurt. When the battle was raging fiercest and the yelling was most terrific we were called to attention, and a beautiful Flag presented to our Regt from the Governor of Fla made by the ladies of Tallahassee. We were commanded to receive the flag in silence." This battle flag used the traditional St. Andrews cross pattern, but bore an unusual "rising sun" design in place of the traditional center star.[21]

The battle of Fredericksburg ended in a complete defeat for the Federals, with the lifeless remains of shattered regiments strewn along the greensward below Marye's Heights. When the Rebels halted Burnside's initial attack near Hamilton Crossing on the Confederate right, the Union commander unwisely decided to advance his second prong in a frontal assault against Marye's Heights. Wave after wave of hardy Federals charged into a murderous fire, and the Army of the Potomac suffered 12,600 casualties. Lee's losses numbered only about 5,300 men. On the night of December 15–16, the Northern troops retreated through a torrential downpour across the Rappahannock, and both armies went into winter quarters.[22]

Lee's and Burnside's forces may have settled into camps for the winter, but ordinary military vigilance still had to be maintained. Men had to stand sentry duty day and night, cut firewood, feed the horses, and perform a thousand other tasks requiring exposure to the cold and wind. This proved especially difficult for most of the Florida soldiers. Hailing from a state that considered forty-degree temperatures frigid and where snow was scarcer than a colony of three-legged dwarfs, Perry's Flowers found surviving the Virginia weather a grueling ordeal. A Virginia artilleryman noted in his diary that two Floridians had frozen to death while on night sentry duty, and Capt. Samuel A. Spencer of Co. I of the Fifth Florida complained: "It has been excessively cold, and I have not been comfortably warm since I got here. . . . I now have but two men [out of forty-five] fit for duty." Spencer resigned by mid-February 1863 after developing pneumonia.[23]

Gen. E. A. Perry sent requests to the Confederate War Department for tents and blankets, but apparently the Florida troops received only a partial shipment of supplies. On February 26, 1863, Lt. Junius Taylor of the Fifth Florida's "Dixie Yeomen" recorded: "We are still here in the woods without anything to protect us from the bitter blasts and snows of winter." Two weeks earlier Capt. Spencer had described the somewhat better living conditions enjoyed by his company. "We have tents, and to each tent the boys have constructed a rude chimney composed of sticks and clay. The chimneys are placed in the doors of the tents, and the sides of the door drawn closely to the walls of the chimney: and ingress and egress is had by lifting the bottom of the tents and crawling in or out."[24]

Despite the hardship and dearth of basic necessities they endured, the Floridians displayed a willingness to help others. A charity drive to assist refugees from Fredericksburg and those whose homes had been damaged during the battle and occupation by the Federals raised large sums throughout the South. The Army of Northern Virginia contributed over $100,000 (in Confederate money), and Perry's Florida brigade and Donaldson's artillery donated $866.75 from their scant resources.[25]

The grim reality of battle, sickness, lack of shelter, and scarcity of food caused a spate of resignations in the Florida brigade, particularly among the officer corps. The Eighth Florida underwent a complete change of its command structure. David Lang finally received his well-deserved promotion to colonel, and William Baya was named the unit's lieutenant colonel. The post of major went to Capt. Thomas E. Clarke, a veteran of the First Florida Regiment and former commander of Co. E, Eighth Florida. To replace Baya, Lt. Joseph Anthony Pacetti, before the war a physician from St. Augustine, was named captain of Company D.[26]

A lowly private who transferred to the Fifth Florida from the Second Georgia in mid-November would aid future historians by publishing a postwar record of his experiences in the Florida brigade. David L. Geer had escaped his father's harsh discipline by crossing the state line to join the Georgia unit. Geer was an indefatigable prankster; the men of the unit often suffered from his rough tricks. For example, one evening he and a partner stole a ram from a nearby farmer and cooked the mutton with suet dumplings. Geer doctored the concoction with an herb that induced both diarrhea and unbearable thirst. All night members of his company beat a course between the slit trenches and the river. The next morning the bleary-eyed sufferers returned to camp to the sound of Geer greeting each with a hearty "Baa!" This was too much for the regimental chaplain, who in a moment of spiritual weakness cursed the unrepentant trickster.[27]

Battered by a year of combat and disease, and often neglected by the Richmond government, the Floridians now had to contend with the boredom inherent in soldiering during the harsh winter. The cold season saw a predictable increase in drinking and gambling. But men will be boys, and winter blizzards provided a more wholesome diversion for the tedium of camp life. The widespread phenomenon of snowball battles spread through the Confederate camps, and the officers apparently encouraged the contests as a safe way to blow off steam and keep the men in fighting trim. The Florida brigade participated in several of these mock battles. Junius Taylor provided an account of the Florida brigade's involvement in one of these engagements. He noted:

Yesterday evening [February 25, 1863] we had a grand battle with snowballs. In the morning [Brig. Gen. William] Mahone's [Virginia] Brigade which is a third larger than ours came over and bartered us for a battle. We accepted the challenge and fought bravely for about an hour, but they were so much stronger than us that we had to fall back inside our lines. After shelling our camp they retired shouting like a set of demons. But the Florida boys were determined not to give up at this, so we sent over and got Generals Featherston's and Posey's Brigades to help us out in the evening. About 4:00 p.m. our three brigades formed a line of battle with colors flying and marched with the two generals cheering us on, making a charge upon the lines of Mahone's Brigade. We drove them from their camp but they fell back upon Wilcox's [Alabama] Brigade and asked them to help them. General Wilcox mounted his horse and soon got his Brigade in line of battle and came down upon us like an alpine avalanche. We stood our ground amid a hurricane of snowballs for about fifteen minutes; then our generals gave the orders for us to fall back in front of our lines, but our opponents charged us so impetuously that we could not make a stand. They ran us through our encampment into a pine thicket on the other side where we made a stand and kept them at bay until darkness put an end to the conflict. So we had to make a draw battle of it, they entirely having the advantage over us, for we were cut off from our camps.

Unfortunately, fake battles would soon be replaced by the reality of bloody combat.[28]

Following the debacle at Fredericksburg and an "equally disastrous venture that came to bear the derisive name 'the Mud March,'" Pres. Lincoln felt compelled to replace Ambrose Burnside. The Army of the Potomac's new commander, Maj. Gen. Fighting Joe Hooker, had a reputation for aggressiveness, bombastic proclamations, and a voracious appetite for prostitutes and liquor. Lincoln's orders to Hooker were direct and pointed: "Beware of rashness, but with energy and sleepless vigilance, go forward, and give us victories." Hooker exuded total confidence in his ability to defeat the Rebels, crowing: "May God have mercy on General Lee, for I will have none."[29]

As the roads dried and spring flowers began to dot the countryside, Hooker commenced his 1863 campaign. On April 27, the Federal leader put his plan into motion. The Union cavalry struck deep into Confederate territory, attempting to cut Lee's communications with Richmond while Hooker led three corps along the north bank of the Rappahannock to Kelly's Ford. He left Maj. Gen. John "Uncle John" Sedgwick's VI Corps opposite Fredericksburg to hold the Army of Northern Virginia in place.[30]

The rapid movement caught the Confederate commander by surprise, and the bluecoats had crossed the Rappahannock and Rapidan rivers before he could respond. Lee left two brigades, totaling only 11,000 men, to hold Fredericksburg (against 40,000 Federals) and hurried west, finally bringing Fighting Joe to bay near Chancellorsville. With Longstreet's corps detached to southeastern Virginia, Lee would have only the divisions of R. H. Anderson and Maj. Gen. Lafayette McLaws and Jackson's corps, a total of approximately 40,000 troops, in the coming engagement. The bluecoats with Fighting Joe numbered more than 90,000 men.[31]

The terrain around Chancellorsville provided one of the few advantages for the Southerners. A military historian described the seventy square miles called the Wilderness as "a nasty, dense thicket of stumps, scrub pines, briers, and brambles with visibility of only a few feet, which made military maneuvering virtually impossible. Here and there clearings offered some relief, but most of the Wilderness was barely penetrable." Lee would use this asset to disguise the size of the force confronting Hooker and to hide Jackson's flank move from the enemy.[32]

E. A. Perry's brigade had been left near Fredericksburg while the rest of R. H. Anderson's division covered two fords on the Rappahannock several miles to the west. On the morning of May 1, Perry's Florida boys received orders and moved from their position on the heights opposite Falmouth. They marched up the Orange Turnpike to its intersection with the Old Mine Road, where McLaws's and the rest of Anderson's divisions were entrenching. Lt. Anderson J. Peeler wrote: "Friday morning, the 1st of May, was one of the fairest & most beautiful I have ever seen and the Spotsylvania Hills, covered with tender clover and grass, seemed to smile beneath the bright sunshine with sur-passing lovliness."[33]

About 11:00 a.m. the Flowers reached McLaws's and R. H. Anderson's di-visions, and Perry's brigade assumed a position north of the Old Mine Road on the extreme right of the Confederate line. A Floridian remembered that "a brisk musketry fire was going on, a number of shells & minie balls passing over our heads" as they took their place in line. Lafayette McLaws exercised tempo-rary command of the Floridians.[34]

The Rebel line confidently moved forward, and at about 12:30 p.m. came into contact with Yankees from Maj. Gen. George Sykes's Second Division, V Corps, advancing toward the east along the Orange Turnpike. After some brief skirmishing McLaws's forces threatened to flank and surround the North-ern soldiers, and Sykes received orders from Hooker to fall back toward Chan-cellorsville. Lee slowed the advance, apparently concerned that the ease of his army's success might be a ruse designed to lure the graycoats into a trap.[35]

By 4:00 p.m. the Army of the Potomac had withdrawn into a defensive posi-tion east of Chancellorsville. Hooker's line ran southwest from the Rappahan-nock River, following the Mineral Spring Road, hooked around the Chan-cellorsville crossroads, and then west along the Orange Turnpike. Southern horsemen notified the Confederate commander that the flank of Maj. Gen. Oliver O. Howard's XI Corps, stretched out along the turnpike, was in the air. By nightfall, the Confederate line extended from Catharine's Furnace to E. A. Perry's position north of the Old Mine Road, about three miles east of Hooker's defenses.[36]

With the enemy threat apparently contained, McLaws sent Perry and Brig. Gen. W. T. Wofford's Georgia brigade "to scour the country between us & the river [Rappahannock], moving in a westerly direction about four or five miles." The Florida troops led the advance, but the excursion resulted only in the capture of six unwary Federal soldiers by Wofford's skirmishers. The Reb-els returned to their lines, "jaded & wornout, scratched & torn by brambles and briers."[37]

During the night one of those errors occurred that have plagued soldiers throughout history. Perry reported that his brigade had constructed a line of rifle pits, being "very much exhausted, owing to the nature of the country through which they had advanced. About 10 o'clock, I received an order to re-trace my steps, and march up the turnpike road to Major-General McLaws' position. I did so, and having arrived with my brigade near McLaws' head-quarters, received an order revoking the former order, and directing me to move my command back to the position I had just left. Having retaken that position, I remained [there] until morning." Adding to their woes, many Floridians had discarded their coats and blankets during the afternoon, and Lt. Peeler recalled that they "suffered from the cold" that night.[38]

Perry's peregrinations had little effect on the battle of Chancellorsville, but while the Floridians stumbled back and forth through the Wilderness, Lee and Stonewall Jackson met to discuss strategy. Ever the gambler, Lee wanted to maintain the initiative, and with Jackson's wholehearted approval, the Confederate commander decided to divide his army. Already outnumbered two to one, Lee resolved to send Jackson's entire corps on a wide flanking movement to strike Howard's exposed right. Lee's two remaining divisions, 16,000 men commanded by R. H. Anderson and Lafayette McLaws, would divert the Unionists by dashing forward, falling back, and keeping the enemy transfixed until Jackson delivered the killing blow.[39]

In the early morning of May 2, Anderson and McLaws resumed the attack. Throughout this day and campaign, E. A. Perry was at his very best—aggressive, confident, and in complete control. Col. Lang recalled: "Being a small Brigade we were made useful in filling up gaps & vacant places in the line & strengthening weak points." In their first action of the day, the Floridians drove Federal skirmishers back to their trenches, the bluecoats retreating without firing a shot. Col. Lang summed up the day's activities, recording that the Florida Brigade "maneuvered back & forth on Gen. Lee's extreme right . . . without being engaged until near night on the 2nd when our pickets engaged the enemy in his defenses but failed to draw him out."[40]

Gen. McLaws, in his after-action report, averred that he was completely in the dark regarding Jackson's mission, and so was Hooker. After marching all day, at 5:00 p.m. on May 2 Jackson unleashed his corps on Howard's XI Corps. Taken completely by surprise, the Union corps disintegrated in the darkening Wilderness and Jackson pressed the attack past dusk. At this moment of triumph the Confederacy suffered an irreplaceable loss. In one of the war's costliest volleys, a group of North Carolina troops fired into the dark at the sound of approaching riders. Stonewall Jackson, who had been scouting in front of his army, received a mortal wound, dying eight days later. Maj. Gen. J. E. B. Stuart, the veteran cavalry commander, assumed temporary command of Jackson's corps.[41]

Unaware of the momentous events happening just a few miles to the west, around nightfall on the 2nd Perry received orders to march to the center of the Southern line to rejoin R. H. Anderson's division. A. J. Peeler wrote that the Florida boys "marched out three miles crossing the Plank Road two miles below Chancellorsville on said road & will here bivouac for the night."[42]

Along the way, the Flowers received an act of kindness from a brigade in their division. A Georgia soldier with Brig. Gen. A. R. "Rans" Wright's brigade recorded:

> Just before dark Perry's Florida brigade passed us on their way to their position in line; they were apparently worn out, having been skirmishing all day with nothing to eat, but they were in fine spirits. This was the brigade that we routed so in the snow-ball battle last Winter, driving them into their tents; some such expressions as these proved that they recognized us: "Hail, snow ballers, You beat us in snow balling, but we will fight together to-morrow." Our men had just received their three days rations, rushed into the road and unmindful of their own wants, emptied their haversacks [and] shared their last hard crackers with the hungry Floridians.[43]

Before daylight on the morning of May 3, the Army of the Potomac still had an excellent chance to win the battle of Chancellorsville. They had a two-to-one numerical advantage, and three of the five corps had hardly fired a shot. Additionally, the bluecoats had strong defenses; the two wings of the Army of Northern Virginia were still divided, though closing fast; and, Lee's most reliable lieutenant lay on his deathbed. The problem for the Unionists was Hooker. For all his pre-battle boasting, Fighting Joe had lost his nerve, abdicating his leadership responsibilities or making foolish decisions. As an early historian of the battle sarcastically observed: "If that was Hooker's idea of how to fight a battle, Lee's mental graph of his opponent's ability must have shown a sharply descending curve."[44]

At dawn, the Florida brigade marched south toward Catharine's Furnace as R. H. Anderson positioned his division to reconnect with J. E. B. Stuart's force. By 7:30 a.m. Perry's Floridians waited a little southeast of the Confederate artillery concentration at Hazel Grove, and perhaps three-quarters of a mile from the strong Federal defenses at Fairview. Peeler wrote that the brigade "formed a line of battle in an open field on the right of & a little to the rear of one of our batteries which had gained an eminence [Hazel Grove was the highest point on the battlefield] & was making a terrible havoc among the enemy with grape and canister, by an enfilading fire down his entrenchments. The enemy was responding briskly with his batteries at Chancellorsville a quarter of a mile distant, throwing grape & shell over us." To the west, Stuart's troops were already assaulting the Yankee line.[45]

The Florida boys waited until Anderson had his brigades aligned, then marched "into a skirt of woods & then advanced in line of battle upon the enemy's entrenchments." Union abatis delayed, but did not stop, Perry's Flowers. These sharpened logs forced the Floridians to crawl through the obstructions, but once they cleared the tangled brush, they surged toward Fairview. "We reached the entrenchments & were halted for a minute or two," Peeler recalled. "We were formed in line of battle perpendicular to it, the right of the brigade, which was the right of the 5th Regt., resting near it. The enemy opened a shower of grape & canister upon us." Perry ordered his men to lie down to avoid the deadly fire from the Union artillery. Lt. Auld, a devout young soldier who would become a respected Presbyterian minister after the war, proudly recounted what happened next. "Our company Regiment and Brigade acted as became true Floridians, although [subjected to a] raking fire of shell and grapeshot. We lay down and loaded and rising on one knee poured it into them until it got too hot for them, when, as the soldiers say they 'got up and got.'" Perry reported the Yankee retreated in considerable disorder. The enemy, he stated, "broke in the utmost confusion, throwing down arms, knapsacks, & c., great number of them running into our lines."[46]

During this phase of the battle the Florida brigade began losing members of its officer corps. Maj. Walter R. Moore, commanding the Second Florida, and Lt. William Lee, commanding Co. A of the same regiment, fell wounded at Fairview. Moments later, Lt. John G. Raulerson, Co. B, Fifth Regiment, had his head blown off by an artillery shell.[47]

The Federal infantry counterattacked, and the Floridians drove forward to meet the threat. However, as Perry's men charged their foes, elements of Brig. Gen. James Archer's and Brig. Gen. George Doles's brigades retreated through the Florida regiments, causing considerable confusion. The Second and Eighth regiments were brought to a standstill, "but the 5th passed nobly on & opened a deadly fire" upon the Federals. E. A. Perry reported that the confusion primarily affected the Eighth Florida, but claimed they "were rallied at once, their *morale* and spirit in no manner impaired." R. H. Anderson lauded the Florida troops, recalling the "heroic little band of Floridians who showed a courage as intrepid as that of any other in their assaults upon the enemy in his entrenchment on the third [of May] and their subsequent advance to Chancellorsville."[48]

By 10:00 a.m., Hooker ordered his army to retreat from Chancellorsville, falling back to a set of newly constructed entrenchments, leaving the division of Maj. Gen. Winfield S. Hancock as the rearguard. The two wings of the Rebel army had now reunited, and an unofficial truce fell over the shattered, smoldering Wilderness. Lee's graycoats had marched and fought for three days without relief, and they were simply exhausted. The dead needed burying, the wounded needed rescuing from the burning forest, but many Confederates busied themselves scavenging the battlefield. Isaac Auld, the religious young Florida officer, took a pair of shoes from a dead Federal soldier, but this "robbery" troubled his conscience for weeks. Most of the Confederates believed the old adage "To the victors belong the spoils," and had no compunctions about taking whatever they wanted from the Unionists.[49]

The respite for Anderson's division lasted only a few hours. Hooker had been badgering Maj. Gen. John Sedgwick to break through Maj. Gen. Jubal Early's Confederates on Marye's Heights, advance up the turnpike, and fall on the unsuspecting Army of Northern Virginia. The plan had a couple of flaws. First, Lee already knew of Sedgwick's breakthrough and had set in motion a plan to stymie Hooker. This included sending R. H. Anderson, with artillery support, up the Mine Road to block a possible breakout from Hooker's salient. Second, expecting Sedgwick, with less than half of Hooker's numbers, to pull the Union commander's fat out of the fire was patently unrealistic. Still, Sedgwick had little choice but to obey his orders.[50]

Uncle John broke through Early's line on the afternoon of May 3, but several brigades, including Alabama troops commanded by Brig. Gen. Cadmus M. Wilcox, held the superior force at bay near the Salem Church. As night fell, Sedgwick found himself in a trap. Early had slipped in behind the Yankees at Fredericksburg; Wilcox, heavily reinforced, still blocked the turnpike; and additional help was on the way to the Rebels from Chancellorsville.[51]

On the morning of May 4, R. H. Anderson's division, including Perry's Floridians, rushed back toward Fredericksburg to help bag Sedgwick. Anderson's troops entered the fighting with Perry's brigade on the division's left flank.

During this engagement the Floridians received orders to charge a Federal battery across an open field. This caused some trepidation among the veteran troops. John H. Robarts of Co. G, Second Florida reported: "I was eight days in the fight [at Chancellorsville] but on Monday evening [May 4] I thought my time had come. I made up my mind to die. There was a battery of twelve guns in a very large field and General Lee ordered the brigade to charge it. The old

Second was in good spirits all through the fight till it come time to charge that battery. I tell you she cooled down. Not a word could you hear from a man's mouth in the whole brigade." Luckily, a mix-up spared the Florida troops further suffering. As Perry's troops began the advance, Rans Wright's brigade cut between the battery and the Floridians. By the time the lines were untangled, the Union guns had been withdrawn.[52]

Sedgwick chose discretion over a suicidal counterattack, and slipped his troops across the Rappahannock using nearby Scott's Ford. With the threat from Sedgwick ended, Perry's warriors retraced their route back to Chancellorsville in a driving rainstorm. Hooker, who had threatened to have no mercy on Gen. Lee, began to withdraw his forces north of the river on the night of May 5–6.[53]

Chancellorsville was a total disaster for the Federals. The debacle could not be blamed upon the common Union soldier; the fault lay with Hooker's catatonic timidity when confronted by a dangerous foe. The battle was a decisive Confederate victory and a tactical masterpiece on the part of Lee and Jackson. A brilliant triumph, but extremely costly for the South, because the Army of Northern Virginia and its commander never quite recovered from the death of Stonewall Jackson. Confederate casualties totaled 13,000, the Floridians adding 109 to Chancellorsville's grisly butcher's bill.[54]

In late May, Lee reorganized the army. Jackson's death made it necessary to change the army's structure from two corps (Longstreet's and Jackson's) to three. This had the additional benefit of increasing the army's maneuverability. Longstreet retained his unit, and Richard S. Ewell and Ambrose Powell Hill became the new corps commanders, with promotions to the rank of lieutenant general. R. H. Anderson's division, including the Florida brigade, was assigned to A. P. Hill's new Third Corps.[55]

5 "The Green and Pleasant Valley of Pennsylvania"

The Route to Gettysburg

Almost before the smoke cleared at Chancellorsville, Gen. Robert E. Lee set in motion plans for the invasion of Pennsylvania. He had apparently contemplated such a move for several months. In February he had directed Jedediah Hotchkiss, a Northern-born engineer and Stonewall Jackson's cartographer, to prepare a map of the Shenandoah Valley, including routes to Harrisburg and Philadelphia.[1]

Despite some official misgivings regarding the safety of Richmond, by June 1, 1863, Jefferson Davis reluctantly gave final approval for the incursion into the Keystone State. Lee shared the chief executive's concerns about the Confederate capital but felt compelled to undertake the gamble.[2]

The commander of the Southern army could offer myriad reasons to invade Maryland or Pennsylvania. First, the chance to forage for supplies in Pennsylvania's rich valleys served the dual purposes of resupplying his troops and allowing Virginia's beleaguered farmers an opportunity to plant and harvest a crop. Second, a victory near Washington might relieve pressure on Vicksburg and the Army of Tennessee, while also encouraging a growing peace movement in the North. Third, the Confederacy still hoped such a victory might even now lead to recognition by one or more of the European powers. More important, Lee believed that he had only two real options—"retire to Richmond and stand a siege, which must ultimately . . . end in surrender, or . . . to invade Pennsylvania."[3]

After gaining Davis's approval for the campaign, the Confederate commander's first problem involved withdrawing his army from Fredericksburg, while holding Fighting Joe Hooker's numerically superior army in place. He decided upon a simple plan. Lee proposed pulling James Longstreet's and

Richard S. Ewell's corps out of line, a division at a time, while leaving A. P. Hill's soldiers in position near Fredericksburg to keep the Army of the Potomac pinned along the Rappahannock. The Confederate commander directed Hill to make "such dispositions as will be calculated to deceive the enemy, and keep him in ignorance of any change in the disposition of [the Confederate] army." If Hooker attempted to follow Longstreet and Ewell, Hill was to pursue him. If the Federals threw a large force across the Rappahannock, the Third Corps was to retreat south along the right-of-way of the Richmond, Fredericksburg, & Potomac Railroad.[4]

On the morning of June 3, Lee began his withdrawal. Hooker almost immediately learned that the Rebel troops were leaving their positions along the west bank of the Rappahannock. He incorrectly assumed that the graycoats were trying to turn his right flank or attempting to cut him off from Washington's strong defenses. Weighing his options quickly, the Union commander concluded that he could best disrupt the Confederate plan by striking across the Rappahannock.[5]

The first engagement of the Gettysburg campaign began late in the afternoon of June 5, and the Florida brigade suffered the first casualties. Under protection of an intense artillery barrage, which a Union soldier claimed "might almost have been heard in Vermont," engineers of Maj. Gen. Sedgwick's VI Corps pushed two pontoon bridges across the Rappahannock near the mouth of Deep Run. The Second Florida, posted as pickets along the south bank of the river, vigorously contested the incursion. Maj. Wesley Brainerd, an engineer with the Fiftieth New York, recalled: "One after another of my men dropped down and attempted to crawl away, some men hit in the arms, some in the body, others in the legs." The Floridians, a soldier of the Thirteenth Massachusetts Regiment informed a friend, "were pretty stubborn about our crossing, but after being peppered awhile with Artillery, they gave way." A Mississippian located on the bluffs overlooking the river plain observed the action. He noted in his diary that the bluecoats charged "with bands playing and much cheering. . . . [They] drove in our pickets and crossed at Deep Run. Constant skirmishing. A few of our men captured." Lt. William Penn Pigman of Co. H of the Eighth Florida recorded: "The Second Regt was on picket and the Yankees made the attack[—]threw over a regiment or two & took 62 prisoners, 4 officers, 58 privates, 3 killed & 2 wounded."[6]

Despite the ease with which Union troops established the bridgehead near Deep Run, Hooker failed to capitalize on his advantage. One reason for the inactivity involved the Florida prisoners. They apparently convinced their captors that the troop movements that Hooker's cavalry and balloonists had observed were nothing more than a shift necessitated by the reorganization of Lee's army.[7]

Pres. Lincoln also weighed in, expressing his concerns. He warned Fighting Joe of the dangers involved in a full-scale incursion across the river. In the delightfully colorful language of the frontier, Lincoln advised his commander that such an assault would leave him "entangled upon the river, like an ox half over a fence and liable to be torn by dogs front and rear, without a chance to gore one way or kick the other." Hooker briefly waffled, then did nothing.[8]

For the veterans of A. P. Hill's Third Corps, the days following the skirmish at Hamilton's Crossing devolved into a period of watchful monotony. Sgt. David Dunham of the Second Florida noted in his diary that the Florida troops were "in good spirits," and that "a battle is expected to commence [as] the enemy have several batteries in position."[9]

The rough, irrepressible humor of the Confederate soldier provided an outlet to escape the boredom. Some of Brig. Gen. Carnot Posey's Mississippians found a set of carriage wheels. They attached a log to them and rolled their fake artillery onto a bluff overlooking the Federal beachhead and in plain view of the enemy batteries across the Rappahannock. Much to the delight of R. H. Anderson's division, the "Quaker cannon" caused "the enemy to shell pretty steadily for some time." Thereafter, picket skirmishing increased slightly, but both the Union and Confederate commanders seemed content to leave matters as they were.[10]

The stalemate at Fredericksburg ended on the evening of June 13. Fighting Joe notified the Union general in chief, Maj. Gen. Henry W. Halleck, of his withdrawal from the Rappahannock to better protect Washington and his exposed right flank. A heavy rain fell the night of the Yankee retreat, and most Confederates did not realize until the following day that the bluecoats were leaving. As luck would have it, the Second Florida had again drawn picket duty during the night of June 13. This fortunate posting allowed the Floridians to get a measure of revenge for their comrades captured eight days earlier. They scooped up approximately twenty prisoners in the confusion of the Union retreat.[11]

The Florida brigade cooked two days' rations, and around noon on June 14, began the westward march to rejoin Lee's army. Hill's corps covered ten miles the first day, camping for the night on the old Chancellorsville battlefield. Many of Hill's veterans took an opportunity to explore the site of their great victory, coming away chastened and depressed by the experience. Skeletons littered the countryside, unburied or entombed in graves so shallow that bones protruded from the ground. A member of Posey's brigade remembered: "Each of us could recall a friend or relative who had gone down in that fierce engagement only a few weeks before. The very place seemed hallowed by their memory and we reverently invoked their departed spirits and recalled their virtues and gallantry."[12]

The dismal, haunted thickets of the Wilderness brought only feelings of horror and disgust for many observers. James B. Johnson, the adjutant of the Fifth Florida, recalled: "[O]ne sight so impressed me I will never forget it. The Chancellorsville [Chancellor] house had been burned, and the top from the ice house, leaving a hole in the ground ten feet deep and fifteen to twenty feet square. This had been filled with bodies, and a thin covering of dirt thrown over it, through which several streams of blue gas were gushing; plainly visible for some distance. And all along the road for several miles we could see here and there an arm or leg protruding where the rains had washed the dirt from shallow graves."[13]

The following day, the Third Corps got an early start. The day was blisteringly hot, but the graycoats seemed glad to be putting distance between themselves and the charnel house at Chancellorsville. Sgt. James Kirkpatrick, of the Sixteenth Mississippi, noted that discarded overcoats and blankets littered the line of march. Still, R. H. Anderson's men made good time.[14]

By nightfall of the 15th, the Southerners had crossed the Rapidan at Germanna Ford, and camped three miles west of the river. The next day they passed through Culpepper Court House, and on the afternoon of June 17, they camped along the northern bank of Hazel Run. The Confederates had marched four days in heat so intense it caused several cases of fatal sunstroke, but Sgt. Kirkpatrick proudly noted: "The men seem generally to keep up & avoid straggling."[15]

On June 19, Hill's corps crossed through the Blue Ridge Mountains at Chester's Gap and entered the Shenandoah Valley. Rain fell on both the 18th and 19th, bringing the blessing of cooler temperatures and the curse of muddy roads. The Rebels passed on through Front Royal, fording both the north and south branches of the Shenandoah River, before flopping from sheer exhaustion in a swampy field south of Cedarville.[16]

All along the line, the soldiers' chief topic of conversation was their destination. Opinions divided equally between Maryland, Pennsylvania, and Washington, DC. The scenes of desolation that greeted them in the Shenandoah

Valley filled many of Hill's veterans with thoughts of revenge. "The idea of making the North feel some of the rigors and hardships of war was uppermost in our minds," a member of the Forty-eighth Mississippi confided, "and we contemplated with satisfaction the green and pleasant Valley of Pennsylvania, teeming with abundance." A Floridian simply wrote: "The men were fired by the sight of bare chimneys and ruined homes all through the [Shenandoah] Valley."[17]

A. P. Hill's Southerners entered Charles Town on the 23rd to a reception they long and fondly remembered. The women of the community lined the roadside, waving small Confederate banners and cheering the ragged graycoats. Frank Fleming recalled: "We met a most enthusiastic reception passing through Charlestown, Va. [Charles Town, West Virginia]—the place where old [abolitionist martyr] John Brown was executed. The town was crowded with ladies waving handkerchiefs and flags to us as we marched through, keeping steps to our fine brass band playing the 'Marseillaise' Hymn."[18]

Lang's brigade received additional cheer with the arrival of soldiers who had been captured during the skirmish at Hamilton's Crossing (on June 5). Those unfortunates had been exchanged in record time, and in the company of Lts. Pigman, Dubose, and Martin, who were all returning from sick leave, had hurried to rejoin the brigade. They overtook their comrades near the Maryland border.[19]

The Florida brigade entered enemy territory singing "Maryland, My Maryland," but their reception in the Old Line State was a stark contrast to what they had enjoyed at Charles Town. The Floridians crossed the Potomac at the same ford they had used on the way to Antietam. If Lang's men saw this as a portent of evil, none recorded it. Confederate sentiment was strongest in eastern Maryland, particularly in the area around Baltimore, and several Rebels from Anderson's division commented on the coolness of their reception in the western part of the state. Dunham noted in his diary, "Everything looks pretty union," while Kirkpatrick, the Mississippian, found "few signs of sympathy since we crossed the [Potomac] river." A Georgian on Rans Wright's staff was even blunter. "We found but little sympathy for our cause in Maryland, and none in Pennsylvania," he recalled. "I believe if Maryland were untrammeled today, she would vote for the Union."[20]

Yet even in rejection the Floridians found cause for laughter. Adjutant Johnson drolly remembered: "Just across the Potomac, I met a lady, Miss Kate Seevers of Baltimore, an enthusiastic rebel. She told me that Marylanders were just waiting to flock to our army, they will join you by the thousands. We had one old man join us and he had a [epileptic] fit and dropped out the first day. That was all I saw of recruits in passing through Maryland."[21]

On June 26, Hill's weary soldiers trooped up the road from Hagerstown, Maryland, to Greencastle, Pennsylvania. They gave a rousing cheer as they crossed the Mason-Dixon line, then trudged north.[22]

A Georgian described this portion of the Keystone State as "a rich and highly cultivated region thickly dotted with neat farm houses. Across the entire state I notice that no property was injured. One can scarcely think that a large army had but recently marched over the ground." Frank Fleming described the area as "a very rich valley." Residents of south central Pennsylvania, whom Fleming denigrated as a "class of low Dutch," gave the appearance that they "scarcely knew a war was going on."[23]

The Florida chronicler noted with pride that most of the Army of Northern Virginia was abiding by the spirit of Lee's General Order No. 72 forbidding pillaging.

> When we reflect on the number of poor fellows in the army whose houses and property have been entirely destroyed by the brutes whose country we are now invading, and who have driven their families from their homes in a destitute condition, we can only wonder they are not guilty of greater outrages. . . . I rejoice that Gen. Lee's order against it [pillaging] are most positive and forcible, and the Sub-generals use every exertion to enforce it, and prevent plundering. The enemy's conduct in our Country is no reason why we should so degrade ourselves as to become guilty of their brutalities by making war upon women children and defenseless citizens.[24]

Not all the soldiers shared those feelings, however noble. "[Brig. Gen. John D.] Imbodden frankly expressed regret at his lack of authority to burn every town and lay waste to every farm in Pennsylvania." R. H. Anderson's division generally satisfied its urge for revenge in pilfering. Kirkpatrick noted in his diary that "many of the boys [Posey's Mississippians] went out on a foraging expedition & returned well loaded. [S]ome came back drunk." Capt. Council Bryan, commanding Co. C of the Fifth Florida, wrote to his wife that chickens had become an endangered species in the area that his troops visited. The temptations of fat fryers and plump piglets undoubtedly proved too strong for many famished graycoats.[25]

After thirteen days of hard marching, Anderson's division settled down for a period of rest in Chambersburg on June 27. Kirkpatrick described Chambersburg, the county seat of Franklin County, as a "place of some note & elegance," but most of Anderson's Rebels found little good to say about the town or its citizens. Dunham recorded that area residents were primarily "Dutch Dunkards" who seemed "very much afraid of our soldiery." Others found the people of Franklin County openly belligerent and full of contempt for the Rebels.[26]

Capt. Bryan recalled that some of the ladies of Chambersburg had convinced their daughters that they would suffer unspeakable degradations at the hands of the Southern army. One young lady asked a Florida officer when the "ravashings" would begin. To his everlasting credit, the Floridian gallantly replied that he would cut off his right arm before he would ever hurt a lady.[27]

In one of the few examples of positive interaction between area residents and the gray-clad soldiers, Lt. Pigman reported that several town women attended the divine services of E. A. Perry's troops. Such religious fellowship was far too rare. All things considered, it is probably fair to say that both groups were happy when they parted company.[28]

The few days at Chambersburg provided Anderson's division with much-needed rest and provisions, but the men soon grew restless. Confederate morale was sky high. A little-remembered incident at Chambersburg further strengthened the perception that the Keystone State would be an easy conquest. Sometime during their stay in Franklin County, some of Lang's troops had a brief skirmish with the Pennsylvania militia. In the action the Rebel soldiers took prisoner three or four soldiers who ran slower than their comrades. Such cowardice in defense of their homes caused Hill's corps to believe that Pennsylvania would be easy to subdue. Francis Fleming caustically observed that the only troops in the area were "raw militia, who have never yet 'smelt gunpowder.'"[29]

On the last day of June, Hill's men finally received orders to cook rations and prepare to march at 4:00 a.m. During the night Longstreet's corps filed past their camp, heading east.[30]

On June 27, from his headquarters near Harpers Ferry, Fighting Joe Hooker had telegraphed a request to be relieved of command of the Army of the Potomac. Pres. Lincoln accepted the resignation, apparently without regret. Hooker, in the words of historian Harry W. Pfanz, "fought his magnificent army poorly at Chancellorsville," and his attempts to intercept Lee's army had proven equally inept. The army and the politicians in Washington had lost faith in Hooker. Worse yet, the general seems to have lost confidence in himself.[31]

Lincoln picked Maj. Gen. George Gordon Meade to replace Hooker. A West Pointer, Mexican War veteran, and son of a prominent Philadelphia family, Meade was tall, gaunt, bald, and something of a curmudgeon. Charles A. Dana, the assistant secretary of war, reported that Meade had the "worst possible temper, especially toward subordinates. I think he had not a friend in the whole army."[32]

When Lee learned of the Army of the Potomac's change of leadership is unknown, but apparently it did not particularly concern Marse Robert. Coddington suggests: "Any benefits the Union army might have gained from the promotion of Meade, Lee felt were offset by the timing of the move. A major change of this sort usually required a period of adjustment for the new commander, in which waste motion occurred with a corresponding reduction in the army's efficiency."[33]

The appointment of Meade little concerned the Florida troops, if they knew about it at all. The élan exhibited by the Florida brigade—and the entire Army of Northern Virginia—as the Pennsylvania battle commenced bordered on hubris. Sgt. John S. Bird of the Second Florida informed his aunt: "We have a mighty foe to contend with tis true. But they are not our equals in battle, if Genl Lee can meet them with one to their three you need have no fear."[34]

6   "Any Man Is Lucky That Comes Out Yet Alive"

The Battle of Gettysburg

The morning of July 1, 1863, dawned hot and humid atop South Mountain. By first light, the Army of Northern Virginia was already on the march, with R. H. Anderson's troops taking the road from Chambersburg to Gettysburg. E. A. Perry's brigade, commanded by Col. David Lang while the general recuperated from a bout with typhoid fever, served as the army's rear guard. The Eighth Florida drew the unenviable task of eating the dust of Lee's forces while tagging along in the back with the wagon train. A few showers sprang up during the day, but the rain did little except briefly settle the dirt.[1]

With the sure intuition of veteran troops, the graycoats seemed to know a battle was brewing. They had confidence in their generals, and past history had proven that they could defeat the Army of the Potomac, even against long odds. A Floridian summed up the feelings of Gen. Lee's Confederates. "[Our] army was full of life and confidence, flushed with recent victories, though we had been on the march for more than a month in all kinds of weather except cold, and part of the time marching day and night on short rations, foot sore, ragged, and some barefoot, [we remained] jovial and in good health, good rifles, and plenty of ammunition, we thought we could whip Meade's army and capture the city of Washington."[2]

At the foot of South Mountain, Anderson halted his division near the township of Cashtown. Anderson noted: "Shortly before our arrival at Cashtown, the sound of brisk cannonading near Gettysburg announced an engagement in our front." They waited there an hour before Dick Anderson received orders from A. P. Hill to bring his division forward, and after summoning the Floridians from the rear, Anderson and his troops headed toward the sound of the engagement. The corps commander assigned Anderson's men to hold the high

ground along Herr Ridge, filling a gap in the line left when Hill had directed
Maj. Gen. Dorsey Pender's division into the fight. There they waited through
the first day of the battle of Gettysburg.[3]

One of Perry's men recorded that they "had one or two little skirmishes with
the enemy," but they must have been very minor indeed, as no mention has been
uncovered from other sources. Another recalled: "We reached the battlefield
on the 1st day's fight at dark and took position in line of battle at the center of
the army and just to the right of town where we lay under heavy fire until the
next day."[4]

Around dawn on July 2, Dick Anderson moved his division southeast to
Seminary Ridge. James B. Johnson, the adjutant of the Fifth Florida, wrote
that "July 2nd was a cloudless day and the heat was intense." The Florida brigade spent the morning waiting impatiently for the inevitable attack. Johnson
recounted: "We knew there was desperate fighting ahead of us and [the men]
chafed at the delay. Some of the men spent the time in playing cards."[5]

Gen. Lee decided to try an *en echelon* assault upon the Union left flank on
July 2. This method of attack, favored by many Civil War generals, called for
a series of brigades to charge, one after another, along the enemy's line of defenses. In theory, the advantage of the en echelon assault derived from the
natural tendency of the generals being assailed to call for reinforcements, thus
allowing later attackers to hit a weak spot or gap and break the line. In reality,
this type of attack seldom worked as planned, but Lee's confidence in his army
made him willing to take the risk.[6]

The Union commander had made the most of the terrain in forming his
army's defensive position. Maj. Gen. O. O. Howard's XI Corps occupied the
northern section of the Federal line, just east of the junction of the Emmitsburg-
Taneytown roads; Maj. Gen. W. S. Hancock's II Corps held the center; and
Meade had directed Maj. Gen. Daniel E. Sickles to connect his III Corps
to Hancock's left, extending the Cemetery Ridge line to Little Round Top.
Sickles instead moved his troops into the rolling ground fronting the Emmitsburg Road. The arrogant general almost cost Meade the battle. Historian
Harry W. Pfanz described the situation as follows: "Meade's army established
a fishhook-shaped line that embraced Culp's Hill on its right, Cemetery Hill
and Cemetery Ridge south two miles to the two hills known as the Round
Tops. . . . At noon Major General Daniel E. Sickles, commanding the Union
Third Corps, committed a dangerous blunder—he advanced his 10,000-man
corps from Cemetery Ridge near Little Round Top to high ground along the
Emmitsburg Road between the [Seminary and Cemetery] ridges."[7]

The Confederate commander's projected offensive would start with the division of Maj. Gen. John Bell Hood assailing the Unionists in the Devil's Den and on the Round Tops. This would be followed by Maj. Gen. Lafayette McLaws's troops attacking the Yankees in the Wheatfield and Peach Orchard, and R. H. Anderson's units would continue the assault upon the III Corps troops along the Emmitsburg Road. Dick Anderson's brigades, facing Meade's strong defenses along Cemetery Ridge, were positioned from left to right, as follows: Brig. Gen. William Mahone's Virginians, Brig. Gen. Carnot Posey's Mississippians, Brig. Gen. Rans Wright's Georgians, Col. David Lang's Floridians, and Brig. Gen. Cadmus Wilcox's Alabamians.[8]

In the early morning of July 2, Lang positioned his brigade on the eastern edge of Spangler's Woods behind a stone wall. Lang later wrote to early Gettysburg historian John Bachelder that the Florida regiments "occupied on the 2nd day July 1863, the line of the eastern edge of the grove [Spangler's Woods], whence we had a full view of the heights opposite, and the enemy's position. Captain Council A. Bryan who commanded the right flank (5th Fla. Regt.), on the evening of the 2nd after the repulse, is positive that his right was on the extreme edge of the grove, while the left of Wilcox's brigade was some hundred yards or more to his right, and rear." Maj. Walter R. Moore commanded the Second Florida, which numbered 242 men. Moore had been wounded at Chancellorsville, but rejoined his unit in time for the Gettysburg engagement. Capt. Richmond N. Gardner directed the brigade's largest regiment, the 324-man Fifth Florida. With Lang in command of the brigade, Lt. Col. Baya led the Eighth Florida, which totaled only 176 men.[9]

Anderson's men had to wait until McLaws's final brigade, Brig. Gen. William Barksdale's Mississippians, became fully engaged with Sickle's III Corps along the Emmitsburg Road. That would be the signal for Wilcox to begin the assault, followed in order by Lang, Wright, Posey, and Mahone. David Lang noted: "About 5 p. m. I received an order from General Anderson to the effect that General Longstreet was driving back the enemy's left, and that Wilcox would advance whenever General Longstreet's left advanced beyond him. I was ordered to throw forward a strong line of skirmishers, and advance with General Wilcox, holding all the ground the enemy yielded."[10]

At about 6:00 p.m. Wilcox's Alabamians began their advance. Lang's Floridians soon followed suit, aligned with the Second Florida on the left, the Eighth Florida in the center, and the Fifth Florida on the right. As they advanced, some of the Second Georgia battalion, acting as Wright's skirmishers, intermingled and advanced with Perry's Flowers.[11]

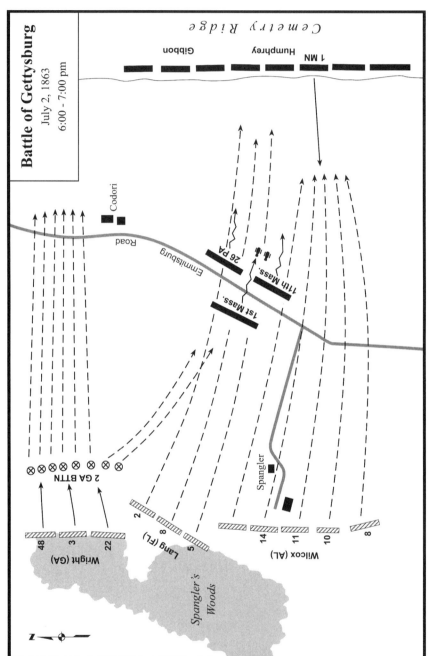

Fig. 7. Battle of Gettysburg, July 2, 1863

Lang's brigade advanced at the "double quick," exposed from the outset to a deadly artillery and musket fire from Maj. Gen. A. A. Humphrey's division along the Emmitsburg Road. Lang recalled that they "moved forward, being met at the crest of the first hill with a murderous fire of grape, canister, and musketry." J. B. Johnson concurred, vividly recounting that the "enemy's guns [were] making great gaps in our lines, and the air seem[ed] filled with musket balls, our men [were] falling on all sides."[12]

Near the Emmitsburg Road the Floridians made first contact with Brig. Gen. Joseph B. Carr's brigade, the right flank of Humphrey's division. The First Massachusetts, serving as brigade skirmishers just west of the thorough-fare, fought with determination, but could not withstand the Florida graycoats' advance. Next Lang's troops engaged the Twenty-sixth Pennsylvania and Eleventh Massachusetts. The Flowers quickly outflanked the Federal units and drove them in considerable disorder toward Cemetery Ridge.[13]

The post-battle accounts of these Union regiments pay tribute to the tenacity of the Florida troops and the ferocity of their attack. A member of the First Massachusetts reported: "The regiment . . . made a stubborn resistance to the advancing enemy, retaining its position until the Confederates were at close quarters and losing many men and some prisoners, being finally forced back. . . . The balance of the regiment formed a line on the extreme right of the brigade and there lost heavily and, with the brigade, contested every foot of the ground while being pressed back." Maj. Robert L. Bodine, commanding the Twenty-sixth Pennsylvania, wrote: "I never before [have] seen such desperation on the part of the rebels, who hurled their columns upon us in masses. . . . My regiment lost 202 out of 376 engaged." A soldier of the Eleventh Massachusetts furnished the following graphic account of his unit's part in the fight: "The left of the division had been forced to fall back, so that the troops were subjected in certain positions to volleys from three distinct points [directions], and the men retreated foot by foot, while thousands pierced by Minie balls, or torn asunder by the explosion of the infernal shell-bullets fell, and saturated the plain with their blood."[14]

Gen. A. A. Humphrey, a West Pointer, kept his men fighting by his example, courage, and iron will, recalling, "[T]wenty times did I bring my men to a halt & and face about [to fire], myself & . . . my staff forcing the men to do it." Despite his efforts, Lang and Wilcox drove Carr's men back. Lang reported, "[T]he enemy fell back beyond their artillery, where they were attempting to rally when we reached the crest of the second hill. Seeing this, the men opened a galling fire upon them, thickly strewing the ground with their killed and wounded. This threw them into confusion, when we charged them, with a yell, and they broke and fled in confusion into the woods and breastworks beyond leaving four or five pieces of cannon in my front." Lt. William Penn Pigman of the Eighth Florida boasted that the Federals were driven "like chaff" for "at least a mile." Unable to stand any longer, Carr's Federals retreated to Cemetery Ridge, rapidly pursued by Lang's men.[15]

Advancing through the field beyond the Emmitsburg Road, the Florida brigade descended a gentle slope, and Lang halted his men in the bottom of a ravine near the base of Cemetery Ridge to catch their breath and re-form. During the brief stop, Yankee fire continued unabated, and the Florida officers hurried to get the brigade properly aligned.[16]

Men such as Lt. John Day Perkins and Lt. Anderson J. Peeler held the line together and moving forward. As the Floridians prepared to again advance, a canister round exploded near Perkins of Co. M, Second Florida, blowing off part of his left foot and shattering a hand. He fell to the ground and lay on the battlefield for a day and a half. To stem the bleeding of his appendage, Perkins coated the foot with mud. Union colonel Regis de Trobriand and his aide found the injured Floridian on the morning of July 4 and took him to the rear. Federal doctors amputated his left leg and thumb, and despite a grim prognosis, Perkins recovered. Peeler also won accolades from his comrades. One recalled, "[A] braver man than Lieut. Peeler never breathed. . . . He dashed up and down the line, hurrahing, and encouraging the men on, and keeping the line dressed on Wilcox. He was wounded by a grape-shot, and stunning him awhile, but after recovering, he advanced, cheering on the men, and setting them an example worthy of imitation . . . until he was again shot down by a minie ball, wounding him seriously in the head, when he was carried to the rear where he fell into the hands of the enemy."[17]

With a breakthrough of the enemy lines seemingly within their grasp, Wilcox, Lang, and Wright sent aides to plead with R. H. Anderson to dispatch Posey and Mahone's troops to help them. The two commanders felt that a vigorous assault by 3,000 veteran reinforcements would destroy the Yankee's position on Cemetery Ridge and ensure a Confederate victory. Anderson reportedly assured the staff officers that he would send in his two remaining brigades, but the Mississippi and Virginia graycoats still had not arrived.[18]

Lang related that as he re-formed the brigade "an aide from the right informed me that a heavy [enemy] force had advanced upon General Wilcox's brigade, and was forcing it back." This "heavy" unit appears to have been the

262-man First Minnesota Regiment, directed by Col. William Colville Jr. Maj. Gen. Winfield Scott Hancock, arguably the Army of the Potomac's finest combat officer, had seen Humphrey's line break apart and did what he could to salvage the situation. To buy time, Hancock ordered the regiment from the North Star State to attack Wilcox's Alabamians in what amounted to a suicide charge. In the haze and smoke of battle, the battalion-sized First Minnesota's determined assault had been mistaken for the attack of a much larger unit.[19]

Lang weighed the odds and decided to resume the advance. The Flowers still thought they could take the ridge, but Hancock had managed to locate the Nineteenth Maine, a relatively fresh unit, and positioned it to halt the Floridians. After the remnants of Humphrey's units stumbled over the prone 400-man Pine Tree State regiment, the bluecoats rose up and fired a volley into Lang's ranks. The Florida commander reported, "[A] heavy fire of musketry was poured upon my brigade from the woods 50 yards immediately in front, which was gallantly met and handsomely replied to by my men." The color bearer of the Eighth Florida fell, and the two sides exchanged salvos at ranges less than fifty yards, while Union batteries poured grape and canister into the thinning ranks of the Florida brigade.[20]

By this time Lang's troops had advanced more than a 100 yards closer to Cemetery Ridge than Wilcox's Alabama boys, who were now retreating. Another aide informed the Florida commander that Wilcox had fallen back and that the Federals had moved far beyond Lang's right flank. Clearly unwilling to stop when victory seemed to be within their grasp, Lang went to the right to check the situation for himself. He "discovered that the enemy had passed me more than 100 yards, and were attempting to surround me." With the brigade unsupported on its right flank and the Floridians in danger of being encircled, Lang reluctantly ordered his troops to fall back to the Emmitsburg Road, some 300 yards to the rear.[21]

During the withdrawal the Federal artillery continued to pound the retreating Flowers. Lt. James Wentworth of the Fifth Florida recalled that the bluecoats "poured a perfect torrent of grape canister and shell after us with terrible effect." Perhaps Lang supposed that they would meet Anderson's promised reinforcements along the thoroughfare, but they found only continued death and destruction.[22]

Lang's battered troops attempted to re-form along the Emmitsburg Road, but the position offered no cover for the Floridians. The land along the pike was flat as a griddle. Reluctantly, the Flowers fell back to their starting point at the eastern edge of Spangler's Woods, and remained there throughout the night. The charge had cost the brigade 300 casualties, about 40 percent of its overall strength.[23]

The July 2 assault had decimated the command structure of the Second Florida. Maj. Moore fell with a wound in the thigh and was later captured. Command then devolved upon Capt. William D. Ballantine, who had experience directing the regiment at Sharpsburg, but Ballantine also fell wounded minutes later. The next ranking officer, Capt. Alexander Moseley of Co. H, fainted from exhaustion on the retreat and the bluecoats later took him prisoner. Captain C. Seton Fleming of Co. G then assumed command of the Second Florida. He would lead the unit on the following day. Another Second Florida officer killed in action was Capt. R. G. Jerkins of Co. B, who had survived a wound at Seven Pines and had been promoted to the captaincy only the previous month.[24]

The charge had also taken a heavy toll on the Fifth Florida. Capt. Gardner suffered a severe wound to his arm, and Lt. Joel C. Blake of Co. K died leading his men. Blake's body was "so completely mutilated . . . that it was never found." Capt. John Frink of Co. F. was also killed at the head of his company, and Capt. William Bailey Jr. of Co. G fell wounded and Union soldiers took him captive. (He would die the following year in the Yankee prison at Hilton Head, South Carolina.) Capt. J. S. Cochran and Lt. J. A. Shaw, both of Co. D, each received mortal wounds during the assault. With Gardner incapacitated, Capt. Council Bryan commanded the unit the next day.[25]

Lt. Col. Baya remained in command of the Eighth Florida throughout the engagement, but the regiment, situated in the center of the brigade, suffered severe losses. Capt. Thomas Love of Co. B went down, shot through both knees, while Capt. Taliaferro B. Livingston of Co. H was wounded and captured. Capt. Love lingered in agony long enough to compose a letter stained with his own blood but filled with comfort and spiritual consolation to his family in Quincy. According to Lt. Pigman, the unit came out of the fight with only four officers "alive and unwounded." The color bearer and the entire color guard had been either killed or wounded, and as a result, the unit's banner was left on the field. Sgt. Thomas Horan of the Seventy-second New York "captured" the flag and received the Medal of Honor for his daring exploit.[26]

The Floridians knew how close they had come to success, and the lack of support they received caused considerable frustration. They had advanced more than a mile under punishing artillery, musket, and small-arms fire and engaged four Union regiments. In the process, they suffered severe casualties, including numerous valuable officers. Little wonder that Francis Fleming bitterly complained: "Had two or three Brigades been sent to support us we could have held [the] position that it cost us so dearly to take."[27]

The Floridians were not alone in wondering why Anderson and A. P. Hill did not send in Posey's and Mahone's large, battle-tested brigades. The survivors of the Army of Northern Virginia began to debate this question as early as the evening of July 2, 1863. No one has really come up with a definitive answer, but there have been a couple of commonly accepted theories. Because of Hill's sickness (an all-too-common event during the closing months of the war) he failed to exercise tight control on his divisional commander. Others tend to place the blame on Anderson, concluding: "Left to his own devices in his first battle under Hill, Anderson was indecisive and sloppy in his actions." Lt. Col. Hilary A. Herbert of the Eighth Alabama later claimed that "Gen. Anderson came out in a letter or interview . . . and said that when Capt. Winn [Wilcox's aide] gave him Wilcox's message Gen. A. P. Hill was not to be found, [and] that Gen. Hill had ordered him to keep two Brigades in reserve & that he had obeyed orders." Whatever the truth might be, there was plenty of blame to go around for both Hill and Anderson, and many soldiers believed their commanders had allowed defeat to be snatched from the jaws of victory.[28]

While the Floridians settled back into Spangler's Woods, the Federals began searching the battlefield. Maj. Bodine of the Twenty-sixth Pennsylvania sent his men out with a specific purpose in mind. "We were armed with the Austrian rifle of an inferior quality and I desired to change them for Springfield rifles . . . without the red tape processes. . . . The brigade we opposed [Lang's Floridians] were all armed with the Springfield rifles. Many of them had gone through the renovating process, and bore the Richmond C. S. stamp." A member of the Eleventh Massachusetts came upon a wounded youth "who was crying, and stated the causes of his grief, that 'Gen. Lee always puts the Fifth Florida in the front.'"[29]

All through the night Gen. Robert E. Lee plotted his strategy for July 3. His plan encompassed a great deal more than the commonly held belief that the Confederate commander sent Pickett's division in a futile frontal attack against the Union center. Three of his units were to advance in a series of coordinated assaults—Lt. Gen. Richard S. Ewell against Culp's Hill; J. E. B. Stuart's cavalry against the rear; and 12,000 men of Maj. Gen. George Pickett's, Brig. Gen. J. J. Pettigrew's, and Maj. Gen. Isaac Trimble's divisions against the Union center. In a precursor to the oft-used World War I strategy, fifty-five Rebel cannon would soften up the enemy line before Pickett's charge. A. P. Hill's Corps would serve as Lee's "only reserve."[30]

Early on the uncomfortably hot morning of July 3, Col. Lang received orders to support Pickett's charge. He reports: "I received orders from General Anderson to connect my right with General Wilcox's left, and conform my movements during the day to those of his brigade. I was at the same time notified that I would receive no further orders." Anderson must have decided on this arrangement after realizing that once the bombardment commenced, communication would be hazardous. The directions for both units would be conveyed only to Wilcox.[31]

Shortly thereafter Anderson directed Wilcox to move his brigade forward and assume a supporting position near Col. E. P. Alexander's line of artillery. As per his orders, Lang brought the Florida units forward as well, taking a position to Wilcox's left, in a depression behind the artillery massed for the cannonade. According to Raymond Jenckes Reid, a member of the Second Florida and a former territorial governor's son, the Flowers built "quite a formidable breast works" from fence rails and used bayonets to strengthen them with dirt. Wright's, Posey's, and Mahone's brigades remained far to the rear.[32]

After the costly attack the previous day, Lang and Wilcox had little confidence in their current situation, mission, or the wisdom of Hill and Anderson. They most assuredly felt little enthusiasm for again charging Cemetery Ridge. Lang related an exchange between the two brigade commanders regarding their probable orders and duties as soldiers. "I called upon Gen. Wilcox," Lang wrote, "and asked what he intended to do if he was ordered to assault after Pickett's division was repulsed, as we both felt confident it would be. He replied, in substance, that he would not again lead his men into such a deathtrap. But said I, suppose your orders are imperative and admit of no discretion in the matter? Then, said he, I will do so under protest. Then I told him my reason for asking this question, to wit, that I had been ordered to conform my movements to his." Lang's writings show he had no illusions of victory on July 3. "[W]e were confident that what Anderson's division had failed to do on the 2nd, Pickett could not do 24 hours later when the enemy had reinforced his line."[33]

The Confederate cannonade, designed to soften up the Union defenses, began at 1:00 p.m. Johnson described the bombardment as "one continuous and awful roar." Raymond Jenckes Reid wrote that "the earth trembled beneath us. We could not raise our heads." When the fire finally slackened, Brig. Gen. J. L. Kemper's brigade, of Pickett's division, passed over Lang's prostrate men and

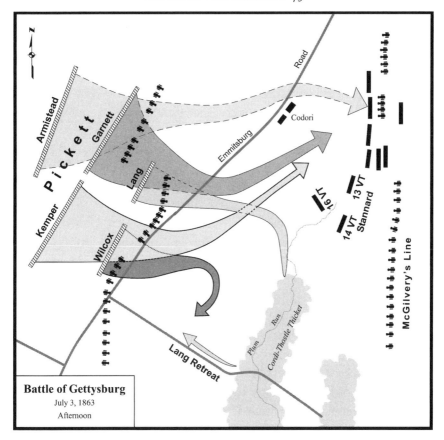

Fig. 8. Battle of Gettysburg, July 3, 1863

began to advance. Once they reached the Emmitsburg Road, "Kemper's Virginians made a left oblique movement," but Wilcox and Lang apparently failed to notice the shift in direction.[34]

It is clear from the Lang letters that Pickett's charge had already failed before the Florida brigade started its advance. Lang later informed Gen. Perry: "As soon as Pickett's Division had retired, we were thrown forward (as a forlorn hope, I suppose), notwithstanding the repulse of the day before, and the repulse of Pickett's whole Division, not twenty minutes before." Wilcox concurred. He reported that his orders were "to advance to the support of Pickett's division . . . [but] not a man of the division that I was ordered to support could I see."[35]

Despite the obvious mistake, the Alabama commander directed his 1,000-man unit to advance. Lang heard Wilcox's orders to move forward, and repeated them to his troops. The Florida brigade, numbering about 400 men, was on Wilcox's left and aligned in the same order as the previous day. The Second Florida advanced on the left, the Eighth Florida occupied the center position, and the Fifth Florida moved forward on the right. Rather than veering left at the Emmitsburg Road, the Florida and Alabama warriors drove straight at Cemetery Ridge, following roughly the same path they had traversed the previous day.[36]

The soldiers in the ranks had even less confidence in their mission than Lang and Wilcox. Lt. Pigman noted that the orders were not well received. He recalled that "knowing what we had to encounter, it was not obeyed with the same alacrity as was the case yesterday." The men had been lying flat in the depression for hours under a blazing sun and deafened by the massive artillery barrage, and some troops discovered they "could hardly go [forward]."[37]

The Floridians advanced unscathed until they neared the Emmitsburg Road. There they began to take heavy artillery fire from "an imposing assembly of thirty-nine Union cannon, under the supervision of Lt. Col. Freeman McGilvery" posted atop Cemetery Ridge. The Federal artillery blasted Lang's ranks with case shot until they approached the ridge, then McGilvery switched to double canister. The accurate Yankee salvos tore great gaps in Lang's lines. Raymond Jenckes Reid observed that "as we raised the Yell they poured a deadly fire of grape and canister upon us. On we rushed. Our men fell fast and thick. At last we were flanked." James Wentworth of the Fifth Florida penned a more vivid description of this phase of the Florida attack. The Flowers charged "amid a terrible shower of shell grape canister, and bullets. It was the hottest work I ever saw. My men falling all around me with brains blown out, arms off, and wounded in every direction." An exploding shell knocked Wentworth to the ground, unconscious.[38]

As the Floridians neared the base of Cemetery Ridge, Brig. Gen. George Stannard's Vermont brigade, of the Union I Corps, was situated in a perfect position to counter the new Rebel attack. One of Stannard's units, the Sixteenth Vermont, had just helped repulse Kemper's Virginia regiments on the right flank of Pickett's division, and now Col. Wheelock G. Veazey, commanding the Vermonters, turned his Green Mountain infantry about and prepared to launch an assault on the Alabama and Florida troops. Stannard's divisional commander, Maj. Gen. Abner Doubleday, watching from the crest of Cemetery Ridge, urged his unit on, waving his hat and shouting: "Glory to God, glory to God! See the Vermonters go in."[39]

Lang saw the Sixteenth Vermont approaching, and sent his adjutant J. B. Johnson to the rear to request artillery support. The gunners informed Johnson that they had expended all their long-range ammunition. Realizing his vulnerability, Lang decided to abandon the attack. The Florida commander sent orders to his regimental commanders "to move by the right flank as soon as they reached the woods in front." The "woods" were a woodlot known as the Codori-Trostle Thicket. Lang apparently hoped that the trees would offer shelter from Federal artillery fire and give him time to prepare his men to either oppose the Federals or withdraw. Wilcox, being sheltered from the Vermont infantry by the Florida lines on his left, quickly ordered his Alabamians to fall back, noting "the enemy did not pursue." They did pursue, of course, just not Wilcox's troops. Gen. Longstreet's "forlorn hope" ended before it had fairly begun.[40]

The Sixteenth Vermont, joined by the Fourteenth Vermont, now turned its full attention on Lang's hapless Flowers. The Green Mountain troops advanced toward the Florida brigade just before the graycoats entered the belt of trees straddling Plum Run. The Floridians entered the woods, taking cover behind the rocks and trees. McGilvery's batteries continued to rain blasts of canister directly into the Codori-Trostle Thicket from a range of about two hundred yards, and casualties kept mounting. Capt. Council Bryan fell wounded and Capt. John Holleyman assumed command of the Fifth Florida. N. W. Eppes carried Bryan from the field and then returned to tote another injured comrade to safety.[41]

The sounds of battle made it difficult for Lang to communicate with his remaining officers. Lang explained: "The noise of artillery and small-arms was so deafening that it was impossible to make the voice heard above the din, and men were by this time so badly scattered in the bushes and among the rocks that it was impossible to make any movement to meet or check the enemy advance." Lang concluded that he had no choice but to retreat. "Unsupported by either infantry or artillery," he wrote, "with infantry on both flanks and in front and artillery playing upon us with grape and canister, [remaining] was certain annihilation." Unfortunately, Lang's order did not spread swiftly enough to reach all the men scattered among the boulders and trees.[42]

The Sixteenth Vermont descended into the woods and slammed into the left flank of the Second Florida. In his after-action report Lang stated: "I ordered a retreat, which, however, was not in time to save a large number of the Second Florida Infantry, together with their colors, from being cut off and captured by the flanking force on the left. Owing to the noise and scattered condition of the men . . . I am afraid that many men, while firing from behind rocks and trees, did not hear the order, and remained there until captured."[43]

The loss of the Second Florida's flag gnawed at the souls of the brigade's survivors until the unit's last veteran died. The beautiful silk banner, inscribed with the honors "Williamsburg" and "Seven Pines" and bearing a unique sunburst design, held a special place in their hearts, and they considered having that emblem taken by the enemy as a blemish on their outstanding record. D. M. Pogue of Co. E carried the flag into battle, and when a cannon round blew off his left foot, he passed the banner to Ruebin Cobb of Co. F. A short time later Cobb fell, wounded, and scavenging bluecoats found the flag lying in the woods.[44]

The Fifth Florida had better luck with their banner. The regiment lost several different color bearers, but during a brief clash with the Vermonters, Lt. Junius Taylor tore the flag from its staff and stuffed it into his shirt. The Fifth Florida's flag was the brigade's only regimental banner not captured at Gettysburg. Lovingly concealed and preserved during Reconstruction, today the banner occupies a place of honor at the Florida State Archives in Tallahassee.[45]

Lt. James Wentworth was not as fortunate as his unit's banner. Knocked unconscious by an artillery round, he awoke, groggily jumped to his feet, and began urging his nonexistent soldiers to give the enemy hell. Wentworth recorded in his diary that a Vermont private approached him and stated that "they would give me hell if I did not surrender." The young officer quickly stood down and was taken captive.[46]

The retreating Floridians had to endure Federal artillery fire all the way back to the Confederate lines. Lang's brigade retreated up a shallow ravine that offered some small protection until it crossed the Emmitsburg Road. The Flowers eventually arrived near Alexander's row of artillery and settled back behind their makeshift defenses.[47]

During the retreat Capt. William E. McCaslan, the acting adjutant of the brigade, remarked to Capt. Seton Fleming "that no matter how one escaped the dangers of any particular battle, he was exposed to the same in the next, and it seemed impossible to pass in safety through them all." These words had barely left his mouth when a cannonball struck his head, killing him instantly. The loss of Capt. McCaslan "[was] deeply lamented by the whole Brigade."[48]

Lang's Florida soldiers lost a further 20 percent in killed, wounded, and captured on July 3. It seemed that any evil that could befall a soldier in combat was visited upon the men from the southernmost state. A small squad of Floridians directed by Lt. Pigman found itself surrounded and surrendered to the Green Mountain troops. Company G of the Eighth Florida suffered severely in killed, wounded, and captured on July 3, and had only five men fit for duty the next day. Capt. Joshua Mizell fell into enemy hands and died the following spring at the Union prison at Johnson's Island, Ohio. Semiliterate John R. Hodges may have summed up the feelings of all the Florida troops regarding the Pennsylvania campaign. Hodges informed his mother that he "was knocked down by a bomb [artillery shell] but I think any man is lucky that comes out yet alive."[49]

The Wilcox/Lang attack came too late to affect the outcome of the battle. Several historians have bemoaned their vain and needless sacrifice. Jeffry Wert observed that "twelve hundred officers and men, exposed to the might of nearly sixty Union cannon in open fields, could not salvage a charge that had already been destroyed." Clifford Dowdey likewise lamented the advance of Lang's Florida unit: "The wreckage of that little brigade, wandering about among the heavy Federal reinforcements after the attack was over, represented the most hopeless waste of all."[50]

For all intents and purposes, the July 3 charge of the Florida brigade ended the battle of Gettysburg. As at Sharpsburg, the Flowers suffered staggering losses. Of the 742 men who marched toward Gettysburg on July 1, 461 had been killed, wounded, or captured. The brigade lost 62 percent of its strength, reportedly the highest casualty rate of any Confederate brigade during the incursion into Pennsylvania. The Second Florida suffered 146 casualties; the Fifth Florida lost 195 men; and, the Eighth had 120 killed, wounded, or captured.[51]

7 "Unwept and Unhonored"

The Retreat from Pennsylvania

The tiny remnant of the Florida brigade, numbering slightly fewer than 300 men, re-formed at its pre-charge position in the depression behind the artillery. No descriptive material is known to exist for Col. Lang's command during the late afternoon on July 3. It must, however, have been a pathetic sight. The slightly wounded, with anguished, powder-blackened faces, joined the healthy few behind the Virginia cannoneers, anxiously peering through the clinging fog of gun smoke for the approach of the enemy.[1]

All about lay the wreckage of the two great armies. The cries, moans, curses, and prayers of the wounded mingled with the rattle of musketry and occasional boom of artillery. The combined stench of the unburied dead and the smell of gunpowder created an indescribably nauseating odor. Both the Rebels and Yankees seemed too weary to continue fighting. "Both armies laid [in] line of battle like two wounded tigers," an officer of Wilcox's Alabama brigade recalled, "tired of the fray, prone on the ground, panting and glaring at each other with bloodshot eyes."[2]

Despite three days of slaughter and the horrid landscape around them, both the Army of Northern Virginia and the Florida brigade remained confident and full of fight. Lt. Col. Hillary A. Herbert, commanding the Eighth Alabama, wrote: "Soon [after re-forming] General Lee . . . rode slowly along our front, the majestic mien of horse and rider, both as calm as a May morning would have tended to reassure us, if reassurance had been necessary. . . . we were not demoralized. Every man of us felt that if the enemy should have attacked our position his repulse would have been as disastrous as ours had been." A common soldier stated the Rebel's feelings more succinctly. "We will fight them until Hell freezes over," he declared, "and then fight them on the ice."[3]

After nightfall, Maj. Gen. R. H. Anderson ordered his division back from its exposed position west of the Emmitsburg Road. But there was no rest for the weary. The Confederates fell back to Spangler's Woods along Seminary Ridge and constructed a defensive line. These works were a "long line of breastworks and rifle pits, extending two and a half miles from the Mummasburg to the Emmitsburg Road. The trees on top of the ridges hid the entrenchments because the Southerners placed them on the western sides of the slopes." Lee undoubtedly hoped Meade might be foolish enough to assault his graycoats the following morning, and he might yet gain the victory.[4]

The blasted battleground may have resembled a suburb of hell, but it literally crawled with activity. Union and Confederate pickets crouched among the dead and dying, and the ambulatory wounded used the cover of darkness to hide their escape. Many men slipped across the killing fields searching for loved ones or close comrades. "Human jackals" used the darkness for the less noble purpose of robbing the dead.[5]

Adj. James B. Johnson, of the Fifth Florida, drew the unenviable duty of leading a small force back onto the battlefield to guard against surprise attacks. "I had to post the picket line," Johnson recalled, "and the dead and wounded literally covered the ground. I ran into a force of Yankees, but they gave back, neither side wanted to make any noise by firing. All night long could be heard the pitiful appeals from the wounded for water, water."[6]

Dawn brought a Fourth of July to Gettysburg that was anything but glorious. Rain fell much of the day in torrents. Many of the soldiers believed that the heavens were crying. Blackened, swollen corpses added to the misery of soggy earth and clothing. Some corpses were now three days old, and the odor of the human and animal detritus caused skirmishers and burial parties alike to retch and gag. A Rebel lieutenant gazed with revulsion at the sight of corpses sitting "upright against a fence, with arms extended in the air and faces hideous with something very like a fixed leer as if taking a fiendish pleasure in showing us what we essentially were and at any moment might become."[7]

A Southern soldier described burying the dead as "the most trying of all the duties of the soldier." Officers detailed men from each company, armed with shovels, to search their area for the dead. The men dug shallow pits and entombed the bodies where they fell. Protecting their fellow human beings from vultures and creeping beasts was the burial party's chief concern. "Sometimes friendly hands cut the name and company of the deceased upon the flap of a cartridge box," even knowing that within a few months "all traces of the dead [will be] obliterated." Not everyone, however, showed such concern for the Confederate dead. A Northern visitor to the battlefield reported: "The rebel dead, almost without exception, are buried promiscuously in single graves or trenches, where they lie unwept and unhonored."[8]

The sorry business of war continued on the Fourth, though it was a sporadic, halfhearted reflex action. Col. Lang reported "a little picket fighting on the 4th," and a member of Posey's brigade noted in his diary: "All quiet on the lines this morning, except a few sharpshooters." The Northern attack that Lee longed for never materialized. A Floridian reported: "On the 4th the enemy showed no disposition to attack us, and we rested."[9]

The Southern evacuation of Pennsylvania began on the afternoon of July 4, with the departure of the Army of Northern Virginia's ambulances and supply wagons. "Ambulances and empty wagons were loaded to their full capacity with the wounded, unable to walk, while hundreds with arms off, or otherwise wounded as not to prevent locomotion," limped along with the column. The sad caravan reportedly stretched for seventeen miles. Lee put generals John D. Imboden's and Fitz Lee's cavalry in charge of protecting the ambulances and supply train.[10]

The Confederates left behind more than 6,000 Rebel soldiers too seriously wounded to be moved. Many of the Florida brigade's most promising officers, including Maj. Moore and Capt. Ballantine, were among those abandoned to the enemy. Surgeons detailed by the Southern army remained to care for the severely wounded. Several officers from the southernmost state were fortunate enough to receive care from Miss Euphemia Goldsborough and other female Southern sympathizers who had rushed to Gettysburg from Baltimore. The rest of Lang's troops, scattered in public buildings and farms around Gettysburg, received competent care from the Federal army's overworked medical staff and charitable organizations.[11]

Among the Florida soldiers left behind was a man who would play a major role in the infamous events of April 1865. Lewis Thornton Powell (also called Payne) was wounded at Gettysburg and captured. After escaping from Federal custody, Powell came under the influence of John Wilkes Booth, who would enlist the impressionable young Floridian in his conspiracy to kill Abraham Lincoln.[12]

The wagons and ambulances containing the Confederate wounded, with their cavalry guard, began their withdrawal from Gettysburg at approximately 4:00 p.m. on July 4. They crossed South Mountain at a gap west of Cashtown before turning south toward Maryland at Greenwood. Hoping to avoid the inevitable traffic jams the wagon train would cause, the infantry and artillery took the shorter route through Fairfield Gap. The foot soldiers and ordinance left as soon as night fell. To delay possible pursuit and deceive the Federals into thinking the Army of Northern Virginia still maintained its position, the graycoats kept fires blazing on Seminary Ridge.[13]

The first night's march proved to be a miserable, harrowing experience for the infantry. Throughout the night rain pelted down in blinding sheets, and the unpaved roads quickly became quagmires. "I soon found that we were in a lane that the artillery and hundreds of wagons and hosts of men had traveled ahead of us," a Floridian recounted, "and the thin mud was in places waist deep. I do not know how many times I fell and went head and ears under." Soldiers who left the roads in an attempt to escape the clinging mud quickly discovered that the difficulty of scaling farmers' cross fences and fording swollen streams made sticking to the thoroughfares easier than blazing new trails.[14]

Despite these difficulties, A. P. Hill's corps made remarkably good time the first night. Sgt. Kirkpatrick reported that the army "marched all night & stopped to rest at the foot of the m[oun]t[ain]s" (apparently the eastern slope of South Mountain).[15]

After three or four hours of fitful rest, Hill's troops began their ascent of South Mountain on July 5 and continued the march to Waynesboro. There they halted for the night. The following morning, mud-splattered and exhausted, Lee's infantry crossed into Maryland, and by the morning of July 7, the Florida brigade arrived at Hagerstown. Here Lang's men found respite, and they quickly began scavenging the area for food and valuables.[16]

While his army relaxed, Lee worried. He realized that the Army of Northern Virginia was trapped in enemy territory. The Confederate chieftain's plan had been to cross the Potomac River on pontoon bridges south of Hagerstown at Williamsport and Falling Waters. The Federal cavalry, however, had destroyed the pontoon bridges at Falling Waters, and three days of heavy rains made fording the Potomac impossible.[17]

Col. E. P. Alexander, Longstreet's artillery commander, reported that he never saw Gen. Lee as agitated, at any time during the war, as he appeared during this time at Hagerstown. After careful consideration, Lee concluded that his only alternative was to prepare his troops for battle, while the Southern pioneers attempted to bridge the Potomac.[18]

The main body of the Army of the Potomac began arriving in front of Hagerstown on July 11, but by then, Confederate engineers had established a strong line of defenses. Anchored on high, hilly ground southwest of Hagerstown, Lee's entrenchments arced along a series of ridges south and east of

Downsville on the Potomac. Conocoheague Creek, a rain-swollen tributary of the Potomac, protected the rear of the Army of Northern Virginia. Lang reported that the Florida brigade formed its line of battle on July 11 "on Salisbury Ridge along Antietam Creek [it was probably Marsh Creek]."[19]

The Confederate commander was obviously still worried about how the defeat at Gettysburg and subsequent retreat had affected his troops' morale. According to Adj. Johnson, "Lee made an address to the army which was read to each command, in which he said, 'We have a swollen and impassable river in front of us and a victorious army in our rear. All I ask of you is the courage which you have shown in every battle, and we will have nothing to fear.'" Actually, "Marse Robert" had no reason to doubt his men's fighting spirit. The Army of Northern Virginia remained confident. "Everyone should be pleased if the enemy should attack us," a Mississippian reported in his diary.[20]

Under intense pressure from Washington, Meade alerted Pres. Lincoln and the War Department of his intention to attack the Rebels on July 14. The bluecoats surged forward at daybreak, but only the Southern rear guard remained. Lee's army was crossing the Potomac.[21]

The evacuation of Maryland proved to be a nightmare for the Confederates. Col. Alexander recalled: "[W]e were marching all night in awful roads, in mud & dark & hard rain & though we had only three miles to go, we were still some distance from the road at sunrise." The heavy rainfall caused the river to rise again. Maj. Gen. Robert Rodes described the scene: "The water was cold, deep and rising. Some small men had to be carried over by their comrades; the water was up to the armpits of a full-sized man." Even with these difficulties, most of the graycoats had crossed the Potomac before the Yankees arrived.[22]

By 11:00 a.m., Union cavalry began to nip at the heels of the Rebels. Enemy pressure intensified on the rear guard, forcing Maj. Gen. Henry Heth to request assistance from A. P. Hill's corps, most of whose members had already crossed back into Virginia. Among the troops that rushed to support Heth was the Florida brigade. Adj. Johnson tersely noted, "We were in the rear guard and we had to fight back the enemy's cavalry two or three times." For once Lang's soldiers escaped without casualties, but some of the "wounded and stragglers" fell into Union hands.[23]

Historians generally view the crossing of the Potomac as the last act of the Gettysburg campaign, but such neat closure leaves part of the story untold. Meade still hoped to capture or destroy part of Lee's army, and he came very close to trapping Ewell's corps in the Shenandoah Valley.[24]

With the arduous crossing completed and the rain-swollen Potomac temporarily separating the combatants, the Army of Northern Virginia moved south a couple of miles and rested (probably near Hainesville). On the 16th of July Hill's corps moved up the Shenandoah to Bunker Hill, Virginia, where it rested for five days. While at Bunker Hill, several sick and slightly wounded Floridians were sent to Winchester for medical attention. With time on its hands, the Florida brigade began the soldier's favorite pastime—guessing the army's destination. "Some suppose we are bound for Richmond," Capt. Council Bryan informed his wife, "some that we will stop at Staunton. I have a leaning on the former opinion." David Lang reported to Gen. Perry (still on sick leave): "Rumors are rife of another crossing into Maryland, but I think it hardly probable."[25]

Meade's army finally crossed the Potomac, and on July 21 the Floridians resumed their southward march. The first day they marched twenty-one miles, crossed the flooded Shenandoah River on pontoon bridges, and arrived at Front Royal near sunset. Capt. Bryan wryly recorded that he "had a good laugh at the stragglers who took a near cut [shortcut] as they supposed and waded two rivers. Good for them."[26]

Though Bryan could find humor in the misfortune of his comrades, the situation faced by the Army of Northern Virginia was no laughing matter. Lee's army was scattered and strung out in a line of march, and Meade recognized a golden opportunity when he saw one. He moved first to gobble up Ewell's corps. Lee had the foresight to station Rans Wright's Georgians at Manassas Gap to guard Ewell's route of retreat. Maj. Gen. William H. French's Federals confronted Wright's troops on July 23, and the Deep South warriors held the gap for several hours against repeated, but somewhat halfhearted, assaults until Ewell's corps reached safety.[27]

On the day of Wright's defense of Manassas Gap, the Florida brigade made a hard march through Chestnut Gap and "camped at our old camp near Flint Hill." Lang's men were issued two days' rations of flour and beef, which they immediately devoured. Their scavenging abilities soon turned up an additional treat. "Some of the boys obtained a lot of wine," Bryan wrote his wife, "impressed at night. They [proceeded] to get gloriously tight. I captured a canteen of it & treated Co. C [Fifth Florida]." Hung over but happy, the Florida brigade continued its retreat at daybreak, traveling over "the worst kind of road" to the Hazel River. The following day, the march concluded when Lang's men "arrived at our old camping ground [with]in one mile of Culpepper [Courthouse]."[28]

As it had fought in the first engagement of the Gettysburg campaign, the

Florida brigade also fought in the last. On August 1, Meade's cavalry drove back Confederate horsemen near the old battlefield at Brandy Station, and A. P. Hill hustled the brigades of Mahone, Posey, and Lang toward the scene of the attack. As the Northern troopers approached Culpepper Courthouse, the Florida, Virginia, and Mississippi infantry intercepted them and drove the bluecoats off after a sharp skirmish. A Floridian reported that Lang's men were "the only brigade of infantry engaged on our side." The Southern foot soldiers pursued the retreating cavalry until darkness forced them to abandon the chase.[29]

Hill described his losses in the firefight as "trifling," but Lang's command suffered 29 casualties, including 6 killed, of 160 engaged in the fight. For the Florida brigade, numbering only 250 men, the loss of 29 men was very significant.[30]

The Gettysburg campaign took a frightful toll on the men from the southernmost state. Still, their spirit and will to fight remained unbroken. Perhaps Capt. Council Bryan's assessment of the Pennsylvania invasion reveals more about the morale, prejudices, and fears of the Florida brigade than any other source. He wrote:

> Our troops are in good fighting order and we are ready for the Blue Bellies any time. I see the Richmond papers gave all credit of the hard fighting in the Centre to Pickett's Division of Virginians, a more cowardly set of fellows never disgraced our uniform than the 2d & 3rd Lines of that Division that went in Battle on the 3rd of July. And Wilcox's Alabamians and the Floridians alone saved the centre from being broken. Gen. Lee himself tried to rally Pickett's Division and could not. When the Secret history of the war is Known, then we will get justice I hope. The men [of the Florida brigade] say that no matter how bravely they act they get no credit for it at home or abroad and I think they are more than half right. The wear and tear of the campaign has made us reckless and if they continue to make our Brigade of 250 men do the work of a full Brigade of 4000 it strikes me there will soon be none left.[31]

8   "Vain Dreams of Glory"

The Newspaper War to the End of 1863

A surly mood seemed to permeate Robert E. Lee's command as it limped along on the retreat from Pennsylvania and Maryland. The Army of Northern Virginia was unaccustomed to losing battles. "Every soldier in our army felt that some great blunder had been made at Gettysburg," a Floridian reported, "and they were sore over it."[1]

Consistent with human nature, a search for scapegoats began immediately. J. E. B. Stuart, A. P. Hill, Richard S. Ewell, and James Longstreet bore the brunt of the punishment dished out by post-battle critics. Even the army's beloved Marse Robert did not escape the finger-pointers. Adj. Johnson remembered: "In going up the steep banks of the Potomac on the South side, a cannon had stalled in the mud[.] I saw General Lee put his shoulder to the wheel and call upon the men passing to help[.] Of course they responded, but for the first time they were silent in passing him[. There was] not a cheer for Lee."[2]

It did not take long for this spirit of acrimony and criticism to filter down to the army's lower levels. The common courage exhibited by Wilcox's Alabamians, Lang's Floridians, and Wright's Georgians should have been enough to silence even the harshest critics, but the Florida brigade soon found itself embroiled in a controversy regarding the failure of the July 2 attack of Anderson's division. In fact, the fight at Gettysburg proved to be merely the prelude to a longer, more painful battle against innuendo and falsehood fought in Southern newspaper columns and military courtrooms. Lang's men were caught in a no-win situation, but they knew they could ill afford to lose this conflict.[3]

The first salvo of the new engagement came from an unlikely source. P. W. Alexander, a respected and normally reliable correspondent for the *Savannah Republican,* authored a widely circulated account of the July 2 action that harshly criticized three of R. H. Anderson's brigades, including the Floridians. Thus, the first report that many Southerners read about Gettysburg contained the following account:

> Anderson's Division . . . was posted in the following order: Wilcox's Brigade on the right, Mahone's on the left, Wright's in the centre, Perry's on the right centre, and Posey's on the left centre. Wilcox was to advance first, to be followed by the other brigades in their order to the left. Wilcox and his unconquerable Alabamians moved out at the appointed time and fought long and desperately. Perry's Brigade (Perry was not present himself) advanced a short distance but did not become fully engaged. Wright went boldly forward, and excelled, if possible, all his previous performances, though at fearful cost to his command. . . . Meanwhile, Wilcox and Wright were struggling with mortal odds against them; but their valor and blood were expended to little purpose . . . [being] defeated by the unpardonable conduct of other portions of the division.[4]

Another army correspondent, signing his dispatch as "A," sent a similar report to the *Mobile Advertiser and Register.* Both columns were reprinted in the *Richmond Enquirer.* That is where these negative accounts first came to the attention of the survivors of the Florida brigade.[5]

Lang's soldiers were understandably outraged at the reports, which stopped just short of calling them cowards. A contingent from the Florida brigade visited both Alexander and "A," eliciting a prompt, if halfhearted, correction from the Savannah writer. The Mobile reporter went further, publishing a handsome tribute to the Florida troops. In part, "A" stated: "[I]n my account of the great battle at Gettysburg, full justice was not done to Perry's Florida Brigade. Its performance was not only creditable, but gallant, as shown by its heavy loss, which in proportion to the numbers engaged, exceeds that sustained by any other [Confederate] Brigade on the field."[6]

Not content with the two corrections, Col. David Lang also penned a letter to the editors of the *Richmond Enquirer.* With obvious pride in his men and anger at the injustice done them, the commander of the Floridians wrote:

> His [P. W. Alexander's] statement as to the disposition of, and orders given to the Brigade is true; but when he says "Perry's Brigade advanced a short distance, but did not become fully engaged," he publishes to the world a misstatement of facts which I cannot pass over in silence. Perry's

Brigade did advance at the appointed time, as ordered, with Wilcox's Brigade; it advanced as far as Wilcox's or Wright's, or any other Brigade that advanced at the same time, and fought bravely and well, until ordered by me to retire, after Wilcox had been forced back by overwhelming numbers and the enemy had advanced, in strong force more than one hundred yards beyond the line I was holding, almost cutting off my retreat. The loss of more than half the men carried into the charge would appear to unprejudiced eyes, that the Brigade did "become fully engaged." Again, in his account of the battle of the 3rd of July, in speaking of the charge of Pickett's Division, P. W. A. omits to mention that Perry's Brigade was engaged, although he mentions the part taken by Wilcox's Brigade; and yet Perry's Brigade moved side by side with Wilcox during the entire day, losing nearly two-thirds of the entire number taken into action. The men I have the honor to command are staid, sober men, most of them having families, who, knowing the perilous condition of the country, entered the service to do all in their power to avert the impending danger; they fight not for vain dreams of glory, nor yet newspaper fame, or notoriety; but they are unwilling to stand by in silence and see their deeds so misrepresented to posterity, as to cause their children to blush with shame, when they read of them in days to come.[7]

The matter should have ended there, but it did not. The catalyst for the escalation of the post-Gettysburg controversy involving the Florida brigade was Brig. Gen. Ambrose Ransom Wright.

There is much to admire about Wright. He evinced a courageous and aggressive spirit on the battlefield and rendered excellent service at Malvern Hill, Second Manassas, Antietam, and Chancellorsville. Unfortunately, a harsh, discourteous temperament marred his exemplary record as a combat officer. The Georgian had a stubborn streak and uncontrolled ambition for personal glory. Additionally, Wright intensely despised R. H. Anderson, his divisional commander, and did little to hide his feelings.[8]

In hindsight, it appears likely that Wright supplied P. W. Alexander, his fellow Georgian, with the original misinformation regarding the Florida brigade's role at Gettysburg. The Georgia general did not stop there. A letter he penned to his wife found its way into publication in the July 23 issue of the *Augusta Daily Constitutionalist*. In this scorching account of the battle, Wright laid equal blame for the failure of his unit to take Cemetery Ridge on Lang's, Posey's, and Mahone's brigades, branding these three units as cowards, and, by inference, implying that Anderson's mismanagement resulted in the butchery of his soldiers. The letter (written in the third person) stated in part:

[L]ooking to the left through the smoke, it was apparent that neither Posey nor Mahone had advanced, and Wright's left was wholly unprotected. A courier was dispatched to Gen. Anderson, informing him of the fact, who answered that both Posey and Mahone had been ordered in, and that he would reiterate the order [but] that our Brigade go on. Before the courier returned, Perry's Brigade on the right gave way, and shamefully ran to the rear. Wright's brigade had now climbed up the side of the mountain, nearly to the enemy's guns, and being left without support either on the right or left, enabled the enemy to concentrate a heavy fire upon it. But the brave men pressed rapidly and steadily on. . . . Just after taking the enemy's batteries, we perceived a heavy column of Yankee infantry on our right flank. They had taken advantage of the gap left in our line by the falling back of Perry's Brigade, and had gotten into the gap left by Perry's Brigade and were rapidly getting into our rear. Posey had not advanced on our left, and a strong body of the enemy were advancing down the side of the mountain to gain our left flank and rear. Thus we were perfectly isolated from any portion of our army, a mile in advance, and although we had gained the enemy's works and captured his guns, we were about to be sacrificed to the bad management and cowardly conduct of others.[9]

Wright felt justifiable pride in the courage of his Georgians and disappointment that such sacrifice came to naught. The Georgia brigadier later admitted that the letter to his wife contained hearsay and camp gossip. Lang's men felt they had several strong arguments to counter Wright's libel. There was some evidence, in fact, to suggest that Wright was not even on the field, but was confined to a hospital during the attack, and the claims of "cowardly conduct" and "shamefully running to the rear" were simply not true. The Floridians advanced to the base of Cemetery Ridge, and fell back only when flanked by the bluecoats—the same course of action taken by Wright's brigade moments later. Lang's losses amounted to more than 40 percent on July 2. Remaining or continuing to press the charge would have accomplished nothing except the total annihilation of the Florida brigade.[10]

When Wright's article came to the attention of the surviving members of Lang's brigade, they were livid with rage. Deeply offended by implications of cowardice, they determined to find the author and demand a retraction. The brigade held an "indignation meeting" and appointed J. B. Johnson a committee of one to seek out the writer and demand satisfaction.[11]

Johnson left a vivid postwar memoir of what happened next.

I rode over to Wright's headquarters. He was an old man [he was, in fact, thirty-seven years old] with very long hair [an unconfirmed story stated that Wright had vowed not to cut his hair until the Confederacy won its independence]. I got down, walked up, and saluted. Wright said, "Young man, what can I do for you?" I replied, "General Wright, I have a paper from Augusta, Georgia, criticizing the Florida Brigade in an article on the Battle of Gettysburg. If you can assist me in finding the author, I will be obliged to you." "Why do you wish to find the author, sir?" "Because," I replied, "it is as false as Hell itself." He turned red, and I saw he was very angry. He said, "Young man, that was not intended for publication. It was a private letter to my wife, from information I had." Now, and right here, he almost sprang from his seat. There were some high officers listening. I turned to Captain [Victor J. B.] Girardey [a future Confederate general], his Adjutant General, and said: "Captain Girardey, will you answer a few questions?" "Yes sir," he said. "Well, where was General Wright when we charged Cemetery Ridge on July 2nd?" "I think he was sick and at the hospital," he replied. "Do you remember to have seen and talked to me that day at the furtherest point your brigade advanced and did we not discuss the advance of the enemy's reinforcements, and that it would be useless to hold the position, and when the order was given to fall back, did our two brigades come out together?" "Yes," he said. "That will do," said General Wright. "I was misinformed. I will write a correction for publication. You can call for it tomorrow." I saluted and returned to our brigade to report.[12]

Probably prodded by court-martial proceedings initiated by R. H. Anderson, Wright published in the *Augusta Daily Constitutionalist* a generous retraction of his previous letter. Admitting that his earlier report contained "grave errors," he averred that it had been "hurriedly" written, and had its basis in camp gossip. In part, Wright declared: "From information received from several of that [Lang's] Brigade, and who were in the charge, I am satisfied that the brigade (which is very small) acted well—that it advanced along with Wilcox's and Wright's brigades and it was overwhelmed by vastly superior numbers, and that even then it only fell back in obedience to orders, and when it was apparent that the day was lost. I learn, also, that it was engaged again on the third, when Pickett's Charge was made, and that it suffered severely in this later charge."[13]

Wright also had an additional chance to defend his post-battle actions because in late August R. H. Anderson had the Georgian hauled before a court-martial hearing. The records of Wright's trial have apparently been lost and what little we know of the proceeding is colored by the loyalties of those involved. A member of the Third Georgia Infantry reported that the brigade commander missed his unit's heroic defense of Manassas Gap on July 23 because "Wright was placed in arrest by Maj. Gen. R. H. Anderson for some order respecting transportation in the Brigade." J. B. Johnson noted that Anderson questioned him regarding the article in the Augusta paper and swore to have Wright court-martialed for writing it. "I am determined," Anderson reportedly said, "that officers must make their reputations with their swords and not by their pens." There is probably truth in both accounts.[14]

If Wright was under arrest by July 23 (the same day the article was published in Augusta and the date of the battle of Manassas Gap), it seems probable that Anderson simply tacked on an additional charge to the existing indictment when the division commander learned about the Georgian's article several days later. In any event, a report in the *Richmond Enquirer* listed the charges against Wright as "disobedience of officers, disrespect toward superior officers, and for matters connected with publications which appeared in the Augusta (Georgia) *Constitutionalist.*" Among those assigned to try the case were Maj. Gen. Henry Heth, presiding, and Joseph B. Kershaw, Cadmus Wilcox, H. H. Walker, and Stephen D. Ramseur, all brigadiers.[15]

Adj. Johnson's memoir, although obviously biased in favor of the Florida brigade, provides an account of the Wright court-martial. The Floridian remembered:

> Some time afterward, while we were in winter quarters, I was summoned to Culpepper Court House as a witness in the [Wright] case. When the case was called up General Wright, who was a lawyer, defended himself. . . . The old general got up and said, there was no law by which you could convict one on the evidence of part of [a] letter; that the balance of the letter might throw a different light upon it. The Judge Advocate agreed with him, and the case was dismissed. General Anderson was considerably worried, and said to me: "I would hate to escape court martial by a technicality, but it will have its effect." General Wright was

a brave, dashing old soldier. I have often seen him charging with his long hair waving. General Anderson in speaking of him said to me: "General Wright is brave and dashing. In fact, sometimes he has too much dash. A little mere [possibly "more"] coolness would bring better results."[16]

If Anderson thought his actions would "have its effect" on Wright, he little knew his man. With typical intransigence, the Georgian refused to let the facts alter his version of what happened at Gettysburg. In his after-action report, dated September 28, 1863, Wright submitted a modified version of his letter to the *Constitutionalist*. While admitting that the brigade on his right [Lang's Floridians] was "forced to retire," he also recorded that "the brigade on our right had not advanced across the turnpike, but had actually given way and was rapidly falling back to the rear." This Wright knew to be untrue, but that apparently did not matter.[17]

There the post-battle conflict over the Florida brigade's Gettysburg actions ended, except for one final, forgotten postscript. A few days after Wright's acquittal, Gen. Robert E. Lee reviewed the troops of A. P. Hill's corps at their camp near Orange Court House. Lee and Hill sat upon their horses on a small rise overlooking the road, and as each unit passed, the Third Corps commander would announce the brigade. As Perry's men neared the natural reviewing stand, Hill turned to Lee and said: "That is the remnant of the gallant Florida Brigade." Thereupon, the Confederate commander immediately removed his hat and remained with his head uncovered in respect until the three small regiments passed. It was a moment the Florida Confederates never forgot. Their beloved chieftain's action did much to restore the Floridian's pride and esprit de corps, for they viewed Lee's compliment as a vindication of their role at Gettysburg.[18]

(In a strange twist of fate, the Floridians had a chance to return the compliment. Shortly before his death in 1870, Robert E. Lee visited Jacksonville, Florida, on his way up the St. Johns River to Palatka. Reporters, who were accustomed to the cheers that had greeted the former Confederate commander all along the route, were perplexed at the reaction of the northeast Florida crowd. At Lee's appearance on deck, "a complete silence fell on the throng," and the men "all lifted their hats and remained uncovered until their former commander retired to his stateroom.")[19]

The end of the Gettysburg campaign brought renewed demands from Gov. John Milton to the Confederate secretary of war for the return of Perry's brigade and yet another controversy for the beleaguered unit. Milton was a strange,

Fig. 9. Gov. John Milton

flawed individual who apparently longed to be a military leader. According to historian Boyd Murphree, "Milton revered his service in the state forces in Georgia, Alabama, Texas, and Florida, wearing with pride his militia rank of colonel and general." He often donned a specially designed "commander-in-chief's uniform," and had pleaded with Jefferson Davis to "give him command of a field brigade." He proposed that Perry's brigade could recruit, refit, and fight bands of deserters headquartered in Jackson County, Milton's home, and west Florida. (He pointedly ignored the more serious problems with Unionists and conscript evaders in east and middle Florida, particularly in Taylor and La-fayette counties.)[20]

The Florida representatives in the Confederate Congress threw their weight behind Milton's effort, but Gen. Lee rejected the proposal out of hand. E. A. Perry, who had rejoined his command a few days previously, was similarly ada-mant, calling on state pride and the history of the Florida brigade: "I feel that the brave Floridians I have the honor to command in Virginia have done so much for the name of their State that it is but justice that the organizations as they now exist should be maintained, that the companies and regiments should be filled, and the brigade strengthened by the addition of other regiments and battalions."[21]

Unfortunately, in December a petition to return Perry's brigade to Florida by several of the unit's officers revived the issue. Lee had had enough. The Confederate commander responded in an uncharacteristically harsh and direct manner. He pointed out that the army needed every man who could shoulder a rifle. He also threatened to reduce the brigade to a single regiment, and noted that if the Floridians were sent home, "other equally deserving [units] could not be denied a similar indulgence, and the army would be broken up." Lee tempered his response by stating: "I should much regret for the brigade to lose its identity. It has served long and faithfully."[22]

This subject might have continued as a bone of contention, but the hardy veterans of the Second Florida effectively defused the explosive situation. Although their term of enlistment did not expire until mid-July of 1864, in January the regiment voted to reenlist for the rest of the war. The Second Florida also issued a manifesto branding as "traitors" those who "entertain the idea of abandoning the cause." This example of selflessness by the "representative regiment," Lee's tough stance, and the beginning of the 1864 spring campaign brought an abrupt halt to the calls for a transfer south.[23]

The Florida brigade, however, still had one fight left in 1863. Throughout October and November, the Yankees and Rebels continued their dance of death through the rolling hills and valleys of northern Virginia, with Lee trying to force Meade to fall back "toward Washington . . . to defend the capital," or at least "to fight the Confederates [on terrain] favorable to the Army of Northern Virginia."[24]

As the Southerners advanced, the Union commander retreated northward and a conviction grew among the graycoats that "Meade was unwilling to face us." A. P. Hill apparently fell victim to that specious opinion. Around noon on October 14, the Third Corps leader spotted the Federals crossing Broad Run near Bristoe Station, and Hill ordered Heth's division to attack them after only a cursory examination. Apparently as a precaution, Hill directed R. H. Anderson to forward Col. David McIntosh's battery and two infantry brigades to assist Heth's troops. In his haste, Hill failed to detect two divisions of the Union II Corps crouching behind an embankment of the Orange & Alexandria Railroad. As Brig. Gen. John R. Cooke's and Brig. Gen. W. W. Kirkland's Rebels charged the bluecoats near Broad Run, Hancock's veterans rose from their position and "slaughtered" Heth's men.[25]

Perry's Floridians and Posey's Mississippians arrived just as Cooke's and Kirkland's survivors began their hasty retreat. Perry's Flowers scrambled through the dense undergrowth bordering the Greenwich Road just in time to intercept a Yankee regiment advancing to flank the fleeing Rebels. Perry reacted quickly to the new threat. An officer of the Fifth Florida described the climax to the action, writing: "Cooke's men could not stand it [the enemy fire] and broke in confusion. The enemy followed . . . [and] as the Yanks made their appearance, Gen. Perry wheeled the 8th and 2nd Florida around, forming a right angle to our line and soon drove them back."[26]

Darkness and defeat ended the engagement, and the Unionists continued their retreat. The Florida brigade suffered three killed and twenty-one wounded, including Lt. Col. Baya, severely wounded in the hip while commanding the Eighth Florida.[27]

The winter of 1863–64 found the Army of Northern Virginia stationed along a twenty-mile stretch of the Rapidan, with the Florida brigade's winter quarters located near Rapidan Station. The ranks of Perry's men swelled to almost 500 with the return of the Gettysburg wounded. Despite the discontent fomented by Milton, the spirit of the brigade and Lee's army remained generally high. The trials of the coming year would require every man available and all the resolve they could muster.[28]

9   "Bloodiest and Weirdest
of Encounters"

The Battle of the Wilderness

The winter of 1863–64 had been a period of hardship, deprivation, and revival for Gen. Lee's Army of Northern Virginia. Severed rail connections to the Deep South, fertile agricultural areas under Federal control, and most farmers either in the army or hiding from conscription agents contributed to the scarcity of food and supplies. The few rations the Rebel soldiers received consisted of poor "blue" beef and parched corn that left the Southerners as empty as if they had not eaten at all. "The one thing we suffered most from," wrote one Confederate soldier, "was hunger. The scantiness of rations was something fierce. We never got a square meal that winter." The soldiers naturally grumbled, but most persevered. Gen. Lee, recognizing the seriousness of the soldiers' plight, advised Jefferson Davis: "Unless there is a change, I fear the army cannot be kept effective, and probably cannot be kept together."[1]

Confederate morale remained high, despite the lack of even basic necessities, due primarily to a series of religious revivals that swept through the Southern encampments near Orange Court House. The reasons for this spiritual awakening were as varied as the men themselves. The graycoats often mentioned fear of death on the battlefield and belief that recent defeats at Gettysburg and Missionary Ridge represented divine punishment for the army's impiety as causes for the renewed fervor. Whatever the reasons, the men of Lee's army constructed forty chapels near the Rapidan River in a matter of weeks. A chaplain exulted: "Such camp meetings were never seen before in America. The bivouac of the soldier never witnessed such nights of glory and days of grandeur. The Pentecostal fire lights the camp, and armed hosts of men sleep beneath the wings of angels rejoicing over many sinners that have repented." Even hard-drinking, sardonic Col. David Lang grudgingly admitted that the chaplains had managed to "make good soldiers of some very trifling material." At least part of the religiosity of the modern "Bible Belt" can be traced to these revivals.[2]

Faith in their comrades and commander also buoyed the hope of the Army of Northern Virginia during the bitter winter. As spring approached, these veteran troops knew that a tough battle lay just ahead. Still, their confidence and morale remained unusually high. Sgt. John F. Sale of Brig. Gen. William Mahone's Twelfth Virginia summed up his unit's sentiment: "I cannot say in truth that they [Mahone's troops] desire a fight but all express a determination to do their utmost when it does come and have confidence in the protection of Providence, their Leader, and themselves." An unnamed member of the Twenty-second Georgia exhibited an even more remarkable example of the esprit of R. H. Anderson's men in an open letter to a Rome, Georgia, newspaper. Encouraging the home folks to remain firm in their commitment to the Southern cause, he urged: "We expect a hard spring and summer campaign, but we are ready for it, for we have no notion of ever being subjugated. This army is generally in the very best of spirits—determined to *sink* or *swim, live* or *die, survive* or *perish* we will battle for our independence—To all of our friends at home, we say, 'cheer up,' for we believe you will have cause to rejoice before this year closes, and at least wait until this army is disheartened before you yield to despondency."[3]

The Florida brigade exhibited a similar high morale. The unflaggingly patriotic and optimistic Capt. Seton Fleming, for example, warned his mother against listening to those Floridians who were "croaking and deploring the duration of the war." With unintended irony (considering his Tory ancestors), he assured her: "Our fathers fought the English seven years, and we can fight the Yankees longer."[4]

Gen. Perry's Floridians, who never truly recovered from the losses suffered during the carnage at Gettysburg, were clearly ready to fight wherever they were needed. Because E. A. Perry had assigned Fleming to serve as a staff officer, Capt. John B. G. O'Neil commanded the Second Florida. Col. Thompson B. Lamar led the Fifth Florida, while Col. Lang commanded the Eighth Florida.[5]

The long-expected campaign began on May 4, 1864. That day, the Army of the Potomac, under its new commander Gen. Ulysses S. Grant, crossed the Rapidan River and advanced into a seventy-square-mile tangle of scrub and second-growth timber known locally as the Wilderness. The Confederate commander responded quickly, sending Lt. Gen. Richard Ewell's Second Corps and Henry Heth's and Cadmus Wilcox's divisions of A. P. Hill's Third

Corps to confront the Federals. Longstreet's First Corps was encamped several miles away near Gordonsville, astride the vital Orange & Alexandria Railroad.[6]

R. H. Anderson's division began converging at Verdiersville near sunset on May 5. The division had been left as the rear guard of Lee's army, scattered at strategic points along the Rapidan. Anderson's orders were to "observe the march of the U[nited] States forces along the Rapidan and oppose any attempt on their part to cross the river in the rear of Lee." Now convinced that no such threat existed, Fighting Dick directed his troops to rendezvous at Verdiersville. The village's location, near the junction of the Orange Turnpike and Orange Plank Road, made it an ideal place for Anderson to regroup his scattered forces. More important, it was only five miles from the Wilderness.[7]

Most of Anderson's men got less than two hours' sleep that night. Shortly after midnight couriers arrived from Lee urging Anderson to resume his march immediately. The battle, begun on the 5th, was still very much in doubt. Lee guessed the bloodletting would continue on the morrow and he would need every available man to drive the bluecoats back across the Rapidan.[8]

Reacting promptly to his orders, by 2:00 a.m. Anderson had his long lines of grumpy, sleepy men stumbling down the Orange Plank Road toward the Wilderness. Brig. Gen. William Mahone's Virginians, numbering about 1,700 men, led the advance. Rans Wright's Georgians fell in behind the men from the Old Dominion. The unit, bolstered by the addition of old men and young boys of the Tenth Georgia Battalion, boasted about 1,650 soldiers. Brig. Gen. Abner Perrin's Alabamians, Anderson's largest brigade with 1,750 soldiers, trailed the Georgians, closely followed by the 500-man Florida unit and Brig. Gen. Nathaniel Harris's tough Mississippi warriors.[9]

Civil War soldiers hated night marches. So much could, and frequently did, go wrong in the dark. Enemy ambushes, getting lost, and stumbling over or into hard objects were very real hazards—or perhaps, there is in each man a remnant of the little boy's fear of the dark. A dogged determination to keep in line and place one foot in front of the other replaced the banter, jokes, and insults that were so much a part of the usual day march. The marchers halted frequently. Usually only an irksome necessity, on the night of May 5 the halts provided a welcome relief. "The men floundered and fell as they marched," a member of Longstreet's corps recalled. "Sometimes the head of the column would lose its way, and during the time it was hunting its way back to the lost . . . path was about the only rest we got."[10]

As if to warn Anderson's division of what awaited it, wounded soldiers clogged the roads. Allowing the "human wreckage" of the battle to pass on the dark and narrow thoroughfare consumed additional time. "We continued to march all night," one of Mahone's Virginians remembered, "and we met nothing but wounded men, some walking, some hobbling on guns used as crutches, some in ambulances. . . . It appeared as if most of the army had been wounded." Using the touch and feel method, covering the five miles from Verdiersville to the battlefield took almost six hours.[11]

As first light began to filter through the canopy of trees covering the Orange Plank Road, Anderson's men picked up the pace of the march. The sound of the cannons' roar and the spiteful rattle of musketry could now be plainly heard. Even the greenest lad in the new Georgia battalion realized that they were heading into a deadly gale. "Rumors of a severe battle the day before . . . were passed from mouth to mouth," a Georgian reported. "Another battle was said to be imminent and we were wanted to keep the ball rolling."[12]

The battle had indeed developed the previous day (May 5), centered along the Orange Turnpike and the Orange Plank roads, the only major east-west arteries through the Wilderness. It is difficult to imagine a more inhospitable place for a battle than this wooded terrain. It affected all aspects of the fight. The area's early settlers had cleared "the original forest of wood to feed the smelting works of Gold and Iron mines in this section. And from every stump where every tree was removed have grown sprouts—then saplings—now trees—as thick as the fingers on a man's hand. Besides, in every space so much as to allow a seed to sprout, Cedar and Chinquepins bushes grow; and interlacing every sprout, bush and tree Muscadine and Wild Grape vines are festooned, making such a network of these growths that a bird can hardly fly through them." Deep ravines and marshy creek bottoms interlaced the whole area, and the region's few small clearings and abandoned fields became the site of some of North America's bloodiest combat.[13]

Lee apparently chose to fight here because the dense jungle would help negate the Union army's heavy advantage in the number of troops and artillery. He certainly would not have overlooked the psychological advantage the Wilderness provided. Both the Southern and Federal veterans remembered that the Army of Northern Virginia had won one of its greatest victories the previous year on the same terrain. The Confederate commander proceeded into the huge forest hoping to hold the bluecoats in place with Ewell's Second Corps and two divisions of A. P. Hill's Third Corps until Anderson's soldiers and Longstreet's First Corps could arrive. With his army consolidated, the graycoats could then destroy Grant's Army of the Potomac or drive it across the Rapidan.[14]

For his part, Grant seemed quite content to fight Lee wherever he could bring the Confederacy's "Gray Fox" to bay. After years of dealing with the likes of Gen. Braxton Bragg in the western theater, there seems little doubt that the Union commander felt confident in his ability to quickly defeat Lee's vaunted army.[15]

The combat on May 5 quickly deteriorated into a two-pronged free-for-all. Along the turnpike, Ewell's Second Corps fought two Union corps to a standstill around a clearing known as Saunder's Field. A few miles south, along the plank road, A. P. Hill with two divisions barely escaped destruction. Despite the danger, both Lee and Hill inexplicably refused requests by Maj. Gen. Henry Heth to reorganize his jumbled brigades or construct breastworks. "Longstreet will be up in a few hours," Hill repeatedly assured Heth.[16]

As the sun arose on the morning of May 6, "red as a ball of fire," Longstreet's First Corps filed onto the plank road to the right of Anderson's division, and the two groups advanced together side by side. The natural competitiveness of both units took over, and a race soon developed. A Georgian remembered: "Just before daylight the head of Longstreet's column, [Brig. Gen. John] Gregg's Texas Brigade leading, debouched into the plank road from the right, [and] we raced neck and neck toward the front." For a while the race was a dead heat, but the Texans finally pulled ahead.[17]

As Anderson's men neared Parker's Store, the sights and sounds of battle dispelled any notion of an easy fight. A sickening spectacle greeted the newcomers. Smoke floated from the forest like a tattered, acrid cloud, restricting the vision of but not quite blinding the combatants. Dead and dying animals and men littered the small clearing. Screams of agony, curses, and prayers were audible above the din of battle. Other unfortunates, dazed and injured, wandered about the Tapp clearing looking for a field hospital. The slackers, cowards, and demoralized soldiers avoided the approaching columns, clinging to the tree line in search of safety. "As we neared the front," one of Anderson's men reported, "we came first upon hospital tents with their harvest of wounded; as day began to break the continuous roar of musketry was almost deafening, then came the ambulances, wagons, litter bearers, limbers, wounded, and some, not all, making for the rear. The panic stricken left the road as they approached the head of the column."[18]

As Anderson's and Longstreet's units filed onto the field of battle, Gen. Lee helplessly watched the demoralization and disorderly flight of Heth's and Wilcox's units. Since shortly after daybreak, Hancock's II Corps had been systematically tearing apart Lee's right wing. Lee, for once, lost his customary composure, screaming harshly at the fleeing troops and ordering the supply wagons to retreat. Only the timely arrival of reinforcements could save the Southern army.[19]

Through the smoke, devastation, and confusion Longstreet's corps advanced with steady stride. Often justly condemned for his dilatory nature, today Longstreet was at his best, acting coolly with promptness and prudence. At the Tapp Farm clearing the dour Georgian formed a line of battle composed of the divisions of Brig. Gen. Joseph B. Kershaw and Maj. Gen. Charles B. Field, anchored along the plank road. Field rushed Brig. Gen. Evander M. Law's brigade, commanded on this day by Col. William F. Perry, to the north side of the road.[20]

To buy time for these units to deploy, Longstreet threw Gregg's legendary Texas brigade straight at Hancock's Yankees. The Lone Star troops hit the bluecoat line head-on, followed closely by Brig. Gen. Henry C. "Rock" Benning's Georgia veterans. Their combined firepower, and that of Perry's Alabamians to the north, finally stalled Hancock's juggernaut.[21]

R. H. Anderson's troops arrived at Parker's Store at 7:30 a.m., but found scant rest for the weary. Almost immediately Longstreet assumed command of the division. He ordered Mahone's brigade to the right to support Kershaw and Field, Wright to A. P. Hill, as he attempted to rally Heth's and Wilcox's jumbled regiments. Longstreet then dispatched Perrin and E. A. Perry to the north side of the plank road to link up with Col. W. F. Perry's hard-pressed Alabamians. Harris's Mississippians were detained along the Orange Plank Road as a reserve.[22]

Col. W. F. Perry encountered the Union Fourth Division of Brig. Gen. James S. Wadsworth almost immediately after leaving the Tapp clearing. About 7:15 a.m. W. F. Perry began his assault. Emerging from the thickets on Wadsworth's left, the soldiers opened fire on the famous Iron Brigade. The two units settled into a slugging match across a deep gully.[23]

Brig. Gen. Alexander Webb's Union brigade arrived to reinforce Wadsworth. Webb quickly discovered what Wadsworth probably already suspected—that W. F. Perry's troops were the only Confederates north of the plank road. The two brigades joined the fight at once, but the Alabamians were too few and too weary to drive away Webb's fresh soldiers. Both sides called for assistance, and a brief lull settled over the battlefield. It was then about 8:30 a.m.[24]

Perrin's brigade reached W. F. Perry first. It had traveled up the plank road from the Tapp Farm perhaps half a mile, slogged across a marshy bottom, and turned left into the woods. E. A. Perry's Floridians followed a few minutes later.[25]

Perrin's men deployed to the right of W. F. Perry's men "on the crest of a little ridge in the thick woods." It was no easy task. Crashing through the undergrowth, they immediately came under fire from the unseen enemy, suffering casualties as they advanced. As soon as his men reached their position, Perrin had them lie down in the line of battle, hoping to reduce casualties. Through the woods, the Deep South soldiers could plainly hear a Union officer shouting orders for his men to move forward.[26]

Meanwhile, E. A. Perry's Florida brigade filed through the heavy brush under a hail of bullets. The troops took position on the left of W. F. Perry's brigade. The Alabama colonel expressed great admiration for Perrin's and E. A. Perry's warriors. "Language can hardly do justice," he later wrote, "to their conduct. They had arrived in the midst of confusion and apparent disaster. Their lines had been formed under fire and in the presence of the enemy moving forward in dense array and perfect order. Such had been the urgency of the crisis that single brigades, and sometimes regiments, as their formation was completed in succession, assailed the foe with almost resistless fury."[27]

Help came for Alexander Webb's bluecoats in the form of Col. Sumner Carruth's three regiments and the units of Brig. Gen. Thomas G. Stevenson and Brig. Gen. James C. Rice, but they launched their charge a little too late. Rather than striking a single battle-weary brigade, they hit three, stretched thin but full of fight. The Rebels unleashed volley after volley, which a Federal recalled "resembled the fury of hell in intensity, and was deadly accurate." For several long minutes the Yankees gave as good as they received.[28]

The troops of one of Carruth's green units, the Fifty-seventh Massachusetts, refused to take cover or fall to the ground, believing they would be accused of cowardice if they did. As a result, E. A. Perry's Flowers cut them to pieces. A recent historian of the Fifty-seventh Massachusetts relates: "The charge disintegrated into spontaneous, miniature battles, and each man fought with chaotic ferocity for himself. The firing was so profligate that some of the boys [members of the Massachusetts unit] drove into it head down and back bent, as if they were in the middle of an intense New England blizzard."[29]

For the soldiers on the firing line, blue and gray, the Wilderness battle was a blind fight. Few saw the enemy. Sight obscured by smoke and tangled woodlands, men groped forward or back, firing at sounds or just in the general direction of the enemy. Officers shouted conflicting orders, and in the confusion men fought Indian-style, crouching and creeping from tree to tree. One of the staff officers from Anderson's division described the battle as "a blind wrestle . . . bloodiest and weirdest of encounters. The Genius of Destruction, tired of the old commonplace mode of killing, had invented the unseen death."[30]

When Webb's assault faltered, Perrin's command impetuously rose and bounded forward like a horde of tattered, powder-blackened fiends, sounding their high-pitched battle cry. The Alabamians tried hard, but it was a bloody, futile failure. Webb's bluecoats stumbled back a little, stubbornly contesting every foot. Postwar accounts claimed Perrin's men drove the Federals an incredible three miles. Such claims were undoubtedly the result of unit pride and failing memory. The best evidence indicates that Perrin's men drove the Union troops back a couple of hundred yards before the unsupported assault ground to a halt, and the Alabama reinforcements slipped back to their original position.[31]

By 10:00 a.m., the fight north of the plank road sputtered to a stop, as if by mutual consent of the exhausted combatants. Only the occasional "pop" of the sharpshooter's rifle and the anguished cries of the wounded disturbed the blood-drenched woodland. South of the plank road, however, the storm tide of battle was just beginning to rise.[32]

Even while the troops of W. F. Perry, Abner Perrin, and E. A. Perry fought north of the plank road, Longstreet discovered that the Union left was in the air, and an unfinished railroad line provided a ready-made avenue of attack. Using the brigades of Mahone, George T. "Tige" Anderson, and W. T. Wofford, Longstreet launched a flank attack that routed Hancock's bluecoats and drove them back to the breastworks along the Brock Road. As the action sputtered to a close, a company of Mahone's Virginians fired a ragged volley at the sound of approaching horsemen, grievously wounding James Longstreet.[33]

Even before the First Corps commander fell, the Confederate attack had run out of steam. A second flank movement had been proposed, but died aborning. For now, the graycoats would have to be satisfied with possession of the plank road. The Union troops, huddling spent and disorganized behind the defenses along the Brock Road, were in no shape to take the offensive. After almost seven hours of slaughter, a lull settled over the Wilderness.[34]

The next threat to the Confederate line along the plank road came from an unexpected source—Maj. Gen. Ambrose E. Burnside's IX Corps. Burnside's army had departed from headquarters at 1:00 a.m. (the morning of May 6), with orders to strike a gap in the Confederate lines between Ewell and A. P. Hill in concert with Hancock's morning assault. Burnside confirmed his well-

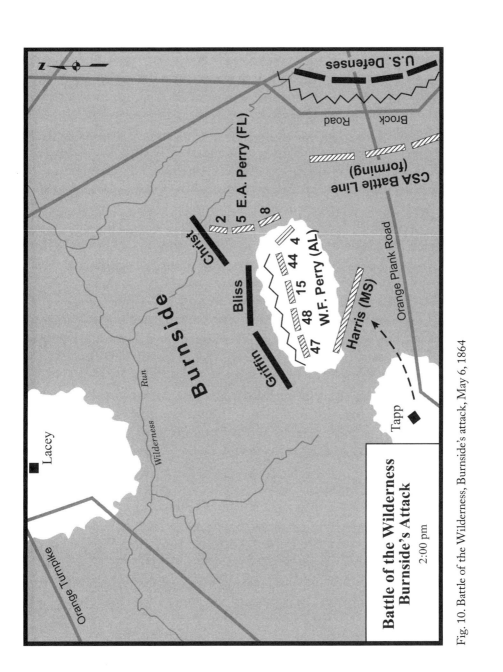

Fig. 10. Battle of the Wilderness, Burnside's attack, May 6, 1864

earned reputation for having "a genius for slowness"; by the time IX Corps arrived, no gap existed in the Rebel lines. Understandably reluctant to charge uphill against an entrenched foe as he had done at Fredericksburg, Burnside decided to shift his command to the southeast to support Hancock. It took the bluecoats from 8:00 a.m. till 1:00 p.m. to cover the two and one-half miles. But around 1:30, weary and bedraggled, "Burnside's Pets" struggled into a small clearing just north of the Confederate position near the Orange Plank Road.[35]

The graycoats opposite IX Corps' new position were ill prepared for the storm about to envelope them. The two brigades—W. F. Perry's and E. A. Perry's—were still holding the area where they had earlier fought Wadsworth to a bloody standstill. (Perrin's men were no longer present, apparently inching through the weeds, briars, and vines toward the Orange Turnpike). W. F. Perry's Alabamians were now on E. A. Perry's left, facing due north. Their position was a good one, located on a hill overlooking a swampy morass. As an additional precaution, the Alabamians threw together a makeshift set of breastworks, which W. F. Perry contemptuously dismissed as a "pile of logs."[36]

The Floridians' luck continued to be all bad. They were aligned at a right angle to the Alabamians, facing to the east (toward the Brock Road). To further complicate the situation, a gap existed between the brigades of the two Perrys. W. F. Perry apparently sensed trouble and quickly began to fill the opening with the tiny Fourth Alabama.[37]

In this position, the left of the Florida brigade projected toward Burnside's hidden bluecoats and more than 100 yards beyond W. F. Perry's line. Although the Alabamian expressed surprise at the Floridian's unorthodox position, almost certainly E. A. Perry had conformed his line to Lee's orders, arranging his soldiers to take part in the pending assault on the Federal's Brock Road defenses. Unfortunately for the Floridians, a vindictive god could not have placed them in a worse position for an attack from the northwest.[38]

W. F. Perry was edgy. He seems to have had a premonition concerning Burnside's presence even before the IX Corps attack began. He threw out skirmishers to protect E. A. Perry's front; sent Maj. William C. Oates, his energetic and intelligent subordinate, forward to scout out the woods in his front; and then hurried to the Florida brigade's commander to try to convince the Floridian to shift his troops into line with his brigade. Further complications arose immediately. About this time a courier arrived from Gen. Lee ordering W. F. Perry to conform his line to E. A. Perry's alignment in anticipation of the Brock Road attack. After a moment's consideration, the Alabamian wisely decided to ignore Lee's directive. A messenger from Oates followed Lee's courier, reporting that the woods were swarming with Yankees and a major attack appeared to be brewing.[39]

The news convinced E. A. Perry. He immediately began putting his brigade in position to form a battle line with the Alabama troops. A scant five minutes would have sufficed to effect the change, but even that time was denied the unlucky Floridians. From the thick woods to the north, Col. Zenas R. Bliss's brigade of Potter's Second Division roared toward the Florida brigade yelping the Yankee's "huzzah" battle cry.[40]

Confused and totally exposed, the Floridians bore the brunt of Bliss's assault. Oates reported that this Federal charge struck the Floridians "squarely in the flank and decimated it at once." W. F. Perry reported that the Floridians "melted away," but the Fourth Alabama's Col. P. D. Bowles, who had a better vantage point than either of the others, reported that he "came up with the Floridians, who were retreating slowly."[41]

Pvt. D. L. Geer of the Fifth Florida left one of the few accounts by a Floridian, and for once, he found little humor in the situation. "We had gotten well into line when Hancock's [actually Burnside's] Corps struck us. Our lines were not connected to our left, so we had it hot right here in this place. . . . Right here some of the boys were killed and most of them taken prisoner. The captain of our company [Capt. John H. Tolbert] was taken and my brother Fred, together with many others. Myself and a few others ran the gauntlet and got out, though they were all around us. We were cut up badly."[42]

A second report came from an anonymous soldier in the Eighth Florida. "[We were] charged by the enemy and was [soon engaged in] the most desperate struggle I have ever witnessed. Our brave boys fought with [their] usual daring. We were flanked and necessarily compelled to fall back, but not without disputing every inch of ground during the engagement. We sustained a loss of 240. . . . Col. Lang, of my Regiment, was present and acted with the usual gallantry that has characterized him on many battlefields."[43]

Though broken, the Flowers were still Rebel soldiers. Bowles recalled seeing a handful of Floridians hunkered down behind a pair of fallen trees, "firing at the enemy at a distance of not more than forty steps. Finally they left this ambush and had not gone more than a few steps when one of them fell, shot in the leg. His comrade deliberately walked back, squatted down and the wounded man put his arms around his neck while he walked off with him before the whole Federal line. . . . It was one of the most heroic acts I ever witnessed."[44]

During this phase of the engagement, the Floridians suffered almost 50 percent casualties, losing 236 out of about 500 men engaged. Of the three

Fig. 11. Lt. Raymond J. Reid, Second Florida Regiment

regiments, the Fifth Florida was particularly hard hit. Col. Lamar had been wounded in both the hand and leg. Scottish-born Capt. James Kinlock, before the war a bookkeeper in Newport, was killed leading the remnants of the "Wakulla Tigers" during the Federal assault. Pvt. Wilbur W. Gramling, along with most of Co. K, Fifth Florida, was captured. Capt. Seton Fleming received two minor yet painful wounds—one in the breast and the other in the abdomen.[45]

Of the casualties, two were more widely lamented than the others. The first was E. A. Perry. As he rode along the line attempting to rally his soldiers, Perry's foot was hit by a minié ball. His wound became infected, soon becoming gangrenous. E. A. Perry had fought his last battle with the Army of Northern Virginia. The second casualty caused almost universal mourning among the Florida brigade. Lt. Raymond Jenckes Reid, adjutant of the Second Florida, took a bullet in the stomach and died the following day. Extremely popular in his own right, he was the only surviving son of territorial governor Robert Raymond Reid and Mary Martha Reid. His mother had organized and served as matron of the Florida Hospital in Richmond, and the tight-knit survivors of the Florida brigade considered her nothing short of an angel of mercy. For the sake of his mother and for his undisputed courage, the Flowers lamented Reid's loss. Commenting on his death, a comrade described him as "a perfect and amiable gentleman, and as brave a soldier as we ever had."[46]

While Bliss's bluecoats chewed up the Florida brigade, W. F. Perry's Alabamians opened a galling fire on Burnside's Pets. Surprisingly few Floridians took the opportunity to scamper off the battlefield, and those who successfully ran the gauntlet fell in with the Alabamians behind their earthworks. Though badly intermingled, the graycoats were veteran troops and exhibited a remarkable esprit. W. F. Perry reported: "The fire of the enemy was returned with the greatest spirit, and the soldiers exhibited a sort of exultant confidence—a feeling I was far from sharing with them."[47]

As the Federals closed the gap, a bloody hand-to-hand struggle exploded all along the barricade. Musket butt and bayonet thrust were countered by sword, lead, and fists. Dead and wounded littered the ground. The dry leaves underfoot caught fire, and smoke enveloped the area, creating a netherworld worthy of Hieronymus Bosch. To rally his disorganized troops, one Union captain actually grabbed his unit's flag and, crawling atop the breastworks, began bellowing "Battle Cry of Freedom" at the top of his lungs.[48]

While Bliss tried to dislodge the mixed ranks of Alabamians and Floridians, Col. Simon G. Griffin's Maine, New Hampshire, and Vermont brigade struck the Confederate left flank. Hit by the fresh assault, the bone-tired troops of the Forty-seventh Alabama were pushed back, folding backward like the closing blade of a jackknife. As more Yankees began pouring around the Confederate flank, W. F. Perry concluded that "nothing was left for us but an inglorious retreat, executed in the shortest possible time and without regard to order." For the only time during the war, the Alabamian claimed, his unit could not hold an assigned position.[49]

As humiliating as Perry found having his brigade broken and forced back, the Rebels still had a will to fight. As W. F. Perry fought to rally and re-form the broken units, Maj. Oates took two regiments and drove through an opening left when the Fifty-first New York retreated. They were buying time with their blood, but their sacrifice paid dividends. Through the haze came reinforcements in the form of Nathaniel Harris's Mississippians.[50]

The Magnolia State warriors had been "laying on the plank road . . . among the enemy's dead and wounded" when W. F. Perry's urgent call for help arrived. R. H. Anderson sent Harris's brigade down the plank road immediately, with the simple orders to *drive the enemy.* In a postwar report to Mahone, Harris related: "Advancing in the direction indicated [by R. H. Anderson], [we] encountered the enemy moving in two columns by the flank, to the rear of the Brigades of Davis [Harris was mistaken], Perry, and Law, with the evident intention of cutting off and capturing them, as those brigades were isolated, both flanks exposed, and owing to the density of the woods, unaware of the enemy in this direction. The enemy was thrown into confusion by the impetuous and unexpected charge of the [Mississippi] Brigade, and were driven in handsome style some distance." W. F. Perry reported simply that the charge "swept them [the enemy] away like chaff."[51]

Harris's assault threw Burnside's green troops back to the tree line, but the battle continued to rage for two hours more. Burnside's Pets just did not know when to quit. W. F. Perry recalled that "desperate and repeated efforts were made by the enemy to dislodge us, but they were repulsed with heavy loss. . . . In this action the enemy suffered heavily, several officers (including a Colonel), and many men being left dead on the field." Finally, the gory fight north of the Orange Plank Road sputtered to a halt.[52]

Elsewhere on the field, the carnage continued. Meade ordered Hancock to launch "a vigorous attack" south along the Orange Plank Road at 6:00 p.m. Lee, however, beat him to the punch. At 4:15 p.m., the graycoats thrashed their way through the thickets and jungle growth, heading right for the barricades fronting the Brock Road. As so often happened during the battle of the Wilderness, the attackers became a disorganized mass in the undergrowth, and the charge lacked the punch necessary for a frontal assault to succeed. Few of the attackers even reached the open field of fire the Unionists had cut in front of their breastworks.[53]

As darkness fell over the Wilderness's scarred and twisted terrain, both armies began building or strengthening earthworks. Gaps were plugged, and corps, divisions, and brigades were reunited and reorganized. Both sides seemed to expect a renewal of fighting at daybreak, and they were determined to be ready. The exhausted combatants were nervous, firing at the slightest movement or noise.[54]

The scene of the battlefield on the night of May 6 beggars accurate description. Screams of agony mixed with "the most intolerable stench from the thousands of unburied dead which ever assailed the nostrils of mortal men." One of Grant's aides, Lt. Col. Horace Porter, left a vivid account of the nightmarish scene. "Forest fires raged," he later recounted, "ammunition trains exploded, the dead were roasted in the conflagration; the wounded roused by its hot breath, dragged themselves along on torn and mangled limbs, in the energy of despair, to escape ravages of the flames; and every bush seemed hung with strains of blood-stained clothing. It seemed as though Christian men had turned to fiends, and hell itself had usurped the place of earth."[55]

The price of the bloodletting had been exorbitant. Union losses are traditionally reckoned at 17,666, while the Confederate casualties are calculated at about 11,000 killed, wounded, and missing. The Federal dead could be replaced, though with inferior soldiers. The Southern manpower pool, on the other hand, was virtually depleted. Only unreliable conscripts, older men, and the very young remained to fill the Confederacy's decimated ranks.[56]

The Florida brigade, R. H. Anderson's smallest unit, suffered the division's greatest percentage of loss. The Floridians had not only lost, once again, a large number of men, but their popular commander as well. Luckily, Col. Lang, who again replaced E. A. Perry at the head of the brigade, was a proven combat officer. They would need all his skills in the days to come.[57]

"One Vast Golgotha"

Spotsylvania, North Anna, and the Arrival of Finegan

The fires, ignited during the Wilderness battle, continued to flare throughout the night of May 6–7. Any movement or noise between the lines brought a hail of bullets from the nervous skirmishers crouching in the darkness near the breastworks, but soldiers, both blue and gray, put aside their fear and animosity to search the field for the wounded. The suffering of the helpless enemy touched even rabid Yankee-hater John F. Sale of Mahone's Virginia Brigade on that night. Sale could not help remembering that "these men had been *bought* to come to our homes and do all the harm one human being is capable of doing to another, still I could not but pity them in their misery. I assisted them by giving them water, making coffee, and other little attentions."[1]

Not all of the searching was of a humanitarian nature. As usual, many stole from the dead and wounded without remorse. Shoes, watches, and money were highly prized plunder, but anything that caught the scavenger's eye was considered fair game. Even some who believed stealing sinful succumbed to temptation. Most of the Southerners were ravenous. One hungry graycoat recorded: "We got out of rations during this battle and could not get to our wagons, but the Yankees had four or five days rations of hardtack and bacon in their haversacks, and we could get them from the dead. I have been so hungry that I have cut the blood off from crackers and eaten them." An Alabamian reportedly lugged a wounded Yankee from the burning woods and would not let the unfortunate Federal out of his sight. When questioned about the Confederate's devotion to the dying enemy, a friend reported: "He had just brought him out of the woods on his back so as to get his boots as soon as he dies."[2]

The battlefield was by all accounts a most unpleasant place. The odor proved almost unbearable. One of Wright's Georgians described it as "the most intolerable stench from the thousands of unburied dead which ever assailed the nostrils of mortal man." The cries of the wounded were deeply disturbing. A Federal surgeon reported that the unfortunates prayed for death, called for Mother, and generally "made the night hideous with their groans."[3]

Dawn brought little relief. Both sides were exhausted. Gen. Lee's veterans, basing their opinion on past experience with Fighting Joe Hooker, John Pope, Ambrose Burnside, and George B. McClellan, felt confident the Federals would fall back across the Rapidan by the next morning. Many bluecoats, for the same reasons, shared the Rebels' assessment.[4]

For some of the Florida troops and others in R. H. Anderson's division, the new day brought an additional hardship. They were part of the unfortunate contingent detailed to bury the "putrid" dead. The rapid decomposition and evidence of horrible burns made this thankless task even more disgusting. One of Billy Mahone's Virginians recalled: "The graves were not over & above deep. The main thing was to bury them."[5]

To his credit, U. S. Grant refused to let his newfound respect for the Army of Northern Virginia and his fervent desire to be clear of the eerie, shattered Wilderness goad him into an unwise action. The Union commander never considered retreat as an option. By 6:30 a.m. Grant had reached a momentous decision. "Make all preparations during the day," he directed George Meade, "for a night march to take position at Spotsylvania Court House with one corps." This move would accomplish two important objectives. It would ensure that Lee could not retire south and destroy the smaller army of Maj. Gen. Benjamin "Beast" Butler, who was advancing on the Confederate capital along the James River. More significantly, this change of base—if successful—would place the Army of the Potomac between Lee and Richmond. All Grant's troops had to do was beat the Southern army to Spotsylvania.[6]

When the dawn attacks the Rebels expected failed to materialize, Lee ordered a series of probes along the line to determine Grant's intentions. Results of the forays began arriving at Lee's headquarters almost immediately. Southern skirmishers generally found the Union defenses abandoned and littered with discarded supplies. The Confederate chieftain sent his cavalry to find the enemy, and turned his attention to equally pressing matters.[7]

The wounding of James Longstreet, the First Corps commander, created problems more significant than most Southerners realized. Lee allowed his commanders considerable latitude in carrying out his orders, and without an able leader to replace Longstreet more than one-third of the Southern army would be crippled. By midafternoon Lee issued orders for R. H. Anderson to replace Longstreet.[8]

Repercussions from this decision trickled down to the Third Corps. Mahone, the senior brigadier of R. H. Anderson's old unit, received the appointment to lead the division. Despite his good showing in the Wilderness fight, this selection apparently resulted from following the order of seniority. Col. David A. Weisiger, the senior colonel of Mahone's old brigade, assumed leadership of the Virginia unit. As if the Virginia army's command situation were not jumbled enough, on the evening of May 7, A. P. Hill reported himself too sick to retain command of Third Corps. Without hesitation, Lee named Jubal Early as Hill's temporary replacement.[9]

The battle of Spotsylvania started with a footrace. Grant's bluecoats began the contest at 9:00 p.m. with the dual advantages of marching along better roads and a two-hour head start. R. H. Anderson, in his initial action as First Corps commander, would be Lee's runner. The decision to send the modest South Carolinian was a matter of chance more than choice. Anderson's troops were "farthest to the right and could start more readily." Upon the outcome of the contest rested the immediate fate of the Confederacy.[10]

The Rebel soldiers encountered awful conditions on this night march. Anderson pushed his troops hard along a track cut through the forest that afternoon by Brig. Gen. William N. Pendleton's troops. The woods on both sides of the rough-hewn track were on fire, and darkness slowed the march to a crawl. Trees littered the trail and stumps jutted from the rough bed to trip the unwary. Still the men of the First Corps trudged through this smoldering landscape, winning the race to Spotsylvania Court House by the slightest of margins.[11]

As the graycoat units were fed helter-skelter into the fight on May 8, the Confederate earthworks assumed their own winding shape, like a bizarre freeform sculpture. The Southern defenses arced, in a wide semicircle, along a series of low hills from the Po River on the left to the Fredericksburg Road on the right. (The breastworks were eventually extended southward to rest on the north bank of the Ni River.) Near the center of the line, perhaps three miles north of the courthouse, a salient jutted due north like a blunted spear point. Most of the soldiers, whether clad in blue or gray, were country boys and they called the bend in the line the "Mule Shoe."[12]

The men of the Third Corps had no inkling of the events happening to the east. About midday on May 8, Jubal Early assumed command of the Third

Corps. Mahone's division once again made up part of the Southern army's rear guard. Early ordered several units, including the Florida brigade, into the shattered woodland to determine if the enemy remained in position. What they found were mostly stragglers and the Federal rear guard. The latter quickly gave ground, offering little resistance. Sgt. Kirkpatrick of Harris's Mississippians described a typical encounter. "Advanced about two miles and found only cavalry. . . . After giving the cavalry a little attention, and finding that they did not belong to the fighting class, we returned to our line."[13]

The Floridians and Alabamians had an even more fortunate experience with Union horsemen. Both units discovered a large number of abandoned horses. Many of the footsore infantry soldiers apparently had visions of joining the cavalry, but found their hopes dashed when their officers decided to give the horses to the artillery. But not all of the animals made it to their assigned destination. Seton Fleming reported: "About midday our pickets brought in 19 captured Yankee horses, which were captured with a small guard and 130 others. I kept one of the horses to use [and] several others [were] kept in the Brigade."[14]

By 3:15 p.m., the results of the reconnaissance convinced Early that no danger existed in the area, and he began the march to rejoin the rest of Lee's army. The Spotsylvania campaign brought a rare period of good fortune to Lang's Floridians in which they served for two weeks as little more than spectators to some of the war's bloodiest fighting.[15]

The Confederate Third Corps had barely cleared the scorched Wilderness when Weisiger's Virginians ran into bluecoats deployed around the Bradshaw Farm. Early's troops, joined by Maj. Gen. Wade Hampton's horse soldiers, advanced to drive the Unionists away and a sharp little skirmish developed. Seton Fleming reported: "Marched some 5 or 6 miles and came up with the Yankees. [We] were thrown into line and advanced on them but did not get engaged. Mahones [actually Weisiger's] did & ran them off." At nightfall, the weary Confederates occupied the farm, sleeping once more among the dead. After a couple of hours, Early moved the groggy, complaining troops a couple of miles to the southeast.[16]

Couriers arrived from Lee by first light urging the Third Corps commander to hurry down "the Shady Grove [Church] road towards Spotsylvania Court House." Early hastened to comply, but it took the exhausted and hungry graycoats six hours to cover the three miles to the Po River. Many of the soldiers moved as if in slow motion. In the established tradition of America's volunteer soldiers, they carped loudly that their rations had not been delivered and about their foolish, heartless officers.[17]

By nightfall they had entrenched along the east bank of the Po, guarding the Block House Bridge. The troops worked all night, and by daybreak on May 10, the Confederate breastworks ran north and south, parallel to the river, for about a third of a mile. Lt. Col. David G. McIntosh's artillery battalion provided support for Early's infantry.[18]

This peculiar alignment was dangerous because it left a wide gap between Mahone and Maj. Gen. Charles W. Field's division, which had previously constituted the extreme left of Lee's army. On the opposite bank of the Po, the Union II Corps waited for daylight to cross the Po at the Block House Bridge. Relying on inaccurate intelligence, Hancock thought he would be facing only Hampton's cavalry.[19]

The battle of the Po, as the May 10 engagement became known, revealed Robert E. Lee at his best. The Southern commander realized the potential for disaster the gap in his line presented, but Lee had a gambler's nerve and a hunter's instinct for the kill. He had, on the evening of May 9–10, ordered Early to take his last uncommitted unit—Henry Heth's division plus three regiments of Weisiger's brigade—on a sweeping march through the humid Virginia darkness to strike Hancock's unprotected flank.[20]

With the first glimmer of light, McIntosh's artillery began raining shells on the Union camps along the Po's west bank. This rude form of reveille seemed to sap the Yankees of any aggressive designs. One of Harris's Mississippians, waiting in the trenches on the Po's east bank, laconically observed: "Enemy troops appeared, started to ford the river above the bridge then withdrew." Heth's greyhounds appeared around noon, slowly but surely driving the II Corps veterans before them. Only some hard fighting by Brig. Gen. Francis C. Barlow allowed the battered II Corps to escape capture or destruction. Sgt. Kirkpatrick reported: "Between 3 or 4 p.m., Heth having struck their flank, came sweeping down parallel to the river on the opposite side. Our batteries played across the fugitive mass with beautiful effect, and many a one rested from his labors forever more. As soon as the [Block House] bridge was uncovered our division crossed over to join the rout, but night came on, before we found an opposing force." Seton Fleming concurred, recording: "[A]bout sunset crossed the creek at Bridge. Stopped a little while in line of battle at [A. R.] Wright's left—then went further up the road about 1 mile from bridge and bivouacked for night."[21]

Throughout the next day, the Third Corps shifted position a time or two, but saw little action. The only excitement the division saw on May 11 came with Federal shelling of religious services held by chaplains of Wright's Georgia brigade. A steady rain began to fall late in the afternoon, and the men of Mahone's division spent a woeful night upon the west bank of the Po. Evening rations had been "a few morsels of corn pone" and a single strip of raw bacon per man. They had wolfed down this meager fare and then collapsed upon the sodden ground. Even without the scant protection of tents or waterproof canvas sheets, they somehow managed to sleep. This was their first full night of rest since May 4, and most simply ignored the miserable conditions.[22]

Long before daylight on the 12th, couriers began arriving from Gen. Lee ordering Mahone's men to hurry toward the Mule Shoe. During the night the Federals, attacking in tight formation, had overrun the Confederate defenders in the salient. A few hardy graycoats held back the Yankees, but they were hard pressed. Lee hurried Mahone's division into the fray as soon as it arrived on the field.[23]

Perrin's Alabama soldiers went in first, fighting their way to the west wall of the salient. Harris's Magnolia Staters followed through the rain and battlefield debris, securing more of the captured breastworks. Brig. Gen. Samuel McGowan's South Carolina troops came next, wresting the rest of the Mule Shoe's western side almost to its apex. For the next twenty hours, which a Mississippian described as "one vast Golgotha," these Southerners held the earthworks against repeated attacks by superior numbers under the most appalling conditions imaginable.[24]

Lang's Florida boys followed Harris, but they were sent to the eastern works of the Mule Shoe salient. Weisiger's Old Dominion soldiers followed the Floridians, and together they waited for the Federal assault.[25]

Grant had directed Burnside to advance his troops simultaneously with the early morning charge of the II and IV Corps, but the IX Corps commander once again lagged far behind schedule. Late in the afternoon, when Burnside's Pets finally arrived, they ran into a hornet's nest. Brig. Gen. James Lane's North Carolinians and Weisiger's Virginians went over the earthworks, attacking the IX Corps' flank. A gory, confusing melee developed, lasting until well after nightfall.[26]

Holding the line, the Floridians were spared the worst of the bloodletting. Seton Fleming related in his diary: "Perry's Brigade placed in line behind breastworks little to right of Ct House where it remained all day.... In evening Mahone and Lanes went out as flankers and when the Yankees made their last assault on our lines Mahone & Lanes Brigades captured 250 prisoners & 2 stands of colors besides guns. Our [the Florida brigade's] loss today slight. . . . Perrys Brigade not engaged but could witness the fight [across an] old field in front."[27]

Around 2:00 a.m. the Confederates began evacuating the Mule Shoe. All afternoon and evening the Confederate pioneers had been constructing a new defensive line along the base of the salient. Behind them the battered graycoats left thousands of dead and wounded.

For the next few days the two commanders maneuvered to gain an advantage, but accomplished nothing more than to increase the already horrible casualty lists. The Florida brigade apparently did not participate in any of the combat, and Seton Fleming's diary has no entries from May 13 till May 20.[28]

On the evening of May 20, Grant abandoned his position near Spotsylvania, moving southeast toward the North Anna River. Lee's troops followed the next day, blocking the way to Richmond by establishing a strong defensive line along the west bank of the North Anna. The new alignment also protected the valuable Virginia Central Railroad and the crossing of the Richmond, Fredericksburg & Potomac Railroad. A. P. Hill returned to lead the Third Corps during this time, though his action at North Anna proved less than exemplary.[29]

When a Union probe drove Wilcox's division away from Jericho Mills on May 23, Lee established a new position, in the form of an inverted "V," atop some high hills overlooking Ox Ford on the North Anna. Though the breastworks were strong, Gen. Lee, sick and exhausted, lacked the ability to strike and destroy the enemy. For the Confederates, the war had already become a strictly defensive struggle. Grant, not knowing the Rebel weakness, worried about the configuration of his army's position. Hancock, Wright, and Warren's corps bivouacked along the south bank of the North Anna, but Burnside's Pets remained north of the stream. The Union commander ordered Burnside to "get over and camp on the south side."[30]

Brig. Gen. James H. Ledlie, alcoholic and totally incompetent, led his brigade across at Ox Ford first. Ledlie decided that driving the Rebels from their entrenchments would bring the fame and glory he apparently craved. He requested permission to attack, called for reinforcements, and ordered the assault on the Confederate breastworks without waiting for approval for his action or for his support to arrive. What followed was a virtual massacre.[31]

Ledlie's 1,500 men could never hope to carry the heavily defended breastworks, and the Confederates knew it. The Floridians taunted the advancing bluecoats, shouting, "Come on Yanks, come on to Richmond." D. L. Geer obviously enjoyed the chance to kill the hapless Federals. "We went into line of battle on a high bluff on the . . . South [actually North] Ann[a] river, and on the other side there was a broad river bottom and it closed up in a field and the woods were within a quarter of a mile from our position. We had eight guns—or cannon—in the works with us. The Yankees were trying to establish a skirmish line in the field and we had a picnic—we picked them up so fast they could not make a line." A Florida officer reported his unit had "a good old time making them 'heel' it away."[32]

The Union artillery tried to cover the assault and retreat of Ledlie's men, but the destruction of attacking bluecoats continued unabated. A member of the Fifth Florida reported that the Yankee "shells shot shrapnel and every other blasted thing has cut all the trees and bushes from around" the Confederate position. Casualties in the Florida brigade were slight, but Capt. Council Bryan recorded an incident in which gnawing hunger cost the small unit several losses it could ill afford. "Five of the 8th Fla," he recounted, "about an hour ago crossed the River to get a yearling that had come down for water (two of the five had stripped off all of their clothing). The Yankees saw them and captured all five."[33]

On May 26 Grant abandoned the attempt to dislodge the Rebels. He swung south toward Totopotomoy Creek. Lee's army trudged south to keep between the enemy and Richmond.[34]

During the last weeks of May, the Army of Northern Virginia began receiving much-needed reinforcements. The divisions of Maj. Gen. Robert F. Hoke and Maj. Gen. John C. Breckinridge arrived first. Both units came to Lee's army with reputations as determined fighters, following the former vice president's impressive victory at New Market and Hoke's successful North Carolina campaign.[35]

The Florida soldiers had also been expecting an infusion of new blood. They had heard that one battalion from their home state would soon arrive, but when they reached Atlee Station on May 28, they discovered three battalions camped along the side of the road. (A fourth Florida battalion had been briefly detained at Bermuda Hundred.) It proved to be a happy reunion of old friends. Seton Fleming reported finding "good many of our friends and acquaintances among them"; while Pvt. George Dorman of the newly arrived First Florida (Special) Battalion, recalled: "We soon began to meet with the Second and Eighth regiment boys, which was a very pleasant meeting of old friends. But, indeed, a very unpleasant place."[36]

Few expected the new troops from the Land of Flowers to be good fighters. Maj. Gen. Sam Jones, commander of the Military District of South Carolina, Georgia, and Florida, warned Richmond, "I greatly doubt if one half of the men ordered will leave Florida, and my order will cause desertion and disorganization." Even a youngster in the Sixth Battalion admitted the new troops were "the odds and ends of the last crop of Florida soldiers." In total, approximately 1,200 troops arrived in the Old Dominion and were consolidated with the 275 members of Perry's old brigade.[37]

The Sixth Florida Battalion and three independent companies were combined almost immediately to form the Ninth Florida Regiment. The unit's nicknames (when known), counties of origins, and commanders were as follows: Company A (Gulf Coast Rangers), Levy County, Capt. Enos A. Davis; Company B (Ocklawaha Rangers), Marion County, Capt. John W. Pearson; Company C (Brooksville Guards), Hernando County, Capt. Samuel E. Hope; Company D (B. F. Guards), Columbia County, Capt. James F. Tucker; Company E, Columbia County, Capt. Green H. Hunter; Company F, Marion County, Capt. A. P. Mooty; Company G, Marion and Alachua counties, Capt. S. M. G. Gary; Company H, Columbia and Baker counties, Capt. Matthew A. Knight; Company I, Hernando County, Capt. William L. Frierson; and Company K, Marion County, Capt. Jacob K. Eichelberger.[38]

The Ninth Florida Regiment had a strong veteran officer corps to lead the new unit. Col. John M. Martin, thirty-two years old, a planter from Marion County before the war, had attended the Citadel and helped to organize the Marion Light Artillery shortly after secession. He had been severely wounded at the battle of Richmond, Kentucky, and sent home. During 1863 he had served as a Florida representative to the Confederate Congress, but Martin desired to return to active service and received a commission as lieutenant colonel of the Sixth Battalion. John W. Pearson, another Marion County planter, apparently served as the unit's lieutenant colonel. Though fifty-two years of age, Pearson had served as a guerilla in the Union-controlled area east of the St. Johns River and had defended Tampa with dogged tenacity before moving to northern Florida to hunt deserters and Unionists in Taylor County. Maj. Pickens Bird, before the war a planter and politician from Hernando County, had previously served in the Third Florida in the Army of Tennessee.[39]

The Sixth Battalion's only combat experience had been at Ocean Pond (or Olustee), but the unit had performed well in that first fight. Early in that engagement the raw battalion had shifted south of the Florida, Atlantic, & Gulf Central Railroad and had opened such a galling fire on the similarly inexperienced Eighth USCT troops that the black soldiers retreated in some disorder.

Fig. 12. Col. John M. Martin, Ninth Florida Regiment

One historian concluded that the Sixth Florida's "enfilading fire was one of the chief factors in causing the initial retreat of the Union battle line."[40]

The ten companies that arrived with Brig. Gen. Joseph Finegan had a somewhat different composition than the veteran troops. More than 400 men from the original units that became the Ninth Florida soldiers were over thirty years old, with sixty-eight-year-old Richard Gany likely having the distinction as the unit's oldest soldier. (He lasted only three months before being listed as AWOL, with the adjutant noting that Gany was "believed sick and unable to report.") Some of the older men may have enlisted as a result the Conscription Act, but many had enlisted in 1861 in militia and coast watch groups. The total count of Ninth Florida troops seventeen years old or younger appears to be very small, with the number of foreign born, Northern born, and those with Hispanic surnames similarly miniscule by comparison to the veteran Virginia regiments.[41]

The First Florida (Special) Battalion also had fought well at Olustee, being part of the advance that finally sent the Yankees in headlong retreat to Jacksonville. Unfortunately, the rest of the unit's history had been less than stellar. The First Battalion companies, counties of origins, and commanders were as follows: Company A, Bradford (formerly New River) County, Capt. John C. Richard; Company B, Suwannee and Columbia counties, Capt. Charles J. Jenkins; Company C, Duval and Nassau counties, Capt. Edwin West; Company D, Hamilton County, probably Lt. William Scott; Company E, Sumter County, Capt. Benjamin O. Grenad; and Company F (Alachua Stars), Alachua County, Capt. John H. Ellis.[42]

Col. Charles F. Hopkins, a native of Georgia and graduate of the Naval Institute at Annapolis, had worked as a civil engineer in St. Augustine before the war commenced. Cool and competent, Hopkins had suffered persecution at the hands of Gov. John Milton (likely because Hopkins's uncle had been Milton's opponent in the 1860 election). The chief executive and Brig. Gen. Joseph Finegan had deflected blame from themselves onto Col. Hopkins for the debacle at St. Johns Bluff in 1862. Hopkins and his unfortunate troops had served several lonely months in exile at Thunderbolt, Georgia, near Savannah, before being recalled. Hopkins's quick thinking had helped secure the Confederate victory at Ocean Pond. Lt. Col. William Washington Scott, a forty-year-old Georgia native, had seen action in the Mexican War.[43]

Like the Ninth Florida, the First Florida Special Battalion had a considerable number of soldiers over thirty years old, even though the unit had also had been organized in the war's early days. It had a few more foreign-born troops than the Ninth, especially in the Jacksonville company. Thirteen-year-old George Meridith seems to have been the regiment's youngest "soldier," but he lasted only three months before his mother tracked him down and took the boy home.[44]

The Second Florida Battalion had originated as part of a plan designed to meet the Confederacy's manpower needs by essentially bribing middle-aged men to join the service. Don Hillhouse provides an excellent synopsis of the convoluted history of Lt. Col. T. W. Brevard's unit.

> The 2nd Battalion companies had seen even less action than Hopkins' Battalion before coming to Virginia. Their origins date from the spring of 1862, when [the Confederate] Congress authorized the formation of companies of partisan rangers for a peculiar sort of mounted guerilla service. The rangers were intended as a mobile strike force, to patrol stretches of unoccupied territory, harass the enemy, and conduct raids when the opportunity presented itself. A provision in the law allowed the rangers to be paid for weapons and munitions taken from the enemy, making the

partisan a kind of land-based privateer. Enlistment was limited to those over the draft age, 35, but the Florida companies appear to have generally ignored this requirement.

Further confusing the situation, the unit went by several designations, including Second Battalion Partisan Rangers, First Battalion Partisan Rangers, and Second Florida Battalion, and the widely scattered companies drew recruits from wherever they were stationed.[45]

The Second Florida Battalion was composed of the following companies, counties of origin, and commanders: Company A, Duval County, Capt. George C. Powers; Company B, Putnam and Bradford counties, Capt. Samuel W. Mays; Company C, Hamilton County, Capt. John Q. Stewart; Company D, Jefferson County, Capt. Marion J. Clark; Company E, Jackson and Washington counties, Capt. Walter J. Robinson; and Company F, Duval County, Capt. Adolphus A. Ochus.[46]

Col. Theodore W. Brevard, before the war an attorney and politician from Tallahassee, was well known to many troops of the Second Florida Regiment. Brevard had originally served as captain of Company D until March 1862. When he failed to be reelected, Brevard returned to Florida and organized the Partisan Rangers. The battalion had served primarily in north Florida, but Brevard had just begun a campaign to clear the valuable cattle country south of Tampa of Federal troops and local Unionists before the situation in Virginia changed that plan.[47]

Records for the Fourth Battalion are sketchy at best. The companies, nicknames, counties of origin, and commanders are as follows: Company A (Henry County Avengers), possibly of Walton County, Florida, and Dale and Henry counties, Alabama, Captain E. A. Curry; Company C (Jackson Guards), Jackson County, Capt. John Tanner; Company D (Bradford Light Infantry), Madison County, Capt. George T. Redd; Company E (Cobb Guards), Jackson County, Capt. George W. Bassett Sr.; Company F (Hood Guards), Leon County, Capt. James M. Shine; Company G (Vernon Tigers), Washington County, Capt. Ephraim P. Melvin; and Company H, Jackson County, Florida, and Houston County, Alabama, Capt. Edward C. Everett. This unit either had no Company B, or all its records are lost.[48]

The Fourth Battalion missed both Olustee and the battle of Cold Harbor. James F. McClellan, the battalion's lieutenant colonel, had served with the Second Florida during 1861–62, but his company failed to reelect him after the

Williamsburg fight. The Fourth Battalion's performance in Florida had led to calls for its "disbandment based on its inefficiency and lack of discipline." The stigma of this recommendation would dog McClellan throughout the remainder of the war. The Tennessee native was forty years old in 1864, and one of the state's best-known attorneys. The soldiers of the Fourth Battalion had elected John Henry Gee, a medical doctor from Quincy, as the unit's major.[49]

Glatthaar notes that the 1862 enlistees included more soldiers who were married with children, and fewer foreign-born men. His statistics match fairly closely Finegan's new arrivals. He also noted that most of these men were farmers, though the rural Florida units included a sizeable number of cattlemen. The arrival of the Second and Fourth battalions brought the first influx of conscripts to the Florida brigade. Most were mature family men in their thirties or forties. The youngest Florida soldier may have been eleven-year-old Daniel Absalom Baker, who made it to Virginia and appears to have fought in some early battles. (Home on sick leave when the war ended, Daniel rode off on horseback to find his older brother James, and wound up saving his sibling's life.)[50]

Brig. Gen. Joseph Finegan commanded the four new Florida units. Finegan, a native of Ireland, had moved to Florida in 1830, accumulating a fortune as a planter, sawmill operator, and partner in Sen. David Yulee's Florida Railroad. He served as a member of the Secession Convention, predictably voting for disunion. Some sources attribute Finegan's generalship to the "political necessities of appointing a sufficient number of brigadiers from Florida." The Irishman proved to be an able administrator, but his actions at Olustee, his one major battle, drew some criticism. A Virginian angrily declared: "Finegan stopped the ordinance train and came near spoiling the whole affair. He ought to be cashiered." To most of the state, however, he remained a hero. The men of the Second, Fifth, and Eighth Florida regiments resented Finegan for purely selfish reasons. The arrival of Finegan almost certainly meant that Col. David Lang would not receive his brigadier's star.[51]

The appearance of the new Florida troops was a source of amusement for some veterans of Lee's army. Geer, the brigade's prankster, recalled: "Now, here was a hard-looking lot of soldiers. They were all smoked from lightwood knots and had not washed or worn it off yet; and being so far down south, they had not received many clothes—only what their mothers and wives had spun or woven for them, and to see their little homespun jackets and most of them with bed quilts instead of blankets. They carried the Florida trademark. One looked like he had eaten a few grindstones and a good many of them looked like they

Fig. 13. Brig. Gen. Joseph Finegan, commanding, Florida brigade

had a pure case of mail [male]-green sickness." One young soldier of the Sixth Battalion agreed. "I can remember," he wrote, "how the old soldiers made mock of our green unsoldierly ways, and dubbed us with nicknames that made us for the time the jest of the army. I cannot blame them. Falstaff's variegated soldiers would have put us to shame." Lee and his staff must have prayed that, in this case, looks would be deceiving.[52]

"Each One a Hero"

Sacrifice at Cold Harbor

The new troops from Florida received their baptism of fire in Virginia almost immediately. Lee's army entrenched along the south bank of Totopotomoy Creek (between Atlee's Station and Pole Green Church), and Ulysses Grant spent much of May 29 probing the Confederate lines for a weakness.[1]

In a foreshadowing of future events, Maj. Gen. John C. Breckinridge's Virginians crumbled under Federal pressure, and A. P. Hill ordered his Florida infantry and skirmishers from Col. David Weisiger's brigade to plug the breach. They easily drove the bluecoats back across the Totopotomoy, and a member of Col. Hopkins's First Special Battalion bragged: "For new troops (at least new to Virginia soil) our skirmishers were conceded to have acted exceedingly well, but they owed much to the experience of the Virginia Sharpshooters, and a small detail of the old 2nd Florida [Regiment]. . . . the 6th Battalion [now officially designated as the Ninth Florida Regiment] did fine service and won credit by charging, with the 8th [Florida] Regiment, the enemy line which had driven back the advance in front of Breckinridge's line, and reestablishing the line."[2]

The Floridians suffered only a few casualties, but Lt. Col. John W. Pearson received a mortal wound in the firefight. The pugnacious old guerilla was formed from the same mold as Nathan Bedford Forrest and William T. Sherman. Pearson viewed war not as an effete Marquis of Queensbury boxing match but as a harsh, bitter brawl with only two possible outcomes—victory or death. While conducting a partisan campaign east of the St. Johns River, he hanged two slaves he believed had disclosed his position to the enemy. On another occasion Pearson had defied the Union navy on Tampa Bay, informing the Federal squadron commander that he did not "understand the meaning of the word surrender," Pearson died on September 30, 1864, at Augusta, Georgia, while trying to return to his Marion County home. A business associate and friend claimed the old guerilla's body and had him interred in Savannah's Laurel Grove Cemetery.[3]

Unable to crack the Confederate line, Grant shifted the Army of the Potomac south toward Cold Harbor. Five roads converged at Cold Harbor, and its location—almost exactly ten miles from Richmond—greatly inflated the strategic importance of the dusty crossroads.[4]

Lee knew the terrain around the tiny village well. Two years previously a major battle of the Seven Days engagements (sometimes called First Cold Harbor, but more commonly referred to as Gaines's Mill) had been contested over the same ground. As with the Wilderness, an eerie, haunted aura seemed to hover over this blood-soaked locale, and both the Federal and Confederate soldiers approached this terrain with a feeling of trepidation.[5]

The new Florida troops literally stumbled over a reminder of the region's gory past. Pvt. George Dorman of Co. A, First Florida (Special) Battalion, recalled: "We stopped in an old field to rest and eat some hardtack and a mouthful of raw bacon. A beautiful spring of cold water was boiling up just down the hill. Of course, that was something appreciated by the Florida boys especially, and we were enjoying the cold water, together with our little rest. Just up the hill . . . some of the boys got to kicking what they thought were gourds about. Upon examination it was discovered that the supposed gourds were the skulls of men, and behold we were drinking from a spring just below a graveyard—where a battle had been fought two years before."[6]

While Joseph Finegan's Florida troops were becoming acclimated to their new surroundings and comrades, the second battle of Cold Harbor had already begun. Realizing the strategic importance of the crossroads village from his earlier experience at Gaines's Mill, Gen. Lee ordered his nephew, Maj. Gen. Fitzhugh Lee, to take and hold Cold Harbor. Occupying the tiny hamlet proved no problem, but holding it was not as easy. By 3:00 p.m., Maj. Gen. Phillip H. Sheridan's Union cavalry, armed with repeating rifles and fighting dismounted, drove off Fitz Lee's troopers. The Confederate cavalry chief called for infantry support, but a late-afternoon assault by Maj. Gen. Robert F. Hoke's infantry failed to dislodge the Federal horsemen.[7]

Robert E. Lee concluded that Grant would concentrate his forces at Cold Harbor before striking west toward Richmond. This offered the Confederate commander an opportunity to take the offensive. Lee hoped he could strike the Unionists while they were strung out on the march, roll them up like a newspaper, and, if all went according to his plan, destroy the Army of the Potomac. The success of Lee's scheme required that the Army of Northern Virginia take and hold Cold Harbor.[8]

Early on the morning of June 1, R. H. Anderson ordered his First Corps to drive off the Yankee horse soldiers. Anderson's plan was simple enough, and should have succeeded. Maj. Gen. Joseph B. Kershaw's South Carolina brigade, one of the Southern army's finest combat units, would assault Cold Harbor from the northwest, while Hoke's soldiers would advance from the southwest and turn the Union flank.[9]

Unfortunately, the Palmetto State soldiers went into action without their capable commander, and Col. Lawrence M. Keitt's inexperienced Twentieth South Carolina spearheaded the attack. The Twentieth South Carolina immediately disintegrated in the face of the enemy gunfire. The panic rapidly spread to Kershaw's other regiments, and they retreated in some disorder and "reflexively started building earthworks." Hoke's division did little better in its part of the operation. It advanced only a few hundred yards, before its commander, "after careful reconnaissance, deemed [the Federal position] too strong to attack." His men halted and also began constructing breastworks, and Gen. Lee's hopes for an offensive victory at Cold Harbor dissipated like the morning mist.[10]

Union infantry began to arrive at Cold Harbor around midday on June 1, with Maj. Gen. Horatio G. Wright's VI Corps relieving Sheridan's exhausted horsemen. Maj. Gen. William F. "Baldy" Smith's XVIII Corps soon followed, and late in the afternoon the bluecoats probed R. H. Anderson's defenses. Wright's infantry drove in Confederate skirmishers and quickly fell back, but Smith's men made better progress. Brig. Gen. James B. Brewerton's division of VI Corps and Maj. Gen. Charles Deven's XVIII Corps division hit a weak spot in the Rebel lines, driving through Hoke's section of the works. Only quick work by Kershaw and Brig. Gen. Alfred H. Colquitt's brigade prevented a Confederate disaster.[11]

The news of Smith's initial success bolstered Grant's hopes for victory, and he concluded that an opportunity existed to pierce Lee's defensive line. He ordered a massive, coordinated assault for the next day (June 2). In his brief stint as commander of the Army of the Potomac, Grant had come to rely upon Hancock's reliable II Corps for his hardest fighting, and the Union commander was loath to begin an assault without Hancock's tough infantry. Unfortunately for the bluecoats, the II Corps soldiers had a terrible night march, and did not arrive at Cold Harbor until the afternoon of June 2. As a result, Grant felt compelled to delay the assault until the following morning.[12]

Both Lee and Grant used the brief respite to prepare for the next attack. The Confederates worked on their entrenchments and shifted troops into position. A modern historian recorded, "Lee's veterans took advantage of this vital 24-hour delay to entrench themselves quickly and effectively, using every creek, gully, ravine, and swamp in such fashion that all approaches to their positions could be covered with a murderous fire." Though not as formidable as the breastworks employed a few weeks later during the Petersburg campaign, the Cold Harbor earthworks had been significantly strengthened from the "ditches" employed on June 1.[13]

A. P. Hill's Third Corps held the Confederate right, R. H. Anderson's First Corps occupied the center, and Jubal Early's Second Corps was deployed on the left. The new troops had been quickly assimilated into the various corps. Hoke's division seemed to fight primarily with Anderson's First Corps, and Breckinridge's troops seemed informally attached to A. P. Hill. The performance of the Kentuckian's infantry at Cold Harbor started in an inauspicious manner. The infantry arrived late on the afternoon of June 2, leaving a wide gap in the Confederate line. Gen. Lee, who was expecting a Union assault at any moment, had arisen from his sick bed and personally sought out Breckinridge, urging him to quickly get his graycoats in position.[14]

The Federal alignment had Burnside (IX Corps) on the extreme right, followed by Warren (V Corps), Smith (XVIII Corps), Wright (VI Corps), and Hancock (II Corps). The Union line stretched from north of Bethesda Church almost to the Chickahominy River in the south. Boatswain Creek, a marshy feeder stream for the Chickahominy, ran through the area where the II Corps veterans faced A. P. Hill's Third Corps.[15]

Mahone's division took up a position several hundred yards behind the breastworks, serving as reserves for Hill's command. The Florida brigade apparently arrived on the field sometime after nightfall on the evening of June 2, setting up camp 200 or 300 yards southeast of the Watts farmhouse, and 250–300 yards behind the entrenchments occupied by Breckinridge's troops. Further to the north, only 100 yards from the Watts residence, the soldiers of the tiny Confederate Second Maryland Battalion pitched their tents in a swale, serving as support for Breckinridge's unit.[16]

The Florida troops immediately began to build entrenchments. The red clay of Virginia made the task of digging trenches difficult, a task exacerbated by the lack of shovels and trenching tools. Pvt. Dorman recalled: "We found out there was trouble ahead of us, so we went to work with our bayonets digging up the old Virginia soil, soon striking into red clay. We would throw it up in front of us with tin plates. We worked all night to get us a little breastworks." The Floridians fell asleep in the new ditches almost immediately.[17]

Promptly at first light (4:30 a.m.) on June 3, more than 60,000 Federals surged forward, but it was hardly the coordinated assault Gen. Grant envisioned. Hancock's II Corps, on the extreme Union left, charged with its usual vigor. Wright's VI Corps advanced, but gingerly and without spirit. The front elements of Baldy Smith's XVIII Corps rushed into the maelstrom of death, but Warren's V Corps failed to join the attack. Burnside, as usual, got his IX Corps troops into action, but not until 8:30 a.m. His troops suffered perhaps 1,700 casualties in their futile assault.[18]

Many veteran Union troops apparently considered the chances of success to be slim, and the likelihood of death much greater. Soldiers, afraid of being buried in an unmarked grave, reportedly sewed name tags on their clothes so that their remains could be identified.[19]

In some cases it took more than orders and adrenalin and patriotism to get the bluecoats to advance. Col. David Lang wrote that some of the captured Federals were under the "majic influence of old rye," and similar Confederate reports lend credence to the assertion. A Union lieutenant with the Eighth New York wrote that a few veterans required cold steel to get them to advance. "The Veteran troops in our Brigade [Brig. Gen. Robert O. Tyler's unit] refused to charge & one Regt. was driven out of the entrenchments by the Provost Gd. At the point of the Bayonet. It was horrible."[20]

All along the line the scene was the same—bloody, useless slaughter. Only on the front held by Breckinridge's units did the Federals manage a breakthrough. Brig. Gen. Francis C. Barlow's division, which had spearheaded the rupture of the Mule Shoe salient at Spotsylvania a few weeks previously, found a weak spot in the former vice president's position and drove through it.[21]

The breach in the Confederate works occurred in the section assigned to Brig. Gen. John Echol's brigade. Col. George S. Patton, an 1852 graduate of the Virginia Military Institute, had temporarily replaced Echols as commander of the unit. During the night, Patton had withdrawn most of his men from a swampy section of the defenses to an "encircling ridge, leaving the breastworks to be held by their picket-line."[22]

Two distinctly different versions of what happened in Patton's sector on the morning of June 3 may be found in the *Official Records* and memoirs of participants. A Confederate participant recalled the battle for the breastworks as "a furious hand-to-hand fight with pistols and clubbed muskets." Winfield Scott Hancock recorded in his after-action report that Barlow's infantry seized the outer line "after a severe struggle and followed into their works under a very heavy artillery and musket fire." Postwar, Breckinridge claimed that of all his battles, he took "especial pleasure" remembering the actions of his troops at "second Cold Harbor."[23]

The Floridians saw a very different picture. Capt. Council Bryan of Co. C, Fifth Florida, in a letter to his wife penned immediately after the fighting ceased, wrote that Patton's "whole line fled panic stricken." Brig. Gen. James G. Martin, commanding a North Carolina unit adjacent to Breckinridge's division, adamantly affirmed that "Echol's Virginia Brigade, on our right, *broke and ran away.*" Geer penned an even more explicit account. "About daylight here came Breckinridge's men running over us like a bunch of Texas steers, stampeded the worst sort. That was always our experience when they were in ahead of us. We had no confidence in them at all." A recent historian of Patton's Twenty-second Virginia summarized the battle of Cold Harbor in a single line: "Breckinridge's troops occupied a swampy segment of the Confederate right center which would have been breached without the aid of General William Mahone's division."[24]

Whatever the truth may have been, the "ragged crack of musketry . . . [and] the boom of cannons and screaming shells" awakened Finegan's Floridians from their abbreviated slumber. David Lang, the brigade's senior colonel and no stranger to fierce fighting, reacted with alacrity. Dorman reported: "Seeing the enemy so near, he [Lang] mounted upon our little breastworks and shouted: 'Charge, boys, charge!' We all rose, and with a yell fired our muskets toward them, and moved forward in quick time." Though far less experienced in combat than Lang, Gen. Finegan proved his fighting spirit at Cold Harbor. Pvt. H. M. Hamill, a boy soldier in the Ninth Florida, recalled that his men dashed toward Barlow's bluecoats "musket in hand, and Gen. Finegan, on horse, was racing up and down the line, crying 'Get ready, men; fall into line and charge.' . . . Gen. Finegan was a born fighter, of hot Irish blood, and I have a vivid memory of how his stumpy figure and fiery horse went slashing to and fro ahead of his men." The Second Maryland Battalion also lunged forward, joining the Floridians in the effort to plug the gap.[25]

One of the finest contemporary accounts of the early morning breakthrough comes from the pen of Council Bryan. "The enemy advanced," he wrote,

in five lines of battle against Breckinridge—whose whole line fled panic stricken over our breastworks and far to the rear—hatless, leaving their

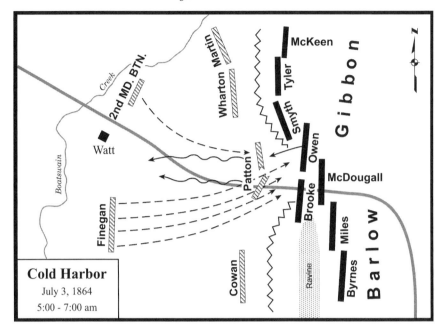

Fig. 14. Cold Harbor, June 3, 1864

guns and anything that impeded their flight—as soon as they had passed out of our way our boys rose with a yell—poured two volleys into the advancing droves of Yankees then jumped the breastworks and charged them—Five [Unionist] to one [Southerner] but each one a hero. They advanced fifty yards to each other[.] The Yankees halt, waver—and run. One more volley and Breckinridge's breastworks so ingloriously lost are ours—the breastworks recaptured and the battle is won. The Yankee dead cover the field—while strange to say twenty will cover the loss of the whole Florida force. The new troops fought like "tigers" and we feel proud of them.

Though no Florida accounts mentioned the gallantry of the Second Maryland Battalion, there can be little doubt that it advanced and matched Finegan's Cracker infantry in the ferocity of the assault.[26]

The section of breastworks retaken by Finegan's brigade, like the one at Spotsylvania, resembled a mule shoe or inverted "U" pushing out from the Rebel line toward the Federal position. Barlow's Federals, exhibiting "a persistency rarely seen, and taking advantage of a slight crest, held a position within

30 to 75 yards of the enemy line [the Florida brigade's position] covering themselves in an astonishingly short time by rifle pits." Probably in a gambit to cover the construction of the rifle pits, the bluecoats made a second attempt to overrun the salient. This time, the assault was easily repulsed. "In about fifteen minutes," a Florida soldier recalled, "the enemy made a charge to recover their lost ground, but they were repulsed by our men with heavy loss. The ground was covered with dead and wounded Yankees, and they were glad to retire."[27]

The Florida and Maryland troops had reestablished their defensive line, but holding it turned into an ordeal to test the mettle of any man. Three problems were readily apparent. First, Barlow's troops, from their hastily constructed rifle pits around the salient, were able to maintain a galling crossfire on the Flowers' position. Capt. James F. Tucker of Co. D, Ninth Florida, wrote:

> The works we occupied had been (it was said) laid out at night, were at the foot of a ridge, formed a sort of angle, and were both enfiladed by the enemy. To such an extent were we exposed to their fire that no one could either leave or approach our part of the line. . . . In this bloody angle or death trap it was almost as much as a man's life to show his head even for a moment. . . . The fire was galling, and came so thick and fast that our colors were riddled and the flagstaff perforated in a number of places. The feeling was that by holding up an open hand Minie balls could be caught as if hailstones.[28]

The second difficulty faced by the men in the trenches was Finegan himself. Somehow, the Cracker infantry's commander had become separated from his command, and while soldiers endured the miseries of trench warfare, Finegan directed his men from the safety of the Watts farmhouse grounds. Communication between the brigadier and his troops was, at best, limited. "Orders from and reports to headquarters," an officer noted, "had to be transmitted by word of mouth or through the medium of a cap box passed from hand to hand, and ammunition was replenished the same way."[29]

Finally, during the early morning charge to retake the breastworks, most of the troops had left their personal belongings and canteens in camp. Very high temperatures, woolen or jean uniforms, and a lack of water turned the usual discomfort of trench warfare into a truly hellish experience.[30]

About 10:00 a. m., Finegan sent orders for Maj. Pickens Bird, commanding the Ninth Florida, to form a skirmish line and drive the Federals from their rifle pits and breastworks. Even the greenest soldier in the trenches that morning realized that a charge by skirmishers across an open field into the teeth of an entrenched, veteran foe was suicidal.[31]

After confirming his orders, Maj. Bird formed his detachment and went forward with a Rebel yell. The results of Finegan's egregious blunder were vividly recounted by Lt. Henry W. Long of Company K, Ninth Florida.

A few moments later the voice of that patriotic soldier and gallant officer [Bird] rang out for the last time, clear and distinct, which was heard above the rattle of musketry, and was of common, "Attention Skirmishers: Forward March!" It being self-evident that obeying that fool hardy order . . . would result in certain death, many of the men detailed refused to respond to the orders. Captain Robert D. Harrison, commanding Company B of the 9th Florida Regiment, when his detail refused to go forward, by way of encouragement to them mounted the breastworks, waiving his sword to enthuse them to obedience, was immediately shot by a federal bullet which disabled him from active service for months to come. Major Pickens Bird had advanced perhaps thirty yards when he was shot down. That gallant officer Captain James Tucker, seeing his Major shot down, leaped over the breastworks, ran to him, and as he rose with the Major in his arms, was himself shot down. . . . Lieutenant [Benjamin] Lane of Company A, seeing Captain Tucker shot down, leaped over the breast works and ran to these wounded officers, picked up Major Bird, and as he mounted the breastworks with him, was mortally wounded.[32]

Bird and Tucker were eventually rescued by the ingenuity of one of their noncommissioned officers. Sgt. Peter N. Bryan, Co. D, Ninth Florida, waited till the fire subsided, then slipped over the breastworks, and by pushing and pulling the wounded officers inches at a time, managed to slide them into the salient. There the badly injured Bird and Tucker lay all day, protected from incoming fire but exposed to the blistering sun. Tucker said they lay among the dead and wounded "like so many sardines in a box."[33]

Throughout the long morning and afternoon, the Floridians crouched in the breastworks, subjected to the glare of the sun and the Union fire. Cries of the wounded for water mingled with the whine of small-arms fire. Eventually, Lt. J. D. O'Hern, Second Florida Battalion, could stand the pleas of the wounded for water no longer. O'Hern collected all the canteens he could lay his hands on and prepared to dash across an open field to a brook almost half a mile away. Warnings by comrades that "a rat could not pass over that field un-

Fig. 15. Capt. C. Seton Fleming, Second
Florida Regiment

hurt" failed to deter the tenderhearted Irishman. O'Hern began his sprint, and
Federal sharpshooters zeroed in on the Confederate officer. The Federal soldiers sensed the purpose of O'Hern's mission; their fire slackened and then
ceased. O'Hern filled the canteens and jogged back to the breastworks, and as
he neared the ditches the Federals gave the Irishman a cheer for his bravery.
Then the deadly business of killing resumed with increased fury.[34]

Late in the afternoon, Finegan sent orders for a second skirmish line to be
formed to drive out the bluecoats from their position in the rifle pits and entrenchments surrounding the salient. Nothing had changed since Maj. Bird's
ill-fated assault, but no one seemed capable of convincing Gen. Finegan of the
foolishness of a second assault. Compounding the tragedy, he chose the remnants of Perry's old brigade, including Capt. Seton Fleming's Second Florida,
for the suicide mission. Once more the men of Florida's "representative regiment," now barely the size of a company, would be called upon to sacrifice for
the cause they loved. Everyone but, unfortunately, Finegan, realized it was a futile gesture, doomed to failure.[35]

Finegan's orders astounded Fleming. Capt. Tucker, lying paralyzed since
Bird's early morning attack, concluded: "Could our brigade commander [Fine-
gan] have seen the situation as we did from our plainer point of view, he would
[not] have permitted a second sacrifice of so many brave soldiers. I have been
told that the order was all a mistake, and was not intended."[36]

Fleming protested, apparently hoping that the order was given in error. After receiving confirmation of the directive, he decided that his only choice, as a soldier, was to obey. He gave Dr. Richard P. Daniel, the Eighth Florida's surgeon, his pocket watch and other valuables (including the diary previously quoted herein), and shook hands with friends, encouraging them to do their duty and make Florida proud. The Floridians were paying a steep price for Finegan's comfortable place in the rear.[37]

The results of the second charge were predictable. Henry W. Long wrote that Fleming "was almost instantly shot to death, as was every soldier who attempted to obey that fatal order." Capt. Tucker watched from the ditch, unable to do anything but pray. "At the agreed signal," he reported, "Capt. Fleming and his brave band of heroic soldiers scaled the entrenchments and disappeared from my view. They did all that brave men could do, but the odds were too great and the same fate that had been meted out to Maj. Bird and his brave men . . . fell to them." Paying tribute to Fleming and his men, Tucker wrote: "To my mind their behavior was superlatively heroic, and I much doubt if it has ever been surpassed." The following evening a party of Alabamians, scavenging the field, found Fleming's body within thirty yards of the breastworks. Also lost in the second charge was Benjamin L. Reynolds, commanding Co. H, Ninth Florida, who fell dead "while cheering his men to acts of heroism."[38]

The second attempt, by Seton Fleming, to dislodge the Federals essentially ended the second battle of Cold Harbor for the Floridians, and they were finally relieved from their "intolerable" position. Lt. Long recalled: "[D]uring the night of the 4th another line of breastworks in our rear was prepared and those occupied by the [Florida] brigade was leveled, during which time we were exposed to the random shots of the enemy, which fortunately for us was not rapid. On the early morning of the 5th the brigade retired to the rear and took its position as a reserve."[39]

The performance of the green soldiers in Finegan's brigade on June 3 won high praise from their comrades. Geer, who had previously mocked their appearance and rough clothing, concluded his account of the battle by stating: "They [Finegan's new troops] played their part as good as the oldest veterans in General Lee's army . . . if they did have on bed quilts and homespun jackets, they made a reputation that morning that proved they were as good as the best we had in our army." The Southern newspapers immediately dubbed the Floridians "the Whirlwind Brigade" for their prompt action. For a short while, they were the darlings of the Army of Northern Virginia.[40]

Pvt. Hamill recalled with obvious pride the tribute paid to the Florida troops after the fighting ended. "[A]way toward midnight, when a lull came to the fir-

Fig. 16. Dr. Thomas Palmer, surgeon, Florida Brigade Hospital

ing, the veteran troops to the right and left of us took up the cry: 'Three cheers for Finegan's Brigade.' I need not say we felt good over it, and I am not ashamed to say we deserved it."[41]

Its moment of fame had cost the brigade dearly. Exact casualty figures are not available, but one contemporary source noted: "The First Battalion lost 75 to 80 killed, wounded, and captured; the 2nd Battalion lost 85 to 90; the 6th Battalion [Ninth Florida Regiment] lost 105." No losses were reported for the remnant of Perry's brigade, but considering the late afternoon charge by Fleming, they must have been severe.[42]

The wounded Floridians were eventually forwarded to the Howard Grove Hospital in Richmond. There they received excellent care from the dedicated medical staff of Dr. Thomas Palmer and Mrs. Mary Martha Reid. Despite the tireless efforts of Palmer and Mrs. Reid, Maj. Pickens Bird died four days after his arrival. His last words were reportedly: "Tell them I died like a Confederate soldier."[43]

Capt. James Tucker, paralyzed by his wound, was sent home to Florida to recuperate. When Tucker married late in the war, he used his uniform as his wedding garb due to the lack of cloth in the state. An insignificant private in Capt. Sam Hope's company of the Ninth Florida named Early Allen was wounded in the chest and sent home to Hernando (modern Citrus) County. The wound refused to heal, and he died several years later, relieved of his suffering at last.[44]

The aftermath of the battle was especially trying for the wounded on the field. The usual tradition of sending a flag of truce to allow for the prompt removal of the wounded failed due to the stubbornness of Gens. Grant and Lee. Grant well realized that sending a flag of truce indicated defeat, and he hesitated to take that step. Gen. Lee, usually the proper Christian gentleman, for once refused to allow the removal without a formal truce. (It was certainly part of his calculations that almost all of the wounded were Federals.) While the two generals dickered, the helpless men lay in the sun amid a stench so horrid that veteran troops retched; watching buzzards pick the eyes out of the dead; and with no water to slake their thirst. By the time the truce was concluded, it was too late for many of the wounded.[45]

12 "We Are Going to See the Elephant Show His Works"

The Siege of Petersburg

On June 8, 1864, the War Department in Richmond issued Special Orders No. 133 consolidating the three remaining Florida battalions into two new regiments. Maj. Gen. J. Patton Anderson, while briefly serving as commander of the Military District of Florida, had recommended merging the battalions into regiments in March, but the advice from the Confederate hinterland did not become a priority until Joseph Finegan's troops transferred to the Army of Northern Virginia. Part of Richmond's earlier reluctance might have stemmed from a desire to keep from opening a political can of worms, but recent events had made the reorganization too important to ignore.[1]

The War Department's decision to build the two new regiments around the First Florida (Special) Battalion and the lightly regarded Fourth Battalion must have surprised observers at the time. T. W. Brevard's Partisans certainly had a better reputation than either Charles Hopkins's or James McClellan's units, but the reasons for Richmond's configuration of the new regiments remains unknown. The sections of Special Orders No. 133 that applied to the Florida brigade read:

XVII. The First Florida Battalion, Lieutenant-Colonel Hopkins, six companies, and the companies of Captains Mays, Stewart, Clarke, and Powers, of the Second Florida Battalion—Brevard's—will constitute the Tenth Regiment Florida Volunteers.

XVIII. The Fourth Florida Battalion, Lieutenant-Colonel McClellan, seven companies, the companies of Captains Robinson and Ochus, of the Second Florida Battalion, and Captain Cullen's unattached company Florida Volunteers, will constitute the Eleventh Regiment Florida Voluneers.[2]

The companies comprising the Tenth Florida Regiment and their commanders were: Co. A., Capt. John C. Richard (pronounced *Ree-shard*); Co. B, Capt. Charles J. Jenkins; Co. C, Capt. Edwin West; Co. D, Capt. Thomas M. Mickler; Co. E, Sumter County, Capt. Benjamin O. Grenad; Co. F, Capt. John H. Ellis; Co. G, Capt. Samuel W. Mays; Co. H, Capt. John Q. Stewart; Co. I, Capt. George C. Powers; and Co. K, Capt. Marion J. Clark.[3]

Politics and smoldering animosities made naming commanding officers for the Tenth difficult. The War Department originally named Brevard to command the Tenth Florida, but Pres. Jefferson Davis, always a stickler for seniority, vetoed the appointment. The new unit's leaders were finalized with Hopkins as colonel, William Washington Scott as lieutenant colonel, and John Westcott serving as major. Scott's prewar occupation, as a merchant in Newnansville, provided little hint of military competence, but the forty-one-year-old Georgia native brought combat experience to the position as a veteran of both the Mexican War and the fight at Ocean Pond. Westcott, a diminutive sixty-one-year-old New Jersey native, had briefly attended West Point, fought in the Second Seminole War, and had served the state as a legislator and as state surveyor general. Additionally, he was a physician, businessman, and railroad entrepreneur, and had helped establish Florida's first Masonic lodge and Jacksonville's first Episcopal church. Despite his advanced age, Westcott's aggressive defense of Tampa in 1863 showed that he possessed a fighting spirit.[4]

The companies composing the Eleventh Florida Regiment and their commanders were: Co. A, Capt. John M. Erwin; Co. C, Capt. E. A. Curry; Co. D, Capt. Adolphus A. Ochus; Co. E, Capt. Andrew Jackson Coffee; Co. F, Capt. John Tanner; Co. G, Capt. George T. Redd; Co. H, George W. Bassett Sr.; Co. I, Capt. Joseph J. Chaires; Co. K, Capt. E. P. Melvin; and Co. L, Capt. Edward C. Everett. No Co. B has been found in records.[5]

As with the Tenth Florida, finding commanding officers for the Eleventh Regiment proved no easy matter. The problem was Lt. Col. J. F. McClellan. The nucleus of the Eleventh Florida would be the Fourth Battalion, which had "earlier been recommended for disbandment based on its inefficiency and lack of discipline," and McClellan suffered from the stigma of his unit's bad reputation. The War Department solved the problem by naming Brevard as colonel, McClellan as lieutenant colonel, and John Henry Gee as major.[6]

Brevard, before the war a Tallahassee lawyer and veteran of service with the

Second Florida, would become the last brigadier confirmed by the Confederate legislature. McClellan, also an attorney before the war, had served as a captain of the Second Florida. Postwar, he led white "redeemers" in the so-called Jackson County War and compiled "the standard legal digest of Florida's laws." John Henry Gee, a physician from Quincy, would have the misfortune to be appointed commandant of the Salisbury, North Carolina, prison. Charged with inhumane treatment of Union prisoners, Gee would undergo a Federal court martial-trial before being acquitted.[7]

The veteran Florida troops welcomed the new troops, but they initially despised Finegan. Their animosity toward "Old Barney" likely stemmed from the two suicide charges at Cold Harbor and the fact that his presence deprived Col. Lang of any chance for promotion to brigadier. On the night of June 6, members of the Fifth Florida got a measure of revenge. Council Bryan reported:

Old Finegan is undoubtedly a fool. . . . He came waddling along the other night and fell into the pit where Capt. Partridge & myself were sleeping—We were both awake & had lots of fun at his expense— pretended we did not know who he was & made him hop around considerably. He was charging around trying to get out and [he] slapped his old irish brogan with my shin—That was too much so I told him if he didn't leave that hole I'd injure the lower part of his bowels with my foot. The old Jack was such a fool he never said who he was but kept "damning the holes" & we had our fun; about one half of our Regt had the benefit of this frolic—He grabbed out after a while & swore the next "man that puts a hole heare, I'll bury him in it."[8]

After a brief respite following their heroics at Cold Harbor, the recent arrivals from Florida got a second introduction to the realities of army life in Virginia. Shortly after midnight on July 11, Finegan ordered members of Col. Hopkins's new Tenth Florida Regiment to man the rifle pits in front of the Confederate breastworks. A member of the battalion described the "picket holes" as a "square hole about four by eight feet and about three feet deep, with dirt or clay thrown up in front. Four men were put in each of these holes every night. One set would have to remain a day and a night before being relieved." Bryan tried to describe to his wife the physical and mental difficulties involved in this hazardous duty. "Where our pickets now are," he asserted, "if the enemy charges us it will be impossible for them to get out. . . . What water they carry in has to last them until they are relieved (24 hours) & it becomes so hot in the tin canteen, you can scarcely drink it. . . . They [the Federals] are not more than 40 yds . . . from us, but there is not much looking around as the bullets are too thick." Bryan added that several of the new troops had been killed or wounded while on picket because "they have been needlessly exposed and are too careless."[9]

The smell of decomposing animal and human carcasses still lying in the sun on the field near Cold Harbor compounded the misery of the troops on the picket line. Yet even in the midst of that enormous tragedy, the soldiers found some black humor. A Union deserter reportedly explained Federal strategy to the Rebels: "Grant intends to *stink* Lee out of his position, if nothing else will suffice."[10]

The members of Hopkins's detail had no way of knowing that the Union troops they thought they were confronting had already begun to withdraw. Grant had decided shortly after the terrible slaughter at Cold Harbor (by June 5) to cross the James River and capture the valuable railroad supply center at Petersburg. In truth, it was his only viable option. Northern Democrats, anti-Lincoln newspapers, and the Union and Confederate soldiers would construe any northward movement as retreat. To strike the Rebels along the swampy Chickahominy River, the next major stream, would risk another bloodletting similar to Cold Harbor and Spotsylvania, with the Yankees attacking entrenched Rebels.[11]

The Union's goal since 1861 had been to capture Richmond, and Ulysses S. Grant realized the importance of Petersburg to the Confederacy. Three railroads, a canal linking the James and Appomattox rivers, and at least twelve roads converged at the "Cockade City," and almost all the supplies for Richmond funneled through Petersburg. Located only twenty-three miles south of the Confederate capital, it boasted a population of 18,000 in 1864. During the conflict, military manufacturing had replaced tobacco and cotton as the city's major industries, and Grant knew that "[i]f Petersburg fell, Richmond was doomed."[12]

Grant's withdrawal from Cold Harbor was little short of a masterpiece of strategy, and the move completely baffled Lee. A Confederate artillery officer admitted: "Marse Robert, who knew everything knowable, did not appear to know what his old enemy proposed to do or where he would most likely find him." For days the Southern commander searched for the Army of the Potomac, but only occasional cavalry skirmishes and brushes with the Union rear guard disrupted the peaceful countryside.[13]

The Army of the Potomac should have taken the Cockade City on the night of June 15. Baldy Smith, with 20,000 battle-tested veterans, confronted Gen. P. G. T. Beauregard with 2,200 "troops," mostly old men and boys of the city militia armed with antiquated weapons. The graycoats were quickly driven from the outer line of defenses of the Dimmock Line, but somehow Beauregard's tenacity and luck—and Baldy Smith's timorous approach—kept the vital city in Confederate hands. The Louisiana Creole promptly summoned the only troops under his immediate command from Bermuda Hundred, but even with 10,000 troops he could not hope to hold Petersburg long without reinforcements.[14]

Beauregard issued increasingly frantic calls for additional soldiers, but his alarms, like those of the boy who had cried wolf once too often, were ignored. Only on June 18 did Lee finally realize that Beauregard was indeed confronting Grant's army. The Confederate commander had already dispatched Jubal Early and the Second Corps to confront a new threat to the Shenandoah Valley, leaving Lee with only about 30,000 men to send to Petersburg.[15]

Ambrose Powell Hill got his troops moving during the evening of June 18. The Third Corps camped at Chaffin's Bluff, but Finegan's men did not arrive there until 2:00 a.m. The Florida troops likely only got about three hours of sleep, for by daylight Hill's graycoats were on the road, crossing the James on a pontoon bridge, hurrying toward the beleaguered Cockade City. "Hill's troops marched furiously," a Hill biographer noted, "along the Petersburg pike, fighting thirst and spitting dust." Straggling was commonplace, with units losing all cohesion as their officers urged them forward, but the sounds of artillery and small-arms fire, as they neared the city, spurred the graycoats to greater haste. The women and old men of Petersburg lined the roads cheering the dusty, exhausted Confederates as they entered the town, but probably few were left when the Cracker infantry staggered through the city streets just before midnight.[16]

Confinement behind breastworks was Gen. Robert E. Lee's worst nightmare. Being pinned down in the Cockade City trenches took away the opportunities for the aggressive tactics that had proven so successful in 1862 and 1863 and were his army's only chance to destroy Grant's numerically superior force. Earlier in the week Lee had informed Jubal Early: "We must destroy this Army of Grant's before he gets to the James River. If he gets there it will become a siege, and then it will be a mere question of time." The Army of Northern Virginia, held in place by the need to protect Petersburg (and, by extension, Richmond), would be restricted to the limited offensive.[17]

The unlikely heroes of the strategy Lee adopted would be Maj. Gen. William Mahone and his Florida, Georgia, Alabama, Mississippi, and Virginia brigades.

Douglas Southall Freeman, the dean of Confederate historians, labeled Mahone's division Lee's "shock troops" during the siege of Petersburg.[18]

Mahone and his Virginians had entered the 1864 campaign with a lackluster reputation. One of Lee's staff officers disingenuously reported that Mahone's "brigade of Virginians had not seen much hard fighting." He conveniently failed to mention that they had had plenty of opportunities to build a far different record. Their "Battle of the Axes" at White Oak Swamp during the Seven Days made them the laughingstock of the army, and at Chancellorsville Brig. Gen. John Paul Semmes declared that Mahone's brigade "never stood a charge in their lives" and refused to let his soldiers fight near the Virginians. The failure of the men from the Old Dominion to support the charge of Lang, Wright, and Wilcox on July 2 caused hard feelings and led to jibes (especially from Wright's brigade) about giving them wooden rifles and giving Enfields to men who would fight. The flank attack in the Wilderness and the slashing dismantling of Burnside's May 12 attack at Spotsylvania seemed to indicate that Mahone and his troops had finally shaken off the doldrums of the first two years and were now ready to build a reputation as a premier fighting unit.[19]

Short of stature and emaciated to the point of starvation—one subordinate described him as "a mere atom with little flesh"—Mahone had a waspish disposition and the ego of a giant. Even his admirers admitted his tendency to be "irritable and in some instances tyrannical," and no one could deny that Mahone was an eccentric of the first order. The VMI graduate and railroad engineer had an unnatural fixation on his digestion, and his headquarters wagon often resembled a rolling barnyard, with a milk cow and chickens to provide the sole ingredients of his diet—fresh milk and eggs. James I. Robertson Jr. concluded that "Mahone was an odd little man, and he was one of the few generals in the Civil War whose star did not shine until late in the conflict."[20]

Mahone's new brigades immediately became aware of their commander's overweening ambition and willingness to build his reputation on their guts and sacrifice. A member of the Tenth Alabama criticized: "Billy Mahone was always volunteering to charge some place or other. He wanted to get his name up for promotion, but he didn't think of us poor fellow's lives, so he came out all right. We didn't like him any how. We didn't want a Virginian over us. For when we done the fighting he would give the praise to his old Va. brigade that couldn't show a good fight. But they were ready to be praised for what other brigades done."[21]

Mahone's division began to enhance its reputation almost immediately. On June 21 Gen. Grant ordered the II and V Corps out of their entrenchments along the Jerusalem Plank Road to damage or destroy the Petersburg & Weldon Railroad (traditionally referred to as simply the Weldon Railroad). As usual, the Federal commander relied upon the II Corps to do his heavy lifting. To divert attention and troops from the railway, the Federal commander sent a strong cavalry detachment under Brig. Gen. James Wilson and Brig. Gen. August Kautz to raid west of the Weldon line.[22]

Late in the afternoon of June 22, Mahone took his Georgia, Alabama, and Virginia brigades up a hidden ravine, striking the II Corps' left flank. The vaunted Federal unit, a mere shell of the force that had fought so valiantly at Gettysburg, Wilderness, Spotsylvania, and Cold Harbor, collapsed like a paper sack. The regiments that did not surrender immediately fled in disorder to the Union lines. Mahone's men killed or captured 2,400 bluecoats and garnered eight battle flags, four artillery pieces, and a huge quantity of small arms. Hancock, "the Superb," who had been on sick leave recovering from his Gettysburg wound, summed up his disgust in general orders, fuming: "[T]he surrender to the enemy of entire regiments by their commanders without resistance was disgraceful and admits no defense." Historian Bruce Catton described the battle as the II Corps' "most humiliating episode."[23]

The following day (June 23), Grant sent Wright's VI Corps out to continue breaking up the railroad. The Fourth and Eleventh Vermont, joined by Col. Timothy Bryan's Eighteenth Pennsylvania cavalry, advanced to the Weldon Railroad, dismantling about a quarter of a mile of rail and destroying a culvert. The officer of the day on the 23rd was Lt. Col. Samuel E. Pingree of the Third Vermont. Pingree arranged the units in a mile-wide "hollow square." He posted a line of skirmishers (90 sharpshooters) west of the rail line; Bryan's dismounted horsemen, strung out along a private road running from Dr. Gurley's house to the railroad, composed the southern side of the square; 200 men from the Eleventh Vermont comprised the northern section of Pingree's formation; and the Fourth Vermont closed the back (eastern line) of the square. After receiving word from spotters, posted in tall pine trees, of a line of dust proceeding south out of Petersburg, Maj. Charles Fleming, commanding the Fourth Vermont, directed his troops to construct a section of breastworks along a low ridge "using newly cut rails, which they found in piles on the ground."[24]

The line of dust indicated the approach of Mahone's division, with all of his brigades, "about 6,000 muskets" in total. (He apparently had left the new Florida troops to man the breastworks, but took Perry's veteran troops to clear the Weldon Railroad.) As the Southerners approached, driving in the skirmishers near the rail line, the men of Bryan's Pennsylvania cavalry grabbed their horses and fled back to the main Union line along the Jerusalem Plank Road. A VI Corps soldier who witnessed the incident observed: "The cavalry had been driven in by a line of infantry skirmishers . . . and it does not appear to be worth anything as far as fighting goes."[25]

Seeing the Yankees fleeing, Mahone decided to try a classic military maneuver—the double envelopment. With Sanders's Alabamians pushing straight ahead, Harris's Mississippians formed the northern pincer and the Second, Fifth, and Eighth Florida completed the entrapment. The Green Mountain soldiers would have been able to retreat, losing just a few stragglers, if they had withdrawn to the main Union entrenchments. Most instead took shelter in Maj. Fleming's temporary breastworks. Even many of those unfortunates might have yet escaped had it not been for Lt. Col. Samuel E. Pingree. Before Pingree fled to the Union army's defensive line, he ordered Maj. Fleming to "hold the line at all hazards."[26]

The Floridians met little resistance advancing through the deep woods. Mahone later claimed that Capt. V. J. B. Girardey, a hard-fighting Georgian on Mahone's staff, led the Florida troops at Gurley's Farm, but the best evidence indicates that Col. Lang again led his old brigade, which now numbered only 166 men.[27]

As the two prongs of the pincers came together, Maj. Fleming and his command surrendered to the Floridians. Lt. Isaac Auld of the Fifth Florida described the day's action as follows:

We left a large detail [the Ninth, Tenth, and Eleventh Florida] on picket at Petersburg, the march was very hot and fatiguing, which caused a number to fall out on the way. [O]ur little Brigade was slipped in behind a bunch who had been cut off and we advanced on them about dusk, and they, thinking we had a large force, surrendered, begging us not to shoot. We all ran up to them through the bushes more like a line of skirmishers than anything else. . . . one of them seeing such a small number of men taking them exclaimed, "Are these all the men you have!" I told him, "No sir! We have a whole line of battle back there, these are only the skirmishers." "Oh, well," he said, "its no use talking, we can't help ourselves."

The unit took 407 prisoners, including Maj. Fleming, and lost only two stragglers for their afternoon's work.[28]

The capture of the Green Mountain troops did not end the battle of Gurley's Farm. Wright's Georgians and Weisiger's Virginians rushed through the growing darkness against the VI Corps entrenchments but were bloodily repulsed. The Floridians were already gone, escorting their prisoners back toward Petersburg. The rest of Mahone's division soon followed. Meade planned on renewing the action the next day, but Grant overruled his co-commander. He decided that his army could use a few days of rest and relaxation.[29]

The Florida brigade was once more the darling of the Virginia press. The *Petersburg Express* recounted the exploit, but, proving that journalistic mistakes are not a new phenomenon, hiked the number of captives and made the incident into a firefight. "About twilight [it reported], Perry's Brigade, now commanded by General Finegan, succeeded in swinging around and brought up in rear of the enemy. A volley or two in their rear put the enemy to thinking and another volley or two brought about a very lively double quick on their part. We succeeded in securing only 483 of the invaders, the remainder running so swiftly that it was found impossible to overtake them." The Floridians cared little at the time for the press or their newly found fame. Most had been without sleep for forty-eight hours, and Pvt. W. A. Hunter of the Ninth Florida claimed that he had not slept for seventy-two hours. Most collapsed into slumber immediately after reaching the trenches.[30]

Mahone's division had temporarily cleared Grant's infantry from the Weldon line, but Wilson's and Kautz's cavalry raiders continued wreaking havoc on the southside and the Richmond-Danville roads southwest of Petersburg. The foray began with the destruction of an engine and thirteen flatcars on the Weldon Railroad. During the next week, the Northern horsemen destroyed sixty miles of rail lines, burned numerous depots and support buildings, commandeered every horse and mule they could lay their hands on, and generally disrupted Confederate communications and delivery of supplies.[31]

The seeds of destruction were planted by the early success of the Wilson-Kautz incursion. Mounds of plunder began to weigh down the Union cavalry's baggage train; slaves flocked to the raiding party, sure that freedom was at last within their grasp; and horses, pushed beyond the limits of their endurance, began to die at an alarming rate. The grand prize of the raid, the high railroad bridge over the Staunton River, also eluded Wilson. A ragtag group of about 300 militia commanded by Capt. Benjamin L. Farinholt held the span until Fitz Lee's cavalry arrived, and a victory by Wade Hampton's veteran horsemen on June 28 at Sappony Church convinced Wilson to return to the Army of the Potomac.[32]

On the night of June 28, Mahone ordered the Floridians and two regiments of Brig. Gen. J. C. C. Sanders's Alabama brigade to march nine miles south to

Ream's Station to intercept the Wilson-Kautz raiders. The Confederate plan was simple enough. Fitz Lee's horsemen would continue pressing the weary bluecoats from the north and Hampton's cavalry would attack the raiders from the south, driving them west into Mahone's infantry, stationed along the Halifax Road. First light found Finegan's men in position, strung out in line of battle just west of the railroad, the Halifax Road, and the remains of the burnt-out depot. The two Alabama regiments (likely the Eighth and Fourteenth Alabama) were stationed on the left and the Floridians posted on the right.[33]

The Deep South infantry had received two days' rations before leaving Petersburg, and many of the foot soldiers were cooking breakfast when, a Floridian later remembered, "a long line of dust, rising in our immediate front" announced the arrival of "the band of robbers [Union cavalry]." The Southerners either wolfed down their food allotment raw or abandoned it as officers hurried them back in line. A Confederate battery, which had accompanied Mahone's column, spoiled the plan to surprise Wilson's troopers when it opened fire prematurely. As the battle opened, Abe Register of Hopkins's battalion announced to his messmates: "Boys, this is one time we are going to see the elephant show his works." (Within hours Register would be dead, blown to pieces by a Federal artillery shell.) Finegan displayed the attributes of a good commander, riding up and down the line encouraging and steadying his troops.[34]

Kautz's division arrived first, and finding Rebel infantry blocking its path, the troops drew their swords and charged straight into the graycoats. Sanders's men received the brunt of the assault, and a soldier in the Fourteenth Alabama vividly recalled the scene years later:

They [Kautz's Federals] then drew their sabers and came right on. Of course, we fired at them, and by this time they were right upon us. I saw a man looking right at me with saber drawn, and by this time we were on one knee with our guns sticking out in front of us to keep their horses from jumping on us. I raised my gun above my head just as the "Yank" struck at me, and his saber struck my gun without doing any damage. One of my friends failed to work his gun just right and got part of his scalp taken off. He immediately turned and ran towards the "Yanks," using very profane language, shooting at them and cursing them as far as he could see them.

By driving straight through the Confederate infantry, Kautz's troopers lost some prisoners and had difficulty floundering through the thick woods and bogs, but reached the safety of Federal lines by nightfall.[35]

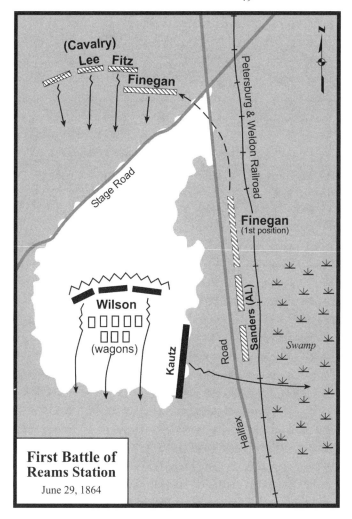

Fig. 17. First battle of Ream's Station, June 29, 1864

Wilson's division, with artillery, baggage wagons filled with plunder, and runaway slaves, drug onto the field near Ream's Station an hour later. The Union raider arrived at Ream's Station convinced that the Weldon Railroad was "in the possession of the infantry of the Army of the Potomac," but quickly discovered he had ridden into a trap. "The situation was critical. Hampton with two divisions of cavalry at Stony Creek Depot, Hoke's [actually, Mahone's] division of infantry at Reams' Station on our right flank, connecting with another large force formed in two lines of battle in our front, and W. H. F. Lee's division of cavalry marching on our left flank, were clear enough indications of the rebel intentions." Instead of charging headfirst into Finegan's and Sanders's infantry as Kautz had earlier done, Wilson decided to abandon his cannons, "contraband," and supply wagons and strike north toward Petersburg along the Stage Road, in hopes of escaping the trap by riding between the foot soldiers and Fitz Lee's cavalry.[36]

Wilson's strategy might have worked, but Finegan guessed his plan and moved quickly north to a position blocking the Stage Road. In a typically laudatory letter written hours after the battle, a Floridian reported the actions of Finegan's troops during this part of the battle.

> [T]he Yankees doubled upon their track, and struck out to their left, hoping thus to cross the Railroad at a point between us and Petersburg. Gen. Finegan, divining their purposes, left a portion of his command to hold the present position [near Ream's Station], and with the rest marched a mile and a half up the road in time to again confront Gen. Wilson. With six hundred and fifty men, Gen. Finegan held him in check four hours, and they were four long and anxious hours. . . . At length, Gen. Fitz Lee's cavalry came to our assistance. In the interim, the raiders had thrown up hastily constructed but quite serviceable breast works. With Gen. Finegan upon the left, and Gen. Lee upon the right, it was decided to charge at once.[37]

Wilson's men had had enough. As soon as the graycoats rushed forward screeching the Rebel yell, the bluecoats bolted from their defenses, riding hard south toward Stony Creek Depot. Leaving anything that would hinder their flight, the bluecoated horsemen spurred their mounts away from Finegan's and Lee's troops. Harassed for days by Confederate cavalry, the beleaguered raiders did not all reach the safety of Union lines along the Jerusalem Plank Road until the evening of July 1.[38]

One group of Floridians had an even longer odyssey. On the midmorning march to block Wilson's move up the Stage Road, five companies of Hopkins's Tenth Florida got separated from their comrades in the dense forests. Col. Hopkins led the rest of his unit during Finegan's and Lee's battle with the raiders, but the Eleventh Regiment's Col. T. W. Brevard, for reasons not entirely clear, found himself with the lost companies. Brevard immediately took charge of the group, keeping it from being captured on at least two occasions. Wandering through the "large hammock" for three days and nights, constantly on the move, the little group finally arrived, "hungry and tired," at Petersburg on July 3. Brevard's men received a hearty welcome from the Florida brigade. Dorman reported: "They began to yell all up and down the line, some slapping their hands, saying 'Boys, we had given you up, and thought you were gone!'" The troops were chagrinned by their little misadventure, Dorman noted: "All we could do was to smile a little and wave our caps."[39]

Confederate casualties at the first battle of Ream's Station are unknown, but were probably fewer than 150, infantry and cavalry. The Federals reported almost 1,400 killed, wounded, captured, or missing for the entire raid. Thirteen artillery pieces were captured, seven claimed by the Florida brigade. (Betraying his ambition, Finegan embarrassed himself and the brigade by straddling one of the cannon, shouting, "Promotion for me!") The Southerners quipped that "after eagerly tearing up the road, [Wilson's men] had been no less eager in tearing down the road" but the Wilson-Kautz raid seriously damaged Confederate supply and communications. It would take the Rebels months to repair the railroad lines, and the Army of Northern Virginia and Southern civilians would suffer weeks of privation as a result.[40]

Unlike most battles, in which the soldiers generally treated enemy captives as fellow sufferers at the mercy of the whims of heartless officers and the stupidity of national leaders, a great deal of animosity existed after the Ream's Station fighting. Southern sensibilities were incensed by the burning of houses, the plunder discovered on the Northern troopers (including a silver Communion service from a Virginia church), and the large number of slaves they had given refuge to. An Alabama officer reported that his men forced Yankee captives to parade through Petersburg carrying black infants in their arms as a sort of poetic justice. Virginia newspapers soon carried long lists of slaves who were to be returned to their masters, but even the unfortunate blacks probably fared better than the captured raiders, who were sent to Andersonville and Libby Prison.[41]

With a lull in the fighting, the soldiers soon began turning ditches into stronger, more permanent, entrenchments. The Confederate fortifications varied in quality, but typically would be about five feet deep; have a firing step, allowing the soldier to step up to fire his weapon and down to load; and, a head log across the top of the breastworks where the defender could fire through an opening between the trench's parapet and the bottom of the log, without having his head shot off. Timber roofs or canvas tent were often used to protect the graycoats behind the breastworks from the sun and rain. In many cases, the Southerners drove felled trees with the butts or branches sharpened and pointed toward the enemy from ten to fifty yards in front of the breastworks as an additional obstruction to an attacking force.[42]

In the past, black slave gangs, either rented from their owners or impressed into service, had often been used to construct defenses, but at Petersburg this dirty job fell to the soldiers. "A rotation system of sorts was devised, in which units spent a specified period on the lines—usually a few days—and then moved to the rear for a day or two before being rotated back into the works, and in which the units often kept part—usually one third—of their strength awake and on guard in the trenches at all times. Details to construct new earthworks, or improve existing ones, were also formed and maintained, often working through the day and well into the night." The soldiers, of course, found "the monotony of this hot & dusty life . . . irksome to the last degree."[43]

The Florida brigade shared in the arduous duty of constructing and guarding the earthworks, and its men also joined in the chorus of letters home decrying their situation. W. A. Hunter of the Ninth Florida complained: "We are out a resting but in stead of resting we have to work and stand guard every day & night which brings it round to me a bout every third day or night to work or stand guard[. O]ur new company is suffering at a fearful rate." The units generally had a permanent camp about a mile from the section of earthworks they defended, and this became their haven in the storm of siege warfare. Still, frequent duty in the trenches, hurried marches to counter Union advances, and days and nights in the picket holes soon took their toll. Hunter informed his wife: "We get to sleep 2 1/2 hours at night and then we don't get to sleep half enough during the day."[44]

Federal bombardment and sharpshooting increased the dangers of life within the trenches at Petersburg. On June 16, the war had taken an ugly turn as the Yankees began shelling primarily civilian targets in Petersburg. This particularly incensed the Confederate soldiers. "The vandals are still throwing shells into the city," a Virginia soldier reported on June 20, "and it is very distressing to see the poor women & children leaving. . . . [It] is enough to move the hardest heart."[45]

The danger to the men in the trenches from artillery fire increased as the Federals increasingly used light, easily moveable Coehorn mortars to shell the Confederate breastworks. Pvt. Dorman of the Tenth Florida remembered years later: "The Federals used a Howitzer or mortar for throwing shells. . . . We could tell when one of them was turned loose. They produced a different sound from the ordinary cannon. We could see the shell going up. In the day time it would look like a rubber ball going in the air; at night it looked like a small ball of fire going. The fuse burning made it easy to be sure at night. They could elevate those short pieces just a little toward us from straight up, and drop those old death-dealing shells almost in our ditches. . . . The boys called them 'Demoralizers.'"[46]

Sharpshooters proved far more deadly than mortars. Dorman explained, "Sharpshooters were men with long-range guns, which would kill a man a thousand or twelve hundred yards [away]—perhaps further—who would secure some elevated position—perhaps a tree—with a spyglass. They could pick men [off] at long taw." Amazingly, the Confederates came to look upon the sniper's deadly craft as merely a minor annoyance. W. A. Hunter reported to his wife: "I am tired of sharp shooting[.] I understand that we got 40 men killed in two days by the sharp shooters; you may think something about forty men being killed [but] here it is no more thought of more than you would think about killing forty flies." A North Carolina officer confirmed Hunter's observation. Maj. W. S. Grady observed that his men had seen "so much of Blood and death that our sensibilities become hardened [so] that we can hardly be said to act & feel like Men." The men even appeared at times to court death. Dorman recalled: "When it came down to sharpshooters and nothing else, the boys were so tired of the ditches they would get out and knock about."[47]

Life in the trenches proved to be a miserable, surreal existence for the Rebels. Life revolved around things that they could not control: food supplies, life at home, the election in the North, the campaign for Atlanta, and the still glimmering, if faint, hope of European recognition. A lieutenant in Colquitt's Georgia brigade explained life behind the Petersburg breastworks.

There are three points of interest each day with us now—early in the morning when the newsboy comes along the line shouting here's your daily paper, when there is a general rush till everyone has satisfied himself in regards to the news—second, later in the day, when the mails come in each man thinks he ought to have a letter and all is astir until he is certain there is none for him—Then third in the Evening when the cooks bring in the rations—then it is that every man is on hand and only retired when he has received his days ration of bread and meat—Occasionally Mr. Grant gets up some excitement addition to the regular routines . . . but if it were not for these, I do not know what we would do but die of Ennui.[48]

The men might temporarily put aside most of these concerns, but the gnawing hunger in their bellies could not be ignored. On rare occasions, such as the days following Hampton's cattle raid, they had food enough, but as the siege dragged on, rations became skimpier in quality and quantity. D. L. Geer explained one of the tribulations faced by the soldiers holding to the cause and Gen. Lee during the bleak winter of 1864: "They reduced the rations to nothing . . . two pints of cornmeal for two days rations, and this meal was corn, cobs and all ground up together. It wasn't fit to feed a decent bug on, yet it was so scarce that we would lay awake at night longing for enough of this cobs and corn ground up together. There was magic in that meal, and the magic was we could not get enough of it."[49]

In the best of times the Confederate Commissary Department had had difficulties supplying even minimal rations and necessities to the soldiers, and the siege of Petersburg hardly qualified as the best of times by any definition. The South, however, had become accustomed to soldiers in the Army of Northern Virginia winning victories despite these deficiencies. "The soldiers . . . exhibited extraordinary resilience in the face of wartime adversity. Not only did they fight tremendous battles and march great distances, they did so eating scanty rations, wearing poor clothes and shoes and sometimes, none at all, and facing supply problems that taxed the most masterful logicians." In fact, sometimes the difficulties spurred them to greater efforts. They knew "if they overran the Yankees, they could eat; otherwise, they went hungry."[50]

The problems faced by the commissary were virtually insurmountable. Large chunks of territory had been lost to the invaders. The loss of Middle Tennessee in early 1862 took the South's major pork-producing region, and the fall of Vicksburg in mid-1863 shut off the flow of cattle from Texas and the Trans-Mississippi. The Confederacy's railway system and manufacturing plants also proved inadequate, and each area that fell to the Federals put additional strain on the tattered fabric of Rebel supply capabilities. The biggest problem, however, involved manpower. Most Southern farmers were either in the army or hiding from conscript agents. As Professor Glatthaar points out: "As civilians they produced; as soldiers, they consumed large quantities of food and other products, but made nothing tangible."[51]

To meet the need for beef, the commissary turned to Florida. In early 1864, the Richmond government established the First Battalion Florida Special Cavalry (known universally, then as now, as the "Cow Cavalry") and assigned Maj. Charles J. Munnerlyn to head the unit. They hunted deserters, fought local Unionists and Federal regiments, and even attacked Ft. Myers, but their primary purpose was to gather and drive the scrawny Florida scrub cattle from the vast herds roaming the south Florida interior to the railheads in southern Georgia. (Confederate sympathizers in the area and experienced cowmen drawn from the Army of Tennessee comprised the original units, but about a hundred veteran cowhands from the Ninth, Tenth, and Eleventh Florida were also assigned to detached duty with Munnerlyn.) They shipped thousands of cows from the southernmost state, but most ended up with the Army of the Heartland or the forces guarding Charleston. As a result, most of the men in the trenches at Petersburg were forced to tighten their belts and endure.[52]

Hungry men can become desperate men, and sometime during this time of starving occurred one of the most famous incidents in the fabled history of Lee's "shock troops"—the theft of Billy Mahone's milk cow. Geer's version of the case of the purloined beef makes his company of the Fifth Florida the "heroes" of the deception, and the Ninth Florida the butt.

Billy Mahone had a fat cow to give him milk. She was kept tied to the wagon, and one night John Koon and A. J. Feagle saw that cow. She was fat, and it was natural to suppose, when there was so much "white mouth" around there, that John and Andrew had a longing to sharpen their teeth on the milk of Billy Mahone's milk cow. So one Sunday night they untied her and led her down a ravine back of the breastworks, and Andrew held her and John shot her. . . . While they were butchering the cow one of Finnegan's brigade came along and they gave him the tripe. When Billy found his cow gone he got mad and cursed and tore up the ground around. A search was made . . . [and] they found the poor devil in the Ninth Florida regiment boiling the tripe. So Billy had caught the thief at last . . . so they made all the privates [of the Ninth Florida] pay $10 and the commissioned officers pay $20. That was the way he punished them, and the Ninth got nothing but the tripe. We had the joke on the Ninth Florida, for we had the beef.[53]

Though the two months since the first battle of Ream's Station had been occupied primarily with skirmishing, bombardments, and sharpshooting, Gen. Burnside had put in motion a plan to end the siege. The scheme was the brainchild of Lt. Col. Henry Pleasants of the Forty-eighth Pennsylvania. Near Elliott's Salient, located atop a high point in the Confederate defensive line, the Union and Rebel lines were only separated by four hundred yards. Pleasants proposed that his unit, which included miners from the Pennsylvania coalfields, tunnel under the Confederate lines and set off a massive explosion. In the resulting confusion and destruction, a large Union force would charge through the ruptured line, breaking the Petersburg stalemate. Because Burnside's white troops had been worn to a frazzle by constant campaigning, the IX Corps commander chose Brig. Gen. Edward Ferrero's USCT soldiers to spearhead the assault. For the first time the Army of Northern Virginia would meet a significant number of African American troops on the battlefield. At the last moment, Grant and Meade determined, for strictly political reasons, to send the weary white troops in first.[54]

At 4:45 a.m. on July 30, Pleasants ignited four tons of black powder directly under Brig. Gen. Stephen Elliot's South Carolinians and Capt. Richard Pegram's Virginia battery. A nearby Virginian reported: "[The explosion produced] a deep rumbling sound, that seemed to rend the very earth in twain, startled me from my sleep, and in an instant I beheld a mountain curling smoke ascending toward the heavens," instantly killing 280 to 350 Southerners. D. L. Geer, stationed less than a mile from Elliott's Salient with the Fifth Florida, reported: "The ground came rolling like water under our feet . . . and then the dead thud, and fire bulge[d] up from the center of the little hill, and many a poor fellow that was strong and lively a second before went up with it. They were thrown up many feet among the dirt and fire, to fall back a mangled corpse among the pieces of cannon, carriages, and caissons, burnt black with powder smoke." A massive crater, measuring 170 feet long, 60 to 80 feet wide, and 30 feet deep, had now replaced the little hill.[55]

The Federal artillery opened all along the line in a massive barrage and the bluecoats stormed into the chasm, but only slowly began advancing toward Petersburg. The remnants of Elliott's Palmetto State brigade opened a ragged, but effective, fire on the Federals clambering out of the crater, rapidly joined by Confederate cannoneers and Maj. John C. Haskell's battery of twelve-pound Coehorn mortars. This did not halt the Union advance, but it slowed it. After a while scattered units, particularly the USCT regiments, finally pushed their way toward the Jerusalem Plank Road through the tangled mass of men in the crater.[56]

Gen. Lee sent Col. Charles Venable to fetch two brigades from Mahone's division. The bantam commander's units were "located less than a mile west of Elliott's Salient, just to the east of where the Jerusalem Plank Road passed through the Confederate line." Mahone chose Weisiger's Virginians and Lt. Col. M. R. Hall's (formerly Rans Wright's) Georgians and led them toward the breakthrough, using a circuitous covered way to avoid detection by the enemy. Several of Weisiger's Virginia regiments hailed from Petersburg, but if Mahone's troops needed additional inspiration they received it when a wounded Rebel stumbled past, pausing long enough to inform the men from the Old Dominion that they would be facing "niggers" who had vowed to give no quarter. At that moment, Union colonel John Bross appeared, leading the Twenty-ninth USCT, and waving the Stars and Stripes. Capt. Victor J. B. Girardey led the enraged Southerners straight toward the black soldiers, driving almost all of the Federals back into the crater. Hall's Georgians followed, attacking on the southwest quadrant of the crater, but both units were unable to clear the crater.[57]

By midafternoon, Mahone had brought up a third brigade, J. C. C. Sanders's Alabamians, in a desperate attempt to clear the crater and reestablish the Confederate line. Mahone used two psychological ploys to inspire the 630 Deep South soldiers—he informed Sanders's troops they would be fighting African Americans and that Gen. Lee was watching from the Gee House and would come and lead them in a second attack if they were repulsed.[58]

The Alabamians scrambled into the frightful landscape without firing, reserving their single shot for a volley after they had closed on the Yankees. They struck at just the right time. The Federals had moments before received orders to retreat, and Sanders's determined assault cracked the thin defensive shell the bluecoats had managed to establish. The "Saturnalia of blood" that followed was nothing short of slaughter, and the black soldiers suffered the most. In the crater the Confederates typically gave the black troops no quarter, killing even those who surrendered, and the USCT's comrades in blue, fearing they would be killed if captured with the Colored Troops, began shooting their black compatriots. Finally, the savagery ended, and what Grant described as "the saddest affair I have witnessed in this war" sputtered to a close.[59]

Union losses are usually assessed at around 3,800 total casualties, and the graycoats suffered losses of about 1,600, including those killed in the explosion of the mine. Two Confederate officers received rewards for their excellent work at the battle of the Crater—Congress approved Mahone as a major general and Capt. Girardey advanced four steps to the rank of brigadier general.[60]

The Floridians took no part in the repulse of the Federals in the crater. Still, several accounts by the Flowers describe what they witnessed during the engagement. Dorman recalled that "we sat under the shelter of our works all day and watched the battle," and counted only five or six wounded in the day's action. W. A. Hunter attempted to describe the sound and sight to his wife, writing: "[O]ur Brigade was not charged by the Yanks so we were not in the fight except the shells they flew all around all the way. I can give you my idea of it[. It sounds like] in the time of a thunderstorm in Florida where there is a great deal of dead pine[. T]hat comes to the nearest to it of anything I ever heard." Dorman described one of the unfortunate casualties: "[A] small man came making his way down the line with a wiregrass hat on his head, smoking a small stone pipe with a short stem. His arm was shot all to pieces, or it looked so. He said, 'Boys I've got it, but I'm taking it coolly.'" Geer reported: "Right in the hottest fire we were ordered to go, but the order was countermanded, and I was glad of it."[61]

Mahone's failure to use the Florida brigade for the assault has led some historians to conclude that the divisional commander doubted its skill or dedication. This supposition ignores the obvious. By withdrawing three brigades in the face of a much stronger foe, Mahone took a tremendous gamble. An aggressive enemy commander could have overrun the lines and turned the Rebel right flank. "While Mahone was weakening the Confederate right," Cavanaugh and Marvel explain, "his remaining two brigades spread out to cover the gap. . . . Warren could have thrown two divisions with twenty-six regiments against those thinly-defended works." With Finegan's troops stationed on the division's extreme left and closest to the Federal lines, withdrawing the Floridians would have alerted the bluecoats to Mahone's actions and invited an attack on that sector.[62]

With the failed attempts in June to take the Weldon Railroad and the late-July debacle at the crater, U. S. Grant decided to make a determined effort to take the Weldon Railroad. The Federal commander ordered Sheridan's horse soldiers, Burnside's IX Corps, and Hancock's battered II Corps to feint against Richmond north of the James River near Fussell's Mill. This would force Lee to withdraw some of his troops from the Petersburg defenses before Grant launched his assault on the railroad south of Petersburg. Among those sent to counter the threat north of the James were three brigades of Mahone's division—Sanders's Alabamians, Girardey's Georgians, and Harris's Mississippians. In three days of fierce fighting, the Federals achieved some initial success, but failed to break the Rebel lines.[63]

Along the Weldon Railroad, the first two days of the battle of Globe Tavern proved a disaster for Grant's troops. On August 17, Warren's V Corps marched to Weldon Railroad and began advancing north toward Petersburg. Beauregard and A. P. Hill responded quickly. The next morning they sent Maj. Gen. Henry Heth's division to punish the Yankees. Heth made good progress, driving the bluecoats back and killing or capturing almost 1,000 Unionists. Upon hearing the news of another defeat along the Weldon Railroad, a Federal staff officer declared: "It is [like] touching a tiger's cubs to get on that road. They will not stand it."[64]

The next day, on August 19, the result was an even greater disaster for the V Corps and one of the war's most confusing battles. This time Mahone joined Heth in attacking the bluecoats. With most of his division north of the James, Mahone commanded Brig. Gen. Thomas Clingman's Tarheels and Brig. Gen. Alfred H. Colquitt's Georgians, as well as Weisiger's Virginians. Mahone utilized the same ravine he had used in the June 22 engagement to slip in behind Warren's soldiers, while Heth hammered the enemy along the Weldon Railroad. Fighting in dense woodland in a pouring rain, Mahone and Heth "achieved one of the war's most amazing feats of arms." Though the Federals outnumbered the graycoats seventeen infantry brigades to five, Mahone and Heth inflicted 3,000 casualties (including 2,700 prisoners), took seven flags, and lost about 600 men. Despite the Rebels' success, Warren and his battered bluecoats retained control of the Weldon Railroad.[65]

August 20 was "the decisive day of the Battle of Globe Tavern." While Beauregard scrabbled together a larger force for a final attempt to clear the railroad, Warren's troops used the lull in the fighting to construct strong breastworks. A Federal officer recalled: "Through the night, cold and rainy, the men labored faithfully, and the morning dawned upon a formidable line of breastworks, stoutly made and tastefully finished." Located on a small hill north of Globe Tavern, in the middle of a large field, the fortifications offered the Union troops an open field of fire away from the tangled undergrowth and dense woodlots that had caused them such misery in the previous fights.[66]

Mahone got four of his brigades (the units from Fussell's Mill having returned) moving at 2:00 a.m. on Sunday morning, August 21. Weisiger's troops, which had fought so well on the 19th, remained behind to man the trenches. By 8:30 Mahone had his troops arranged along the Vaughn Wagon Road. Harris's Mississippians, commanded this morning by Col. Joseph M. Jayne, faced north, with Finegan's Floridians, Sanders's Alabamians, and Wright's Georgians, augmented by detachments from Brig. Gen. Alfred M. Scales's North Carolina and Brig. Gen. Edward L. Thomas's Georgia brigades, facing east toward the Union lines. Mahone quickly surveyed the area from the woods along the east side of the cornfield, but apparently had no idea that the bluecoats were strongly entrenched near Globe Tavern. According to the plan devised by A. P. Hill, Heth would again assault the Federals from the north, Mahone's "shock troops" would charge from the west, and Brig. Gen. Johnson Hagood's Palmetto State brigade would advance upon the Yankees from the southwest.[67]

Around 9:00 a.m., Finegan's Floridians led the assault, advancing into the

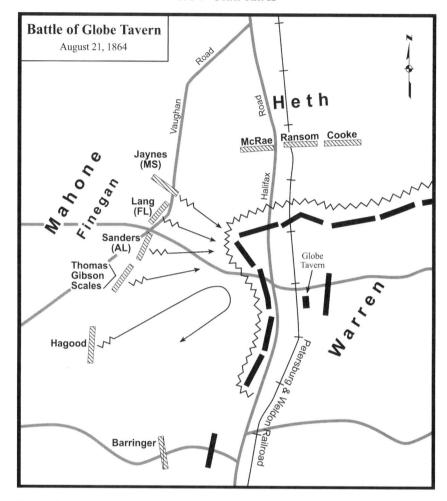

Fig. 18. Battle of Globe Tavern, August 21, 1864

cornfield surrounding the Federal entrenchments. The Union skirmishers scrambled back toward the breastworks, but about fifty proved too slow and were taken captive. Within five hundred yards of the fortifications, a storm of grape, canister, and small-arms fire engulfed Finegan's men. The Floridians immediately fell back into the woods, but this temporary confusion "created a panic among the supporting lines." Quickly rallying, the Flowers joined Sanders's and Harris's men in the assault on the V Corps position. An officer of the 8th Alabama, veteran of the Sharpsburg's "Bloody Angle," Spotsylvania's Mule Shoe salient, and two days of fighting at Gettysburg, reported: "The command [Mahone's three brigades] advanced through an open field and when within about 500 yards of the enemy's works he opened on our command with grape and canister. . . . The fire poured on our ranks was the *most severe of the war* [emphasis added]."⁶⁸

While leading his Alabamians, Brig. Gen. J. C. C. Sanders fell mortally wounded. Thereupon Finegan took charge. According to the Irishman's most recent biographer,

> The Floridians opened the attack on Mahone's left, spearheaded by Colonel Lang's consolidated Florida regiment [the Second, Fifth, and Eighth] and by Colonel Brevard's Eleventh Florida regiment. Strictly by bad luck Finegan's men came up to about a hundred yards in front of the Federal breastworks of Brigadier General Edward Bragg's Iron Brigade . . . a superb unit of Westerners from Indiana, Wisconsin, and Michigan. General Finegan, mounted to the rear of the Florida brigade and to the front of the Mississippi brigade, kept sending more companies of Floridians and Mississippians to Lang's forward position, but the Florida/Alabama front line was torn to pieces by the musketry and canister of the Sixth Wisconsin and Twenty-fourth Michigan. When elements of all thirteen regiments in Finegan's left front sector began to break and run to the rear in panic, the Irishman rode forward and momentarily re-established his line with the able assistance of Lang, Brevard, Colonel J. Horace King of Alabama and Colonel Joseph M. Jayne of Mississippi. When the Iron Brigade was reinforced . . . Finegan's three brigades fell back in confusion, suffering heavy losses.

Despite the determination exhibited by the Deep South soldiers, the Federal position proved too strong, and Finegan's men retreated to the safety of woods near the Vaughn Wagon Road.⁶⁹

Two brief accounts by semiliterate Florida soldiers survive to give some sense of the combat at Globe Tavern. Pvt. Young Hunter of the Ninth Florida wrote his mother on August 22 to inform her of the wounding of his father, W. A. Hunter. "[W]e were charging the Yankees breast works," he recorded, "when he [W. A.] was wounded an[d] about the time he was wounded we ware ordered to fall back[.] I went to Pa and brought him out to the River[. W]e made two charges and had to fall back both times[. W]e lost a great many men both times . . . it was the hottest fight I have been in yet[. T]he [Y]ankees were well fortified and we had to charge through an open corn field[. T]he shell grape canister an[d] minie balls came as thick as hail." An unidentified soldier of the Ninth Florida repeated much of the same material but affirmed that Finegan's Floridians got within fifty yards of the breastworks.[70]

Heth's graycoats enjoyed some success north of the earthworks, but Johnson Hagood's command advanced into a trap and was cut to pieces, loosing 449 out of 740 men carried into the fight. Mahone clamored for more troops to renew the assault, but night fell before the reinforcements arrived, and darkness brought a halt to the bloodletting. As a result, Grant retained control of the Weldon Railroad, seriously curtailing the flow of supplies reaching the Army of Northern Virginia at Petersburg.[71]

The Florida brigade lost approximately 100 men in the fight at Globe Tavern. Among the killed was Capt. James G. Spann, a South Carolinian serving on Gen. Finegan's staff for just more than one month. Col. Brevard "received a heavy blow" when he discovered that his younger brother, Lt. Mays Brevard, had been killed almost at the breastworks, commanding his company. A flowery Victorian-style tribute stated that Lt. Brevard "was conspicuous in every battle," leaving "a proud name in the annals of the State."[72]

For the first time since their arrival in Virginia, the Ninth, Tenth, and Eleventh Florida had assaulted a strongly entrenched foe and failed to achieve their objective. Due to the initial "panic" created by their early retreat, the Cracker infantry, along with Johnson Hagood's battered brigade, received the lion's share of the blame for the failure to capture the Globe Tavern works. Putting the best possible face on the three-day battle, some Southerners noted that Union casualties totaled 4,300, as compared to 2,000 Rebel losses. Others were not fooled. Perhaps the best assessment of the Globe Tavern engagement came from Capt. Fagan of the Eighth Alabama. "We accomplished nothing," he concluded. "Such *brilliant* movements as these will so deplete our army that Grant will soon take Richmond."[73]

By the next morning the Florida brigade had settled back in the trenches, where another sort of depletion was rapidly sucking the life from the proud Army of Northern Virginia—desertion. The next seven months would see the trickle of soldiers taking "French leave" become a full-fledged hemorrhage.[74]

Patton Anderson had prophesied in April that ordering the Florida troops to Virginia would "cause desertions and disorganization." A few had remained in their home state, conducting a guerilla campaign against the Unionist invaders, but the vast majority had obeyed the order. By June, as the dreary reality of life and death in the trenches became the soldier's daily ritual, Confederate troops, including the Florida troops (particularly the Ninth, Tenth, and Eleventh regiments), began to desert with increasing frequency.[75]

An officer summed up his opinion of the reason for the rash of soldiers leaving the Army of Northern Virginia in mid-July, writing: "There have been more desertions of late than ever before. The hard life they lead and a certain hopelessness which is stealing over the conviction of the best and bravest will have some effect in inducing demoralization hitherto unknown." These factors, plus others peculiar to the Floridians, helped to spur the great number of desertions by Finegan's troops.[76]

Hardships were certainly a part of life in the Petersburg trenches. The food that reached the troops was of such abysmal quality that it was barely fit for human consumption and of a quantity that barely kept them alive. Shortly after his arrival in the Old Dominion, W. A. Hunter had complained: "Our rations is getting very short[. W]e don't get more than half as much as the men want." The problem only got worse as the siege wore on, and constant gnawing hunger certainly contributed to the high desertion rate. A Ninth Florida soldier went over to the Yankees, explaining that the *weekly* ration for his entire regiment consisted of one-quarter pound of bacon, three-quarters of a pound of cornmeal, and a little sugar and coffee. Recalling Geer's description of cornmeal with the cob ground into it, and the rancid Nassau pork, which the soldiers nicknamed "Nausea Bacon," it is difficult to imagine how the Richmond government expected the Southern soldiers to fight on such an appallingly inadequate diet. Gen. Lee, ever mindful of the condition of his men, pled with the Commissary Department to provide adequate victuals for his army. "There is suffering for want of food," he wrote. "The ration is too small for men who have to undergo so much exposure and labor as ours." His plea went unheeded, and conditions further deteriorated during the winter of 1864–65.[77]

Cleanliness may be next to godliness, but in the trenches it was next to impossible. Soap became increasingly difficult to obtain, and for men forced to live for days at a time on the dirt, this lack of basic hygiene led to sickness and lice. The men sought to combat the vermin that afflicted them by holding their uniforms close to the fire, using heat to kill or drive away the pests. The soldiers often burned their uniforms in the attempt, and replacement clothing proved almost impossible to obtain.[78]

Sickness was the scourge of the new Florida troops. Horrid rations, vermin, filthiness, and cold weather all contributed to the long sick lists. As autumn turned to winter, the men from Florida suffered severely from the frigid temperatures. Even some of Perry's old brigade had frozen to death during the winter of 1863, but Finegan's men found winter in the Old Dominion almost unbearable. Dr. Thomas M. Palmer, surgeon in charge of the Florida ward of the Howard's Grove Hospital in Virginia, made an impassioned plea to return the troops to Florida for the winter when an inspection report indicated that almost half of the Tenth Florida was either sick or on special detail. The Ninth and Eleventh Florida fared little better. A few days earlier W. A. Hunter had related: "There has been as many as seventy five reported on the sick list in one morning[.] I understand Dr. Palmer says if we are not sent back to the south we will all die."[79]

In his letter Dr. Palmer tried to explain the reasons for the unit's poor physical condition. "The composition of this brigade," he wrote, "will also prove that it cannot be efficient in this climate under the fatigues which they are necessarily compelled to go through. First, it is composed of men over conscript age; second, men within conscript age who have been discharged from other commands in Virginia and Tennessee because they were unable to stand the hard service; third, boys under eighteen, a large number of whom have taken measles and will be unfit for service here for months, and if they are furloughed they have to come back and go through the same acclimation as if they had never been here: all these facts go to prove that this brigade cannot do service in Virginia." Palmer's pleas fell upon deaf ears, and the desertions continued apace.[80]

Letters from home certainly contributed to the high rate of desertions among the Florida soldiers. With morale sometimes higher in the army than on the Florida home front, women often begged their husbands to return to their hearths and alleviate their suffering. Such letters placed the soldier in the uncomfortable position of choosing between duty to his family and loyalty to his comrades and cause.[81]

An example of this can be gleaned from the letters of W. A. Hunter. While Hunter and his son Young were in Virginia, one of his strong slaves, named Dane, became threatening to W. A.'s wife and daughters. After several epistles offering what advice he could, the elder Hunter finally wrote: "Try to scare Dane and if he wont behave him self you must kill him or sell him[.] Be sure to keep the children safe[.] Tell Melissa & Sue to shoot him." Such reports induced some soldiers to find a way, however ignoble they considered desertion to be, to get home.[82]

By late 1864, the number of Florida soldiers taking French leave had become a source of humor for the Federals and a source of constant concern for Finegan, Mahone, and A. P. Hill. A Pennsylvania soldier recorded: "So many deserters now came in every night from the Florida command that they became a source of considerable annoyance to the staff officers at brigade headquarters, who were awakened at all hours of the night to receive them. One of the officers, in a spirit of fun, sent a polite note one evening to Finegan, requesting him to 'come over and take command of his brigade, most of which was apparently on our side of the entrenchments.'" The fiery Irish commander was not amused, and called an artillery barrage on the Pennsylvanians that lasted all night.[83]

Lack of strong regimental leadership certainly contributed to the epidemic of desertions, and Finegan must take some of the blame for that. Due to sickness and battle casualties, both the Ninth and Tenth regiments had several vacancies in their upper command positions. In Hopkins's unit, by the end of September the elderly Maj. Westcott found the strain of active campaigning too strenuous and received orders to return to Florida. Col. John Martin's Ninth Florida had had neither a lieutenant colonel nor a major after Cold Harbor. Hopkins nominated Capt. John C. Richard, an able officer from Starke, to replace Westcott; Martin suggested Capt. James Tucker to take the place of crusty, valiant Lt. Col. John W. Pearson, and Capt. Sam Hope to fill Maj. Pickens Bird's office. Finegan apparently wanted to fill the position with "an outsider," and Martin and Hopkins bitterly opposed the move. As a result, the positions remained open, and efficiency suffered as a result.[84]

By midwinter, the flood of desertion had become so desperate that conscientious officers posted guards to watch pickets they suspected might take French leave, but on at least two occasions the "guards" joined the suspects in going over to the enemy. The Florida soldiers went into winter quarters near the Boydton Plank Road, three miles from the sector of the lines that they were ordered to protect. Several of the deserters used their lonely vigils as the perfect opportunity to escape to the Federals.[85]

Finegan, an able administrator who cared deeply about his troops, requisitioned supplies and pointed out the deficiencies in the Commissary Department to A. P. Hill. Like the rest of the Florida brigade, Finegan despised the Virginia cold. He and Col. Lang tried unsuccessfully to get wages for his troops (which they had not received for six months), and sought decent clothes for the men. The Third Corps leader sloughed off the complaints with the obvious and rather coldhearted response that he could do nothing about any of the problems.[86]

Rather than improve conditions, the Rebel army and government leaders tried to instill fear instead. Most brigades, including Finegan's, witnessed at least one execution of a comrade. This did not have the intended effect; the men, who had all struggled with the same demons, tended to identify with the victims. The killing of John "Shorty" Griffis, a Bradford County Cracker, left those who witnessed it with a deep admiration for the little man. A witness recalled:

> It was a cold evening, and the wind moaned through the barren limbs. . . . There were two "Stobs" (or stakes) driven through the frozen clay to tie Shorty to. The moaning of the cold winds and the prayers of poor Shorty for his wife and little children, as he was being tied between the two stakes were pitiful. He did not seem to care for himself; he thought of no one but those he loved; he said they would starve and have no one to care for them. When the guards finished tying him, the long cap was pulled over Shorty's face so he could not see the detail that were to shoot him. . . . Shorty was praying for his wife and little children, and his last words were, "God have mercy on my poor wife and children." That prayer was his last. It was carried away with those moaning winds and echoed back to us as it went over the barren hills, and it were the screaming bullets that had stopped Shorty's prayers, and Shorty was no more.[87]

All the members of the Florida brigade, like the simple Bradford County farmer, faced an untenable choice. "Much of east Florida was already in Federal hands, and here Union sentiment prevailed. West South, and Middle Florida were overrun with deserters, conscription evaders, refugees, and fugitive slaves." A spirit of defeatism seemed to grip an increasing number of the state's residents, and the letters from home almost certainly reflected that loss of hope. The situation was even worse in the army. "Soldiers constantly went without. They were often partially clothed and barefoot, their diet was unappetizing, insufficient, and lacking in proper nutrition. Even as late as 1864, some troops marched off to battle with barely serviceable weapons, some with none at all. . . . And then, to make matters worse, many of their families at home were suffering." Add to this the bitter cold, and you had a recipe for desertion.[88]

Despite the soldiers having a myriad of reasons to take French leave, the records reveal that three out of every four Floridians associated with the regiments in Lee's army during 1864 and 1865 served their cause to the end. Those percentages are somewhat misleading. An analysis of the records of all Florida soldiers still with the army in Virginia during 1864–65 shows that the rate of desertion by members of the Ninth, Tenth, and Eleventh regiments totaled one deserter for every three men. In the regiments of E. A. Perry's old brigade (the

Second, Fifth, and Eighth Florida regiments), less than two of every ten soldiers took French leave.[89]

The Floridians who remained loyal to the Confederate cause covered the spectrum of Southern society. For example, 3rd Sgt. Peter Boyer Perry of Co. F, Ninth Florida, was a forty-one-year-old veteran of both the Mexican War and the Third Seminole War. As a member of the famed South Carolina Palmetto Regiment, Perry "claimed to be . . . the first [U.S. soldier] to plant the flag of the United States upon the walls of the City of Mexico." He surrendered at Appomattox, and it literally took an act of Congress to grant this veteran of three wars a pension for his service in Mexico. Pvt. David Bartow Johnson of Co. B, Tenth Regiment, had also served in the Billy Bowlegs War. Though wounded three times at Cold Harbor, Johnson never missed a roll call, and like Perry mustered out at Appomattox. George Washington Mayo, a twenty-eight-year-old private in Co. K, Eleventh Florida, stood only five feet tall. He was shot in the breast at the battle of Globe Tavern, and the doctors had been unable to remove the projectile. Union troops captured Mayo as he struggled to follow his comrades on the long trek to Appomattox with the bullet still lodged beneath his shoulder blade. Charles Slater had been born in Liverpool, England, in 1798. In March 1865 he received his discharge for "old age and debility." But he was loath to leave his comrades; the Federals caught him in Richmond, and he died of diarrhea at the Newport News Union prison. These men, and other Floridians, continued to battle for a Confederate nation long after common sense must have told them their cause was lost. Perhaps the oddity is not that so many deserted, but that so many remained in the ranks.[90]

From August 21 through the late fall of 1864, the Floridians saw no combat except for occasional night raids to scoop up Federal pickets. The only break in the tedium of siege life during this period occurred when units from Mahone's division and Hampton's seemingly indefatigable cavalry fought at Burgess' Mill in late October. The bantam Virginian again attempted to drive through a gap in the Yankee line, but this time, Mahone walked into a trap, escaping only after many irreplaceable men had been killed, wounded, or captured. Once more, Mahone left the Floridians to guard the breastworks and they did not fight in this engagement.[91]

As 1864 came to a close, the Floridians joined Mahone's division in a race to once again drive Warren's V Corps away from the Weldon Railroad. On December 7, the Federals left Petersburg, heading for Hicksford and Belfield, the former on the north and the latter on the south bank of the Meherrin River, where they destroyed sixteen miles of rail and burned a wagon bridge. There they encountered Hampton's dismounted cavalry and the Home Guard, entrenched along the north bank of the Meherrin. Lee sent A. P. Hill, with regiments from Mahone's, Heth's, and Wilcox's divisions, south to intercept and defeat the bluecoats. Hill led his soldiers on the forced march south.[92]

The weather turned bitter, and Hill's Rebels marched toward the Meherrin in a sleet storm. A member of the Eighth Alabama reported, "The roads had been badly cut up by passing wagon trains and were now frozen hard. The weather was intensely cold, and the men and officers suffered agonies from sore feet." C. O. Bailey, a veteran of the Seventh Florida Regiment, concurred. In a letter home, Bailey related: "We had an awful time of it—the ground was frozen all the time[. I]t had rained a hard rain a few days before we started and the roads were badly cut up and then being frozen it was just like walking on sharp rocks. . . . it was so cold that the breath of the men would turn to ice on their beard as they marched along. As I did not have any beard my breath froze on my blanket that I had around me." It was reported that a few of Hill's men had no shoes during the winter march.[93]

When the men arrived, they found that the Federals had already departed. Bailey summed up the whole trip, stating, "[W]e just marched down to within about 4 miles of Belfield stayed there one day and turned around and started back the next day." On the return trip an anonymous Floridian loudly contrasted the bitter Virginia weather to conditions in his native state. "Ain't Florida a great place?" he rhetorically queried. "There the trees stay green all the time, and we have oranges and lemons and figs and bananas and it is the greatest country for taters you ever did see."[94]

The Federals called this operation the "Apple Jack Raid" because during their retreat toward Petersburg they discovered and consumed several barrels of apple brandy. In their drunkenness they purportedly burned and pillaged several buildings. A few bluecoat foragers were captured, presumably by Hampton's horsemen, and summarily executed.[95]

The Floridians had one final operation before the New Year. On December 30, the Tenth Florida was sent to do provost duty between the Appomattox River and Dinwiddie Courthouse. The unit marched a total of forty miles, spent a cold day and night on alert for stragglers and deserters, and returned to winter quarters on New Year's Day.[96]

13 "There Are Some True Men Left"

To Appomattox

The conditions of the troops further deteriorated during the final months of the war and desertions continued unabated. Food supplies shriveled until they were almost nonexistent. "I get so hungry," a South Carolina soldier wrote to his family, "that it makes me sick. I stand it much better than I thought I could, but I don't know how long I will hold out at it. . . . Our men can not and will not stand it much longer." Earlier in the war, packages from home, often filled with edible treats and clothing, had been a morale booster. By 1865 they rarely made it to the troops. Postal authorities reportedly pilfered those few boxes that ran the gauntlet through Union-occupied territory. Even the highest officers suffered want. When an Irish Member of Parliament visited Gen. Lee, he shared one of the two biscuits that comprised the Confederate commander's entire supper.[1]

Lee continued to issue constant pleas for improved rations for his soldiers, but to no avail. The Commissary Department proved incapable of meeting even the most basic needs of the graycoats, and that led to other problems. Hungry men became more susceptible to disease and infection, and weakened, feeble men made poor warriors. Inadequate clothing also contributed to the men's debilitated condition, and even Pollyanna would have had trouble being optimistic about the South's chances for victory. Starvation, coupled with despair, had long since opened the floodgates of men leaving the army. In one night, two hundred men—the equivalent of two full companies—went over to the enemy. In just three days, from January 19 to January 22, fifty-six soldiers deserted from Hill's Third Corps, including twenty-seven from the Florida brigade. During the same month, "the 10th Florida lost 29 men to desertion, or about ten percent of the unit's aggregate present."[2]

Despite the wretched conditions, most of the army suffered and persevered, waiting for a new spring campaign. Each soldier likely had his own reason for staying with the Army of Northern Virginia, but one reason seems to predominate. Many soldiers feared that taking French leave would bring dishonor to their families. Dorman related a conversation he had with Pvt. William A. Driver before a minié ball to the elbow ended Dorman's military career. In a quiet moment Driver told Dorman, "We are actually suffering for something to eat. And look at my almost bare feet. We can get out of this." Dorman recognized the validity of the argument, but replied: "Billie, we can not think of doing such a thing. If we are permitted to live to ever see this thing ended, how could we ever go back and face our people at home." Other reasons probably included personal honor, love of country, hatred for the Yankees, and devotion to Robert E. Lee. The latter reason was a potent deterrent to desertion. Even the cynical D. L. Geer later wrote that Lee "was the only mortal man I ever thought I could ever pay homage to."[3]

In perhaps the ultimate example of grasping at straws, on February 9, Secretary of State Judah P. Benjamin proposed acceptance of blacks into the Confederate armed services. Gen. Lee sent a circular among his troops requesting input into the idea of establishing several CSCT divisions. Many of the troops put the cause of Southern independence before their defense of slavery. Others saw the measure as confirmation of "their belief that the Confederacy was no longer worth fighting and dying for."[4]

Only one known document gives an indication of the Florida brigade's reaction to Gen. Lee's circular. Lt. A. J. Peeler, who had been exchanged after more than a year's captivity at the Union prison at Johnson's Island, reportedly penned a letter to Secretary of War John Breckinridge "recommending that black men be used as soldiers." Considering all that the Floridians had sacrificed to the cause, perhaps Peeler spoke for a majority of the troops from the southernmost state. Small numbers of black soldiers eventually were sworn into Confederate service and began training, but they never saw field service with the Army of Northern Virginia. Ironically, Benjamin's speech came only two days after one of Lee's army's last offensive victories.[5]

U. S. Grant had received incorrect intelligence in early February of 1865 that supplies for Petersburg and Richmond were being shipped to the beleaguered cities along the Boydton Plank Road. After a few days of dry weather, on February 4, he decided to send Col. J. Erwin Gregg's cavalry and three infantry divisions from Warren's V Corps and two divisions of the II Corps to the area around Hatcher's Run. The Union commander's apparent objectives were to capture the wagons and destroy the supposed Rebel supply lines along the Boydton Road. If the Union troops could also gain control of the South Side Railroad, Petersburg's last link with the fertile regions of southwest Virginia and North Carolina would be broken. On February 5, Gregg easily reached his objective but found only a few wagons, which he destroyed.[6]

Maj. Gen. John B. Gordon's battered, war-weary Second Corps veterans of the Shenandoah Valley held the ground north of Hatcher's Run near Dabney's Saw Mill. Lee hurried Henry Heth's more reliable Third Corps division to reinforce Gordon. By midafternoon, as the Union troop concentration continued, the Confederate chieftain also ordered Mahone's division out of the Petersburg trenches to support Gordon. Mahone was ill, so Old Barney Finegan, the division's senior brigadier, assumed command of all five of Mahone's brigades during the battle of Hatcher's Run.[7]

Late on the afternoon of February 5, Brig. Gen. Thomas A. Smyth and Brig. Gen. Gershom Mott's Union divisions advanced up the Duncan Road north of Hatcher's Run. Around 4:00 p.m. Heth's and Brig. Gen. Clement A. Evan's units probed the enemy positions, and Heth discovered a gap between Smyth and Mott. Before the graycoats could exploit the opening, the II Corps commander rushed Col. Robert McAllister's brigade into the breach. After some heavy skirmishing, the Confederates fell back and dug in for the night. Finegan's unit arrived during the fighting, but was not engaged.[8]

The next day, with the Federals entrenched along the Duncan Road, the fighting shifted to the area around Dabney's Saw Mill, south of Hatcher's Run. It appeared at first that Finegan's men would miss the combat. Shortly after noon, Gen. Lee had ordered Old Barney to return to Petersburg. The men started back toward their winter quarters, carping loudly about the icy weather and the insanity of life in the army.[9]

While Finegan led his men back toward Petersburg, things began heating up along the south bank of Hatcher's Run. Around 1:00 p.m. Warren sent Brig. Gen. Samuel W. Crawford's brigade west along the Vaughn Wagon Road probing for the Rebels. A mile or so past Dabney's Saw Mill, Crawford found them in the form of Col. John Hoffman's Virginians. Both commanders immediately called for reinforcements. Crawford could expect, and soon received, several brigades in his fight, but Gordon had only the remnants of the Second Corps to keep the Federals from breaking the Confederate line. Lee and A. P. Hill, observing the fight from a nearby hill, immediately ordered Finegan back to Hatcher's Run.[10]

Until Old Barney arrived, Confederate hopes rested upon a fragile reed.

Roughly handled in the Shenandoah Valley, the Second Corps had earned a well-deserved reputation for an unwillingness to fight. An eyewitness sarcastically reported, "Up to this time, Gordon's Valley troops had made no fight; they had attempted to save the Confederacy by the old maneuver of running, not fighting."[11]

John B. Gordon, one of the South's finest combat leaders, was having no more of that tactic. Ably assisted by the dashing Brig. Gen. John Pegram (commanding Maj. Gen. Edward "Allegheny" Johnson's old division) and Clement Evans, Gordon took charge of the engagement. "The fight was Gordon's," the eyewitness averred, "and he was going to fight it out, so he ordered a charge. His men accordingly went at it. But after a little the line wavered, then fell back; however, they did not fly, their brave men and officers had resolved not to do that. Gen. [William] Terry is said to have ordered an officer from behind a tree, and not being obeyed, to have run his sword into him." Twice Gordon and his commanders charged toward Dabney's Saw Mill, dominated by an immense mound of sawdust, and both times they took the ground before being repulsed.[12]

As the exhausted Second Corps prepared for the third assault, Finegan arrived with his entire division. Wearing a "citizen coat," a beaver hat, and carrying a walking stick, the Irishman conferred briefly with Gordon, then set his troops in the center of the attack force. Finegan arranged his troops in three lines: Weisiger's Virginians and Brig. Gen. William H. Forney, commanding Sanders's Alabamians, in the first; Harris's Mississippians and Wright's Georgians, now led by Brig. Gen. Moxley Sorrel, in the second; and the Florida brigade, directed again by Col. David Lang, in the third line. As the charge began, Finegan rode beside the men from the Old Dominion shouting: "On ye go brave lads; on ye go; on ye go."[13]

The Florida brigade lay down, waiting its turn. Writing years later in his pension application, Pvt. Robert F. Davis recalled: "I was in the second [actually, the third] line of battle & . . . was lying down on the field . . . under the direction of our Capt. when the enemy enfiladed our line with a brisk fire from cannon. Nearly every time it fired the shells hit a large white oak near my co." Struck by shrapnel or flying oak splinters, Davis missed the rest of the battle.[14]

The Virginians and Alabamians had little trouble in driving Crawford and Brig. Gen. Romeyn B. Ayres's Yankees before them. Crawford's men had been fighting for hours, but they were driving Pegram's division when Finegan's first line hit them. Lt. Col. William H. Stewart of the Sixty-first Virginia, reported, "[A]s we formed a line of battle across a small farm patch, the enemy

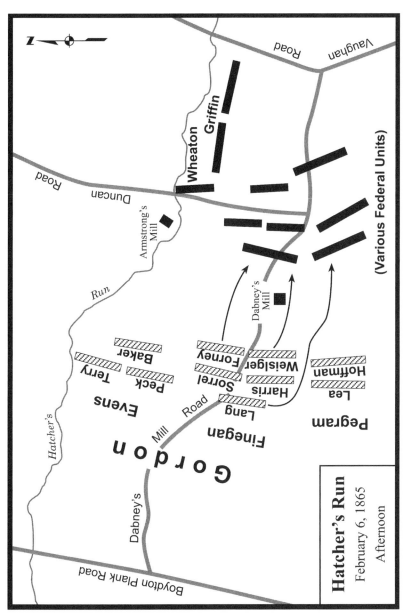

Fig. 19. Hatcher's Run, February 6, 1865

were driving Pegram's men pell mell out of the woods, when we charged with a great yell and turned them [the Federals] to run like lightning through the woods for apparently a mile." An Alabama officer recorded: "We drove them back easily, and did it handsomely, nothing easier." For the third time that day the Confederates crouched in the trenches east of the sawdust pile.[15]

Union reinforcements began arriving almost immediately. Brig. Gen. Ranald McKenzie's brigade began filing onto the field near Dabney's Mill. Finegan, "utilizing the excellent sense of timing that he had already demonstrated at Ocean Pond," sent in his Georgians and Mississippians before the Federals could get into a proper line of battle. McKenzie's troops fled panic-stricken.[16]

An hour before nightfall, Brig. Gen. Frank Wheaton had brought order to the disorganized Union brigades and readied them for another attempt to take the worthless mill. The Florida brigade's time had finally arrived. "Just as it seemed likely that the Northerners would retake the mill again, Finegan came galloping up on his right (south) flank from west to east with the four small regiments of his own Florida brigade, waving his beaver hat and yelling encouragement to his troops." A Richmond newspaper reporter, who was with Weisiger's brigade, noted that Finegan's improvised third wave, in support of the Virginians and Mississippians on the Confederate right, staggered the Union left again, driving them back in some disorder. "The Whirlwind Brigade" had again proved it would fight.[17]

Still, it seemed the battle would never end. More bluecoated reinforcements arrived, and by nightfall, the Federals had once again taken the mill and the trenches that had been so bitterly contested all afternoon. In the end, superior numbers had proven too much for the Southerners to overcome, and had also shown how feeble some of the butternut units had become.[18]

The next day the Yankees conducted a series of sorties against the Confederate defenses but found no opening to exploit. A terrific winter storm hampered their offensive operations, and the Federals spent much of the day burying the dead. Lee seemed quite content to allow the Federals to claim control of Dabney's Saw Mill. The Union troops fortified their position along the Duncan Road, stretching the line Lee's army had to protect by another three miles. The Southerners had, however, saved their vital Southside Railroad supply line.[19]

Union casualties probably numbered around 1,500 men: killed, wounded, or captured. Southern losses are generally estimated to be about 1,000. Casualties for the Florida brigade appear to have been light. The Tenth Florida reported only three slightly wounded (including Pvt. R. F. Davis), one killed, and one seriously hurt—Lt. Col. William W. Scott. Scott was shot in the arm, which the doctors soon amputated. This left both the Ninth and Tenth Florida with neither lieutenant colonels nor majors, and little hope of having them appointed. Col. T. W. Brevard of the Eleventh Florida reported: "I have not been injured in the recent affair on the right—though I have lost some very good men—My best officer Capt. [Gabriel J.] Floyd was killed on the 5th inst. He was the son of Col. Robert Floyd of Apalachicola."[20]

The Richmond newspapers lauded Finegan's conduct during the battle, but Old Barney's days with the Army of Northern Virginia were numbered. In January, Florida governor John Milton had again begun fomenting to have Gen. Finegan returned to the southernmost state. Finegan had powerful friends, including his business partner David Yulee, a former U.S. senator; as a result, the transfer received congressional approval by January 23, 1865.[21]

The Irishman sought to justify the move, explaining, "I am between fifty-four and fifty-five years of age, and have been in the State and Confederate service about four years, and have not in that time been absent one week from duty. While the application has not been made at my solicitation, it would be agreeable to me if I could be transferred to a climate more congenial to my health and age, and where my intimate knowledge of the country and people would enable me to render more service than I can possibly do in command of a small brigade." Despite his fervent desire to be back in the Land of Flowers, Finegan's sense of duty proved too strong, and the Florida Irishman refused to leave his "small brigade" leaderless. With Mahone still on sick leave, Old Barney fought along the icy, snow-covered banks of Hatcher's Run with his ticket home in his pocket. When Mahone returned, on March 20, Finegan began the trip to Florida.[22]

The departure of Finegan left an opening for a brigadier general to command the Florida unit. Under intense prodding from Mahone, T. W. Brevard received the nomination. Writing on March 10, Mahone opined: "The condition of this Brigade in *tone*, discipline, and organization demands vigorous attention, and the services of the best man at its head to save it from utter disorganization. Col. T. W. Brevard, 11th Fla., is the only officer in the brigade worthy of the trust of the charge, and I regard him as one of the most promising officers of my knowledge. I would therefore ask and urge his appointment as a brigadier general at once—the sooner the better." By March 28, the recommendation was approved, making T. W. Brevard "the last of the 425 Confederate generals duly appointed by the President."[23]

It is interesting to conjecture why Mahone chose Brevard and rejected the hard-fighting, reliable Col. David Lang. Certainly it is not because the Elev-

Fig. 20. Brig. Gen. T. W. Brevard,
Eleventh Florida Regiment

enth Florida had fewer desertions than the other regiments in brigade. The Eleventh suffered as many soldiers abandoning the cause as the other units, and Cpl. Washington Waters, with obvious disgust, noted: "when he [John Raybon] left here there was fifteen left at the same time and the next night seven more left and there is one company that eighty-five has left[.] . . . the men all thinks that the battalion will be burst up and I hope it will." Brevard displayed courage in the few battles in which he had been engaged, and showed considerable ingenuity in leading the lost companies at First Ream's Station. Lang, by contrast, had a proven record that included Fredericksburg, Gettysburg, Cold Harbor, and each of the fights around Petersburg, often as brigade commander.[24]

The answer likely lies in Mahone's attitude, rather than any special insight into Brevard's character. Lang seems to have displayed an acerbic, sarcastic, even cynical demeanor, which certainly could not have appealed to a man with an ego as large as Mahone's. Also, it could not have hurt Brevard's chances for promotion that he had been a prominent Tallahassee attorney, married to the daughter of a former Florida governor. Lang, by contrast, was a young surveyor from the hinterlands. Whatever the reason, it would matter very little in the final weeks of the war.[25]

While the political shenanigans played out in Richmond, the soldiers in the trenches continued to suffer. The appointment of a new commissary general brought some relief. Food, better in quantity and quality, began filling the soldier's tin plates. This change came too late. Brevard confided to his mother: "The army is more feeble hearted than I have ever known. It is absolutely indispensable that change speedily for the better or the Army will become as desponding as the people out of it."[26]

Perhaps the best description of the condition of the Florida brigade during the last month of the war came from Maj. Robert Stiles of the Richmond Howitzers. Confessing the easy duty of his artillery unit, Stiles watched in horror the arrival of Mahone's men after months of "manning a very trying part of the Petersburg line." Stiles reported: "We thought we had before seen men with the marks of hard service upon them; but the appearance of this division of Mahone's, and particularly of Finnegan's Florida brigade, with which we happened to be most closely associated, made us realize, for the first time, what our comrades in the hottest Petersburg lines were undergoing. . . . We were shocked at the condition, the complexion, the expression of men, and the officers, too, even the field officers; indeed we could scarcely realize that the unwashed, uncombed, underfed, and almost unclad creatures we saw were officers of rank and reputation in the army."[27]

Those sentiments were echoed by a former member of the Ninth Alabama Regiment who went to visit his old unit at Mahone's position near the Howlett Line. "A mere handful remains of the little band," he lamented; "they have been wasted by the storms of battle and by disease, and even the few remaining look weary and worn. . . . I find our ranks so thinned that when in line of battle along the works, the boys are scattered eight feet apart. Hardly a skirmish line, yet when the battle comes, they will have to meet solid lines."[28]

In an effort to improve the military situation, a desperate Gen. Lee tried a risky strategy. On March 25, the Confederate commander sent John B. Gordon and the Second Corps in an early morning attack on Fort Stedman. Lee hoped to force Grant to contract his lines, and possibly even destroy the Union supply depot at City Point. With shorter lines, Lee hoped he could dispatch troops to aid Gen. Joseph E. Johnston in the Carolinas. The attack, observed by Pres. Lincoln, who happened to be visiting Grant's headquarters, started well, but Union forces soon overwhelmed the Confederates. The bluecoats suffered total losses of slightly more than 1,000 men; estimates of Rebel losses ran from 2,800 to 4,000 irreplaceable soldiers.[29]

Billy Mahone's division was still stationed along the Howlett Line when

Lt. Gen. Phillip Sheridan and Warren's V Corps broke through Maj. Gen. George Pickett's line at Five Forks on April 1. The previous evening the Confederate commander had telegraphed Mahone to send him one brigade if possible. Mahone sent Harris's Mississippians, who reported to Lee early on the morning of April 2. By that time, the Federals had begun a general assault on the Petersburg line.

As the Rebels' defenses crumbled, just buying time for his scattered army to reunite became the first priority of Gen. Lee. The Confederate commander stationed Harris's soldiers and some of Cadmus Wilcox's division in Fort Gregg and Fort Whitworth, with orders to hold at all hazards. Despite suffering severe casualties, the Mississippians held their position until Gen. James Longstreet arrived. The First Corps leader established an interior line that ran from Battery 45 to the Appomattox River, saving the Confederate army to fight another day. D. L. Geer offered the requiescat for his Mississippi comrades, who were overrun by "superior numbers—so overwhelming that [it] passed all effort on the part of the few starved and ragged soldiers, of whom many died in the last ditch, still trying to uphold the reputation they had so nobly won in days past and gone."[30]

Mahone's division left Petersburg in the early morning darkness of April 3. Thugs and outcasts looted Richmond, setting the capitol afire, and, Geer reported, "[W]e marched away from there in the light of the burning cities." As they headed toward Chesterfield Courthouse, the sky flashed into sudden brightness as the James River Squadron ignited the Drewry's Bluff magazine. Mahone later remembered that the explosion "lighted the heavens and fairly shook the earth in all that region." Every soldier knew for certain, Geer recalled, that all was lost.[31]

At Chesterfield Courthouse Mahone discovered the road and grounds crowded with women, children, and slaves fleeing Petersburg. Determined to maintain military discipline, Mahone gave his troops time for a quick breakfast and then put them to work collecting any military material that had reached that point. While they were busy following orders, Adm. John R. Tucker arrived with 2,000 Confederate Marines. The Rebel leathernecks impressed Mahone, who described them as "well-clad—armed with cutlass' and navy revolvers, every man over six feet and [the] picture of perfect physical development." The naval unit moved on quickly, but not before a drunken Marine officer "commandeered" a horse from one of Mahone's staffers.[32]

Leaving Chesterfield Courthouse, Mahone led his division up the road, camping for the night at the house of a Capt. Flournoys. From there they crossed the Appomattox River at Goode's Bridge, holding the span in the belief that R. H. Anderson's corps would be using it on the retreat from Richmond. Sometime during the afternoon Mahone received orders from Gen. Lee to proceed the next morning to Amelia Courthouse.[33]

Arriving at Amelia Courthouse on the morning of April 5, Mahone met Gen. Lee for the first time since the retreat. It saddened Mahone to observe Lee wearing a "full uniform. . . . He wore all his best clothes—including his gold spurs and magnificent sword and belt. It impressed me that he anticipated some accident to himself and desired to be found in that dress." In their far-ranging discussion, the Confederate chieftain informed Mahone of his intention to diminish "the number of Corps and division commanders in this army." With the death of A. P. Hill on April 2, Mahone had begun reporting to Longstreet.[34]

After noon the Rebels began leaving Amelia Courthouse, heading toward Farmville. On the road, the Confederates began running into Federal cavalry, and Longstreet's troops clashed with Sheridan's horsemen near Jetersville. Mahone's division traveled all night, apparently serving as the army's rear guard.[35]

Early on the morning of April 6, Mahone's division arrived "in the usual good order" at Sayler's Creek, where one column of the Army of Northern Virginia had halted. At Lee's request, Little Billy detached a portion of the Florida brigade "at Marshall's Corner to guard against any cavalry forays from the logging road that wandered east from there, towards Gill's Mill." T. W. Brevard, still unaware that he had been promoted to the rank of brigadier, commanded a force composed of the Fifth, Eighth, and Eleventh Florida regiments. The going was slow for Brevard's men as they slogged along beside "the long line of slow-moving wagons, some of them stalled forever in the deepening mud."[36]

No known Florida brigade account of Sayler's Creek exists, but the men must have put up a stubborn resistance. Roger Hannaford of Pennington's brigade, Custer's division, reported: "A mile or so farther, we came on the 2nd Cav Div, & from them learnt that it was indeed Lee's wagon train. A portion of their Div had attacked it, & had been repulsed. . . . we soon came to a lot of their wounded. . . . the effect of such a sight on a lot of men just going to attack the enemy is exceedingly bad." The Cracker infantry may still have been full of fight, but they were too few to meet so many of Sheridan's crack horse soldiers. Hannaford continued: "[We] took off through the fields . . . on the gallop, gradually making for the train, yelling like Indians. . . . we soon flanked the train guard, who had been hastily drawn up in line to oppose us. This done we came on the wagon train where there was not a single guard."[37]

D. L. Geer had often sworn that he would never be taken captive, preferring death to a Yankee prison, but at Sayler's Creek he fell into Union hands. Quickly assessing the situation, the Floridian spotted a nearby fallow field, thickly covered with pine saplings. He motioned with his head to a comrade, indicating his intention to make a break for the evergreens, but the other soldier, obviously thinking the undertaking too risky, shook his head. Geer dashed into the cover of the young trees, correctly deducing that the Federals could not ride their horses into the thicket and that they would not follow him on foot. After several harrowing adventures, Geer rejoined the Florida brigade the next night at Farmville.[38]

Upon hearing of the disaster at Sayler's Creek, Gen. Lee hurried Mahone's division back to the scene of the combat, ordering Little Billy to spread his men in line of battle. Seeing the disorganized, discouraged masses of fleeing graycoats, the Confederate chieftain whispered, "[M]y god has this army dissolved." Mahone replied, sweeping his arm toward his troops, "[H]ere is a division ready to do its duty and he [Lee] returning to himself said yes Genl [Mahone] there are some true men left." Although Lee wanted Mahone to take his infantry and clear the field of "those people," luckily nightfall brought an end to the engagement.[39]

Mahone's division crossed the High Bridge during the night; the next afternoon found it entrenched in a semicircle near Cumberland Church, three miles north of Farmville. In an effort to buy his fleeing army more time, Lee had given Mahone orders to destroy the High Bridge, but for reasons unknown, the span remained intact and the Federal pursuit continued. Mahone stated: "I suppose my division then numbered some thirty five hundred muskets and the troops had lost none of their discipline and willingness to do [their] duty. My line was short and did not cover the ground I desired so had to prolong it by placing [Col. W. T.] Poagues battalion of artillery on the right." The line still contained a gap, but Mahone would fight with what he had.[40]

Maj. Gen. Nelson Miles's II Corps division had followed Mahone, crossing the Appomattox River via the High Bridge or a low wagon bridge. By midafternoon Miles had deployed his battle line along the low ground northeast of Cumberland Church, near a marshy rivulet ominously named Bad Luck Creek. Miles sent his men in frontal attack around 2:30 p.m., but Mahone's division bloodily repulsed the Union charge.[41]

Around 4:30 p.m., Miles again ordered his troops to assault, and swung Col. George W. Scott's brigade against the Confederate left. Miles had discovered the gap in Mahone's thin line, but before his troops could exploit the opening,

Col. John R. Tower's veteran Eighth Georgia (and perhaps other elements of Brig. Gen. Tige Anderson's Georgia brigade) rushed in to plug it. Caught in a crossfire from Mahone's left (Weisiger) and Anderson's troops, Scott's Yankees hastily retreated, leaving the ground strewn with their dead and wounded. Mahone's division, with considerable help, had won the Army of Northern Virginia's last victory.[42]

Union losses likely numbered about 800 men, while the Confederates suffered perhaps 250 casualties. In what can only be classed as a "moral victory," Fitz Lee's cavalry, protecting the wagon train, captured Brig. Gen. J. Irvin Gregg. Brig. Gen. Thomas A. Smyth, who had often fought so well against Mahone, received a mortal wound at Cumberland Church. He died two days later, "the last Union general killed in the war."[43]

That night Miles sent two items through Confederate lines, neither of which pleased Little Billy. The first was a miniature of Mahone's wife. While the Virginian appreciated receiving the keepsake, it meant that the Union general had captured his milk cow and baggage wagon. An artilleryman saw Mahone later that night "in a towering passion abusing and swearing at the Yankees."[44]

The second item had greater importance than Little Billy's digestion. Gen. Grant sent a letter to Lee suggesting a parlay to discuss terms for the surrender of the Army of Northern Virginia. Upon receiving the note, Lee passed it to several aides and James Longstreet. Longstreet read it and reportedly muttered, "Not yet." A flicker of hope must have yet remained in the two generals.[45]

All the next day the Confederate army struggled westward. The men hoped to find rations at Appomattox, but when they reached the hamlet, they learned that the Union horse soldiers had captured the supplies, Brig. Gen. Reuben L. Walker's artillery unit, and much of Brig. Gen. Martin Gary's cavalry. More important, the Union forces blocked the escape route to the west. Lee and his army were trapped.[46]

The Southern commander toyed with the idea of trying to break through Sheridan's troopers, but with options gone and his army falling apart, Gen. Lee bowed to the inevitable. At around 2:30 p.m. on April 9, 1865, Lee and Grant, with a few staff officers, sat in the parlor of the Wilmer McLean residence and Lee surrendered the Army of Northern Virginia. For the remnant of the army, the dream of Confederate independence was now dead.[47]

The ragged Rebels received the news with tears, shocked disbelief, and numerous prayers for God to strike them dead. An Alabama officer reported that on April 10 "General Mahone ordered his division to be formed in a [hollow] square and then made a short speech. He said, in part, that he wanted us to accept the surrender in good faith—to go home and make as good citizens as we had soldiers." Monday and Tuesday (April 10 and 11) was spent paroling the artillery and cavalry. "In this way," Hillhouse explains, "the thousands of broken down and starving horses could be quickly dispersed to find fodder while the paperwork for the infantry was prepared." The Federals fed their old enemy, and the various Southern units seemed to hold together as if by force of habit.[48]

The Florida brigade appears to have been one of the last units paroled. The men shouldered arms, marched down the Lynchburg Stage Road between two columns of Federal troops, and stacked their rifles and hung up cartridge boxes and other military accouterments. Many units left their battle flags, as ordered. Others could not bring themselves to part with the beloved emblem and found ways to carry home the banners they had followed across so many bloody fields.[49]

After stacking arms, they marched to tables, where they gave their names and units. This information was copied, in duplicate, and signed by their commanding officer. The bluecoats kept one copy of the parole and the soldier received the second. A pass, signed by the commanding officer, allowed the soldier to go home. The Union government generally provided train or ship transportation to the major city nearest the paroled soldier's home.[50]

D. L. Geer, likely cringing at such a bitter memory, left the only known Florida account (sketchy though it is) of the surrender process. He recalled: "We camped and stayed right by the road where we stopped that morning, for we had to wait for our paroles. The officers were paroled first—those commanding brigades first, and then they paroled the privates. We had to wait there until the fourth day at 1 o'clock when we got ours."[51]

The Florida brigade, commanded by Col. Lang, surrendered 64 officers and 441 men at Appomattox. The men from Perry's old brigade numbered about 150. That number would have been considerably higher had not much of the Fifth, Eighth, and Eleventh Florida been captured at Sayler's Creek. Those unfortunates, and stragglers caught at Farmville, Amelia Courthouse, and other points along the line of retreat, had a much harder route than the Appomattox parolees. The captured Floridians were considered prisoners of war and shipped to Union prisons. It would be months before some of these men would be allowed to take the oath of allegiance and begin the long journey home.[52]

Confederate soldiers in Florida and throughout the South received paroles from Federal occupation forces at most county seats. Wounded men, those prevented from returning to their units due to Federal occupation of large areas of the South, state militia, home guards, and those who simply had preferred not to return thus were forced to sign the oath. A few, like Pvt. Isaac S. Butler of Co. K, Tenth Florida, arrived home in Thomasville, Georgia, from Appomattox and was once again forced to take the oath.[53]

Not all soldiers made it home without problems. When a USCT soldier denied a party of Floridians the use of a spring near City Point, the ex-Rebels were incensed. When the black soldier hit Pvt. Hartwell Koon of the Ninth Florida, the ex-Rebels sprang into action. The privates, who had no weapons, beat the unfortunate bluecoat senseless and an unnamed Ninth Florida officer ran the Union soldier through with his sword. Barely escaping the black soldier's comrades, they wandered for weeks before reaching Florida.[54]

All across the South a similar scene was repeated in a thousand homes. Families would watch the roads, waiting, praying that their loved one would come home. A Tallahassee woman described the situation in her household. "I was watching Eddie [a young child]," Susan Bradford related, "and did not know there was anything to see, when Father said, 'There they come.' Entering the front gate . . . were three Confederate soldiers. Poor fellows; they were pitiful. Thin and so browned by exposure, until they were hardly recognizable. Footsore and weary, on they came." They had gone to war, four years earlier, naively confident that any Southerner could defeat any three, or five, or ten Yankees. In Greek tragedy such hubris always received its punishment, and for many of the Florida Rebels, the final act was just beginning.[55]

Thereafter

Only a week and a half after Appomattox, a former Florida soldier gained no-toriety for his involvement in one of the most infamous crimes in American history. Federal authorities arrested Lewis Thornton Powell, a former member of Co. I of the Second Florida, for his participation in the plot to assassinate Pres. Abraham Lincoln and members of his Cabinet.[1]

Powell had been shot in the wrist at Gettysburg and captured, but he es-caped from a Union hospital in Washington and spent a year as a member of Col. John Mosby's partisans. Powell deserted to the Yankees in January 1865, took the oath of allegiance (using the alias "Lewis Paine"), and loitered around Washington, becoming a crony of the actor John Wilkes Booth. On the night of April 14, 1865, Powell attacked Secretary of State William Seward with a knife, severely maiming the abolitionist but failing to kill him. Captured three days later at the house of co-conspirator Mary Surratt, he was tried at Wash-ington, DC, and hanged on July 7.[2]

Opinions regarding Powell were diverse. A few admired the former Florida soldier's stoic demeanor, and the *New York Herald* reported: "If the crime of Paine could be forgotten there was much in the young man's character to be admired." His defense attorney, vainly attempting to prove his client insane, stated: "He lives in the land of imagination where it seems to him legions of Southern soldiers wait to crown him as their chief commander." An ex-soldier who knew Powell believed "it was his nature to be easily influenced for either good or evil." Whatever the truth, Powell remains as much an enigma today as he was when he sat in the dock and unemotionally faced the gallows.[3]

Powell was one of 15,000 men Florida supplied to the Confederate war ef-fort, and one of the more than one-third of that number who never returned

Fig. 21. Lewis Powell after 1865 arrest

to the southernmost state. Those who did come home included amputees, men disfigured by wounds, and the psychologically and emotionally scarred. All of the veterans found themselves living in a new and—for many of them—difficult era. As Dr. Rable observes: "Civil wars produce political, social, and economic upheaval, leaving in their wake deep bitterness among both the victors and vanquished. After Appomattox the South's political leaders saw themselves entering an era of revolutionary changes imposed by the national government, which many viewed as an outside power."[4]

As the Florida soldiers arrived home, they discovered that a great deal had changed. Many of the state's resources had been lost—contributed to the war effort or taken by one of the warring factions that struggled for control of the various districts. Their homes were often destroyed or in disrepair and their unplanted fields overgrown with weeds and saplings. Some of the returning veterans quickly relocated to places that seemed to offer more opportunities to improve their lives. Most Floridians could not bring themselves to abandon the state they had fought for, and these men began rebuilding their farms and way of life.

Lewis Powell and John Wilkes Booth apparently thought that the murder of Abraham Lincoln would somehow aid the dying Confederacy. The assassination had just the opposite effect. Lincoln's plan for the postwar era (though hardly finalized) seemingly involved immediate reconciliation between the North and South while protecting the rights of African Americans. The new president, Andrew Johnson, initially seemed to be the former Rebels' worst nightmare. A Unionist Tennessean, Johnson had long been an opponent of the planter aristocracy and defender of the yeomanry. He had openly declared his desire to "punish and impoverish" the leaders of the rebellion, break their "social power," and "remunerate" Southern loyalists for wartime losses from the property of "wealthy traitors."[5]

Johnson's idea for Presidential Reconstruction called for using Unionists to form governments in the states of the former Confederacy. He appointed William Marvin, a native New Yorker who had served as a Federal judge at Key West during the first years of the war, as Florida's seventh governor. Johnson, however, feared giving African Americans any political power more than he wanted to punish the ex-Rebels. The first state legislature elected after the war, according to a Florida informant to Sen. Charles Sumner, was comprised of "four-fifths rebel officers, from Brig. Gen. Joseph Finegan down to a corporal." Not surprisingly, Marvin, and most of the other newly minted chief executives, quickly enacted black codes. According to Eric Foner, Florida's version, "drawn up by a commission whose report praised slavery as a 'benign' institution deficient only in its inadequate regulation of black sexual behavior, made disobedience, impudence, and even 'disrespect' to the employer a crime. Blacks who broke labor contracts could be whipped, placed in the pillory, and sold for up to a year's labor." Marvin even volunteered the dictum that freedmen should refer to their old owners as "Master."[6]

Many of the state's former Confederates and prewar Unionists were thrilled with this arrangement, but Presidential Reconstruction (which some pro-Confederate historians have labeled "the Era of Good Feelings") was an anathema to veteran abolitionists in Congress like Charles Sumner and Thaddeus Stevens. With more than enough votes to override any veto by Johnson, the Radicals and their allies in the House and Senate enacted a series of acts that swept the new state governments into the dustbin of history. "As a direct result of southern intransigence on [ratification of] the Fourteenth Amendment," the first and second Reconstruction acts of 1867 declared existing governments in Florida and nine other Southern states illegal, divided those states into military districts under the control of a Federal general, and mandated full rights of citizenship for the freedmen. The new Republican bloc in

Florida derived its real power from the presence of Federal troops, and that, along with the political supremacy of African Americans, grated like broken glass on the hearts and souls of most ex-Confederates. Both the freedmen and former Rebels used the same phrase to describe the new situation—"The bottom rail is the top rail now."[7]

Many white Floridians found ways to fight the new Republican Reconstruction. The "Redeemers" fought back with terror (whether called the Ku Klux Klan, Young Men's Democratic Clubs, or another name) and with their political savvy, often directed by the officers who led them during the war. Violence and virtual anarchy became the rule in many rural areas. In Jackson County, for example, more than 150 people, primarily freedman and outspoken Republicans, were killed, and when Col. John Hately, who had developed a reputation as a "turncoat," was murdered in 1869 in Hamilton County, the killer apparently went unpunished.[8]

Orange County presents an excellent, if extreme, case study for the rural areas of the state during the Reconstruction period. In 1871, during the height of the Barber-Mizell feud, there were forty murders in Orange County (home of modern Disney World and Universal Studios). Only ten ever came to trial, and not one resulted in a conviction. Arsonists burned both the courthouse and jail, but no suspect ever spent a minute in jail for the crime. As a result, it is impossible to tell if these crimes represented a continuation of the feud or just random attacks on the symbols of law and order.

Members of the Barber and Mizell families had both served in the Eighth Florida, and both patriarchs had had children killed at Gettysburg. After the war, the Mizells allied themselves with the Republicans. John Mizell became the Orange County judge and appointed his brother David as sheriff. In his official capacity, David had already taken much of the Barbers' cattle herd to pay a Reconstruction tax, and when he went to serve another warrant, the sheriff was shot and killed from ambush. No one saw the killer, but Judge Mizell led a posse that seized Isaac Barber. The men in the posse tied Barber to a tree and the twenty officers emptied their six-shooters into the unfortunate man. Shortly thereafter one of Moses Barber's grandsons also fell into Mizell hands and mysteriously drowned in Lake Conway with a plowshare tied to his neck. The vigilante violence escalated until a threat to send in Federal troops finally ended the killing.[9]

By 1876 Federal troops remained only in Florida, South Carolina, and Louisiana. The presidential election that year pitted Democrat Samuel J. Tilden against Republican Rutherford B. Hayes, and according to early returns it appeared that Tilden had won the election. Both Republicans and Democrats in the three occupied states sent in election returns to the U.S. Congress verifying that their candidate had won. What followed was political maneuvering by both parties where "conscience was no restraint," and the Southern Democrats essentially sold their votes in return for the removal of Federal troops from their states. The Republicans, in turn, sold out their political allies—the freedmen. A pro-Confederate historian's book on the era ended with the ominous, but truthful, words: "Reconstruction in the South was over . . . except for the consequences."[10]

Predictably, Florida whites often looked to former Confederate veterans as leaders of the new social order. Many ex-officers assumed governmental roles. Three members of the Florida brigade in Lee's army became governors: Edward A. Perry, two-term governor William D. Bloxham (the first captain of Co. C of the Fifth Florida), and Francis P. Fleming. For the next four decades, service in the Confederate military was a virtual requirement for other local and state offices.

An early departure from the ranks of former Florida brigade survivors was Capt. *Richmond Gardner* of the Fifth Florida. His wounding and capture on July 2 at Gettysburg was followed by imprisonment at Johnson's Island, Ohio, until just before the end of the war. During his first winter at Johnson's Island, Gardner suffered from "neuralgia brought on by his wounds and the severity of the climate." After his parole, Gardner returned to Leon County, marrying the sister of John Alexander Cromartie in 1865. (Cromartie had served in Gardner's Co. K.) The couple "lived in their quiet home on Lake Iamonia" until Gardner's final illness. He died in December of 1875.[11]

At the end of the war, *Joseph Finegan* returned to Fernandina, where he served for two years as a state senator for Nassau County until Reconstruction laws disbanded the legislature in 1867. Leaving Florida, Finegan moved to Savannah and became a cotton broker. He later returned to central Florida, where he owned a large orange grove and sold town lots until his death. Old Barney passed away in October 1885 at Sanford, Florida, but was buried in the Old City Cemetery in Jacksonville.[12]

The gangrenous wound of *E. A. Perry* at the battle of the Wilderness ended his career as a combat officer. He commanded a minor post in Alabama until the war's end, then returned to Pensacola and resumed his practice of law. His family and law practice, along with his pastimes of reading and fishing, occupied his time for the next twenty years. A committed Democrat, he supported William Bloxham in the latter's successful run for governor in 1880. Four years

later the Democrats, fearing the return of Radical Republican rule, nominated the popular Perry for governor. The old general came out in favor of calling a Constitutional Convention to replace the Reconstruction Constitution
of 1868. The voters overwhelmingly supported this campaign issue, and they
elected him the state's fourteenth governor by a narrow margin.

Perry took office in January 1885 and appointed his cabinet, which included
his old comrade in arms David Lang as adjutant general. Besides the adoption
of the 1885 Constitution, Perry's administration pushed through money for
education, tourism, and small pensions for Confederate veterans. His term saw
tragedy as well. Fire destroyed half of St. Augustine in 1887, and a severe epidemic of yellow fever swept through Florida in 1888.

Perry suffered from poor health during the latter part of his term, which
came to an end in January 1889. He retired from public life to the comfort
of his Pensacola home, and later that year made a trip to Texas, hoping to improve his health. After suffering a stroke, Perry died in October 1889 in Kerr-
ville, Texas. The Yankee, whose name would forever be associated with his little
Rebel brigade, was only fifty-eight years old when he died. His funeral drew
huge crowds, including scores of his former soldiers and then governor Francis
Fleming. He is buried in Pensacola's St. John's Cemetery.[13]

In the decades after the war, *James Hamilton Wentworth* enjoyed a distinguished career in the fields of law, education, business, and the ministry. Following his capture at Gettysburg, Wentworth survived two of the North's most
infamous prisons—Fort Delaware and Johnson's Island. Wentworth returned
to Florida and lived at Shady Grove in Taylor County. Prominent in his county,
he worked as a schoolteacher, attorney, and county judge. He also married three
times and raised a large family. From 1869 to 1873 he served as Taylor County
superintendent of schools, and later as chairman of the board of county com-
missioners. He moved to Escambia County around 1885 and became a missionary Baptist minister. He outlived all three of his wives and died in December 1893 at Pensacola. He, too, is buried in the St. John's Cemetery.[14]

Wounded and captured at Gettysburg, *Walter Raleigh Moore* spent over a
year as a prisoner at Johnson's Island before being paroled. He returned to the
Florida brigade late in the war and assumed the colonelcy of the Second Florida.
Moore commanded Florida's "representative regiment" during the surrender at
Appomattox. Unfortunately, he apparently never wrote a memoir or sought the
spotlight, and his outstanding war record is little known, even in the state he
served so steadfastly.

When the war ended, Moore returned to his farm in Columbia County near the banks of the Suwannee River. Always dedicated to the memory of his fellow Confederates, Moore accompanied David Lang and William Ballantine on the 1895 trip to Gettysburg. He also stayed active in veteran affairs, serving as commander of the E. A. Perry Camp of the United Confederate Veterans in Lake City. Moore died in October 1898 at Wellborn, Florida. He is interred at the Huntsville Methodist Church, just outside of Lake City.[15]

William Baya is another forgotten hero of the Florida brigade, and one who suffered greatly for the cause. Severely wounded in the hip at Bristoe Station in October 1863, he received a second injury at Weldon Railroad the following August and spent four months recuperating. He was captured at Saylor's Creek and eventually released from Johnson's Island in July of 1865.

Back home, Baya moved to Jacksonville and worked in the grocery business. He also married and raised six children. The old soldier stayed active in military affairs, despite his wounds, serving as a brigadier general in the Florida state militia. He worked actively in the United Confederate Veterans organization. Baya died in July 1903 and is buried in Jacksonville's St. Mary's Cemetery.[16]

In a letter to his wife in June 1864, *Council Bryan* wrote: "If the good Lord spares my life through this war, many happy days may yet be added to us, at our little house in Florida." Bryan resigned his commission in November 1864 after being elected to the Florida House of Representatives. He returned to his wife and their "little house," his prayers having been answered. After the war, Leon County citizens once again elected Bryan clerk of the circuit court. He lived and served his state for the next four decades, undoubtedly content with his quiet life. Bryan died in 1907 and is buried in the Old City Cemetery in Tallahassee.[17]

William Duncan Ballantine was captured at Gettysburg and subsequently imprisoned at Fort Delaware and at Morris Island, South Carolina. At Morris Island, the Federals held Confederate prisoners under artillery fire, and the Southern press labeled the unfortunate hostages as the "Immortal 600." Like W. R. Moore, he gave dedicated service, being wounded four times during the conflict and commanding his regiment on more than one occasion.

After the war, Ballantine returned to the southernmost state and became involved in veterans' affairs. He also wrote a valuable account of the Pensacola company's journey to Richmond. At one point the New York native served as commander of the Florida division of the United Confederate Veterans (UCV). After Reconstruction he became involved in politics and served on the staff of a Florida governor. He died at his home in Fernandina in March 1907.

His obituary, prepared by fellow members of the UCV, contained the following poignant observation: "Comrades, we are fast passing away. Realizing this, let the life and services of our beloved comrade be an incentive to duty in every walk of life for the few remaining years left us."[18]

Prior to the death of his beloved brother Seton at Cold Harbor, *Francis P. Fleming* transferred to the Florida brigade in the Army of Tennessee. Postwar, he seriously considered moving to the Confederate colony in Brazil but chose instead to practice law in Jacksonville. He became a founding partner in the firm of Fleming & Daniel, practicing with former captain J. J. Daniel, the first captain of Co. G of the Second Florida. In 1871 Fleming married Florida Lydia Pearson, daughter of Bird Pearson, a former Florida Supreme Court justice. The union resulted in three children: Francis Phillip Jr., Elizabeth, and Charles Seton (named for the uncle he had never met).

Fleming later entered politics as a steadfast Democrat and Southern Nationalist. Succeeding his old comrade, E. A. Perry, Fleming became the fifteenth governor of Florida in January 1889. Fleming immediately began to deal with the pressing problems of the day, most notably the yellow fever epidemic sweeping across parts of the state. In early 1889, he called a special session of the legislature to create a state board of health—his administration's greatest achievement. He sought to curtail the power of the Republican Party, recalling its "misrule" during Reconstruction, and set aside state land in south Florida for the remnants of the Seminoles living in the area.

At the expiration of his term, Fleming returned to his law practice in Jacksonville. In addition to writing the memoir of his brother, which was published in 1884, Fleming was instrumental in reviving the moribund Florida Historical Society and worked tirelessly to improve the lot of Confederate veterans. Fleming died in December 1908 after a lengthy illness and is buried in the Old City Cemetery in Jacksonville.[19]

Despite his serious wounds at both Fredericksburg and Sharpsburg, *David Lang* survived the War between the States and lived a long, useful life. He returned to Florida and resumed his career as a civil engineer, moving around the northern part of the state with his family. He also became, in the late 1800s, an important figure in Florida politics.

Lang appears to have remained in Virginia for some time after the surrender, probably to let the situation in the Southern states calm down, but also to seek solace in marriage. While serving in Virginia he met Mary Quarles Campbell, daughter of Dr. Joseph Decatur Campbell. Lang had written to Campbell in 1864 to ask for his daughter's hand in marriage, while still serving with the Florida brigade. The couple married in 1866 and Lang, accompanied by his eighteen-year-old wife, returned to the southernmost state.

They settled briefly in Houston where their first child, Robert Campbell Lang, was born in December 1866. Over the next several years the couple had three more children: sons Joseph and Paul Virginius and daughter Helen Augusta. The Langs are listed on the 1870 census as still living in Suwannee County, but at some point the young family moved to Madison and later to Cedar Key, in Levy County.

Like so many officers of Perry's brigade, Lang became involved with state politics. He served an eight-year tenure, from 1885 to 1893, as adjutant general of the State of Florida during the gubernatorial administrations of his friends and former comrades, E. A. Perry and F. P. Fleming. During the period that he led the peacetime militia, Lang finally received the well-deserved rank of general. When the legislature approved the Constitution of 1885, he sought increased funding for training camps and additional pay for active-duty militiamen. Lang also set about reorganizing and training state troops, laying the foundation for Florida's modern National Guard. While serving the public interests, Lang suffered a harsh blow in his personal life, when his beloved wife Mary fell ill and died (in 1889) at the age of forty-one.

Lang's dedication to his fellow Florida soldiers never faltered. He maintained an active involvement in veterans' groups, such as the United Confederate Veterans and the Confederate Veterans of the First Florida Brigade. He generously responded to requests by early historians to reconstruct the events of several major battles. Lang corresponded with John Bachelder about the futile charges at Gettysburg and wrote to Ezra Carman detailing the Floridians' involvement at Antietam. Lang also aided the fledgling Fredericksburg National Battlefield Commission.

He served as private secretary to two Florida governors, Henry L. Mitchell from 1893 to 1897, and Bloxham from 1897 to 1901. During this time, Lang viewed the rise of the Prohibition movement with trepidation, and he reportedly buried casks of whiskey throughout the Florida Panhandle in case the antiliquor forces achieved power. Lang was serving as cashier of the Florida State Hospital in Chattahoochee at the time of his death.

As America geared up to fight "the war to end all wars," David Lang was one of the few remaining survivors of the small group of men who had commanded a brigade in Lee's army. He had been only twenty-five years old when he led his small unit of Floridians at Gettysburg, and the unreconstructed Rebel survived the terrible events of July 1863 by more than half a century. The proud and grizzled warrior died in December 1917. Lang is buried next to his wife, Mary, in a dignified plot in Tallahassee's Old City Cemetery.[20]

Lang's death signaled the beginning of the end. The few aging Florida brigade survivors still living began to depart this "vale of tears" for their eternal rest. By the late 1920s most of them were deceased.

The end came in the middle of the twentieth century with the death of *Edward Jackson Hilliard* (1841–1943), almost certainly the Florida brigade's last surviving veteran. His extraordinarily long life covered a period of tremendous changes. He was born in December 1841 in Ware County, Georgia. Hilliard's family moved to Florida when Edward was three years old, and he spent the remainder of his life (except for his years in Lee's army) in Polk County. He enlisted as a private in Co. K of the Eighth Florida Regiment and was wounded in the hand at Sharpsburg. Promoted to the rank of fourth corporal, Hilliard was again wounded at Gettysburg and captured. Imprisoned at Point Lookout until exchanged in November 1864, Hilliard received a furlough to south Florida. He tried to rejoin his unit but could not due to Sherman's March to the Sea, which had made transportation to Virginia difficult. He got as far as Madison when he learned of Lee's surrender at Appomattox. He signed the oath at Madison and returned home to Polk County.

The remainder of Hilliard's long life accurately reflected the advance of civilization in south Florida. He worked first as both a cattleman and farmer. He married twice and raised his family at Fairview, just east of Fort Meade. Hilliard served as a Polk County commissioner from 1898 to 1900, moved to Frostproof in 1912, bought a five-acre orange grove, and built a large house in town. In his long life, the old soldier saw his home county change from a frontier backwater sheltering hostile Seminoles to a haven for retirees and snowbirds from the North.

In 1938, the ninety-six-year-old Hilliard, escorted by his grandson Clifford Manley, returned to the Gettysburg battlefield. Traveling by train, they made the trip to attend the seventy-fifth Blue-Gray Reunion, where Pres. Franklin D. Roosevelt dedicated the Peace Monument. As Hilliard was one of the few Confederate veterans who had actually fought at Gettysburg, he received special attention. *Life* magazine photographed Hilliard with the governor of Pennsylvania in the vicinity of the Rogers' House, where he had been captured. The journal also intended to publish a lengthy article about the former Florida soldier, but dropped the story in favor of coverage of Hitler's invasion of Poland.

About a week before his death, Hilliard remarked to his great-granddaughter's husband, a soldier: "You have joined man's army, [but] pretty soon, I'm going to join God's army." Outliving both of his wives, "Uncle Ed" Hilliard died in January 1943 at 101 years of age. He is buried at Pleasant Grove Cemetery in Fort Meade.[21]

Hilliard's life had spanned an extraordinary period in American history. Raised in the era of musket and bowie knife, he had been a youth during two of the last Indian wars fought east of the Mississippi River. Hilliard fought to defend the Jeffersonian vision of rural America, but lived to see the United States develop into an industrial giant. He died during the midst of a second world war and with the horror of atomic warfare just around the corner. With Hilliard's passing, the last link was broken and the story of the Florida brigade came to an end.

Perhaps the words of the *Richmond Enquirer*—the most unlikely and ironic of sources—offered a fitting tribute to the men of the Florida brigade in Lee's army. In early 1864, the paper gave rare acknowledgment of the Floridians' sacrifice, reporting: "We hope that this Brigade, now a small but Spartan band, will not be allowed to lose its identity as *Florida* troops; but that its decimated ranks will be filled up by the new levies about to be raised in that State, and that volunteers will join this Brigade, which has done faithful service in the Army of Northern Virginia, and won a name and a fame for the gallant little State of Florida."[22]

The men of the Florida brigade cared deeply about their reputation and how they would be viewed by posterity. Col. Lang had demanded clarification of the unit's record at Gettysburg so that the children of his men would not "blush for shame, when they read of them in days to come." The survivors also wanted vindication for the spirits of their family and comrades resting in the blood-drenched soil of Virginia, Maryland, and Pennsylvania. They Floridians were certainly not the best brigade in Lee's fabled army, but they generally fought bravely and don't deserve neglect. If their story has been accurately told, perhaps now they can truly rest in peace.[23]

Acknowledgments

This book had its genesis almost thirty years ago when Mary Beth Williamson, my aunt, undertook the daunting task of exploring the dark thicket of the Waters's genealogy. Knowing my interest in the Civil War era, she assigned the task of researching that aspect of family history to me. I soon discovered that all eight of my great-grandfathers fought for the Confederacy, four of them in Florida units. I found a plethora of secondary source material on my grandsires from Georgia and South Carolina, but I also discovered that virtually nothing had been published on the Rebels from the southernmost state. Naively confident, I set about to rectify that situation.

Early in my quest I discovered two kindred spirits. They both were excellent researchers, published writers, and good friends. Don Hillhouse of Orange Park, Florida, and Dr. David Coles of Farmville, Virginia, deserve much credit for this book. They encouraged me when I wanted to quit and shared the fruits of their research. Both of these men have made significant contributions to the scholarship on Florida's Confederate troops. David Coles, along with David Hartman, compiled the extraordinary six-volume *Biographical Roster of Florida's Confederate and Union Soldiers,* and I believe David's master's thesis on Ocean Pond (Olustee) is still the finest study I have read of that engagement. Don Hillhouse's articles and his self-published *Heavy Artillery and Light Infantry* (Tenth Florida Regiment) are excellent examples of perseverance and scholarship. I used his book extensively in the final chapters of this volume.

Several other people deserve a chapter of praise, but perhaps they will settle for a line or two. It may be possible to write a decent history on an Army of Northern Virginia subject without the help of Robert K. Krick, but I scarcely see how. Thanks to "General" Krick, former chief historian at the Fredericks-burg National Battlefield Park, for allowing a lowly private from the "Citrus Squad" to rummage through his file books and pick his brain for information. (My only regret is that he has, as yet, failed to "see the light" and convert to the way of true sports enlightenment—Atlanta Braves baseball and Florida Gator football.) Robert Krick could have almost certainly added several additional volumes to his impressive list of publications if not for his generosity in helping other historians.

His son, Robert E. L. Krick of the Richmond National Battlefield, is proof of the old saying that "the fruit don't fall far from the tree"— both in knowl-edge and in generously providing aid to researchers. Bobby took me to both the North Anna and Cold Harbor battlefields, giving me fair warning about the voracious appetites of the Old Dominion ticks. In addition, he shared a valu-able set of Second Florida letters for the Seven Days period and read a draft of the Seven Days chapter, tactfully pointing out several valuable sources and several stupid mistakes. Thanks to both of these true gentlemen of Southern history.

Other members of the National Park Service have also been extremely helpful. Scott Hartwig at Gettysburg allowed Don Hillhouse and me to hunt through the park's files, fielded panicky e-mails, and pointed two neophyte his-torians to the sites of the Florida brigade's greatest suffering. Dennis Frye at Harpers Ferry; Eric Mink at Fredericksburg; Mike Andruss at Richmond; Jim Ogden at Chickamauga; and Chris Calkins at Petersburg all provided valu-able information or advice. *Smithsonian* magazine recently named Ed Bearss, the dean of National Battlefield Park historians, a living national treasure and I agree wholeheartedly. He kindly helped me even when I was too green to know which questions to ask. The citizens of our country would be a lot less upset with government bureaucracy if all public servants were as dedicated and com-petent as the National Parks historians.

The late Dr. Samuel Proctor, a history professor at the University of Florida and author, taught me as an undergraduate, accepted my first article for publi-cation in the *Florida Historical Quarterly,* and even encouraged me to submit a second essay to that excellent journal. Words are inadequate to express the con-tributions he has made to Florida history. Dr. Proctor truly deserves the title of "dean of Florida history." I met Canter Brown Jr. through Dr. Proctor, and Canter also provided encouragement and tips regarding the academic style of writing.

I utilized several valuable collections of War between the States materials in both Florida and Georgia. The Robert Manning Strozier Library at Florida State University, Tallahassee; the P. K. Yonge Florida History Collection at the University of Florida, Gainesville; and the State Library and Archives of Florida in Tallahassee, all provided important information. The State Library deserves accolades for making a great deal of useful information available on the World Wide Web. Unfortunately, I must sadly report that the use of items at P. K. Yonge was almost impossible several years ago—it is now considerably less irksome. Dr. Lewis "Nick" Wynne of the Florida Historical Society, Cocoa, Florida, provides a welcome contrast to the "Don't mess with my fiefdom" attitude. Nick is kind, generous, helpful, and always a joy to talk to. Thanks to him for giving me permission to use my *Florida Historical Quarterly* articles in this volume. The University of Georgia Library in Athens contains a treasure trove of Civil War–era newspapers on microfilm that also proved extremely helpful.

I believe that Robert L. Baldwin of Harrisburg, Pennsylvania, is the "unsung hero of Florida Civil War history." His unstinting search for Florida Confederate photographs has helped to uncover an amazing number of images from the southernmost state. He has kindly made his collection available to the authors, and has literally put a face on the men of the Florida brigade.

Any number of other writers, researchers, individuals, and historians have aided in this project, including Gordon Rhea of Mount Pleasant, South Carolina; Bruce Allardice of Chicago; Dr. Joe A. Akerman of Madison, Florida, and his son, J. Mark Akerman of Greensboro, North Carolina; Dr. Joe Knetsch of Tallahassee; Leland Hawes of Tampa; Ted Savas of Eldorado Hills, California; Kyle S. VanLandingham of Riverview, Florida; Bill Walker of Mandeville, Louisiana, who graciously permitted us use of the Johnson narrative; Jim Johnson of Port Richey, Florida; Jim Studnicki of Tampa; Annagayle McClure of Littleton, Colorado; Stacy McCain of Washington, DC; Alfred Young of Burtonville, Maryland; John Horn of Oak Park, Illinois; and Col. John J. Masters Sr. and Lt. Col. Greg Moore, both of St. Augustine, Florida.

Richard Ferry of McClenny, Florida, has made numerous contributions to the preservation of our Florida heritage and deserves the praise of a grateful state. Jonathan C. Sheppard of Tallahassee has completed an excellent history of the Floridians in the Army of Tennessee. He opened my eyes to the intense rivalry between the various districts of Florida before secession, and helped with tips and sources for the final chapter of this book.

Each of these individuals has been a tremendous help with this project and deserves more than this brief mention. I hope that two others—Warren

Wilkinson of Georgia and Massachusetts, and Vince Murray, a journalist with the *Ocala Star-Banner*—are smiling down from heaven, remembering the good times we shared in researching this volume.

The excellent staff members at the University of Alabama Press have been extremely helpful in the publication of *Spartan Band.* Thanks to them for their faith in this project and dedication to Southern history. Copyeditor Robin DuBlanc deserves a special vote of thanks for her wonderful work on this book and gentle good humor in dealing with a writer who insisted on taking every wrong turn.

Three people generously agreed to read the manuscript, and they deserve not only my thanks but also my admiration for their intestinal fortitude. My brother Robert A. Waters, an oft-published author from Ocala, Florida, has encouraged me through the years, and more than once helped me traverse the shoals of the publishing industry. Despite our closeness, he can always be counted on to give me an honest opinion. Larry Stephens of Cave Spring, Georgia, is a new friend, but a valuable source of support. He can truly work miracles. His excellent regimental history, *Bound for Glory: A History of the 30th Alabama Regiment, CSA,* is a wonderful book. As librarian at Georgia Highlands College, he has helped me track down obscure material (quickly) and been a true "Barnabas" (Son of Encouragement). Dr. Keith Bohannon of Carrollton, Georgia, has been a friend for more than twenty years. (I think he was still a teenager when we first met.) He is a noted historian and a distinguished scholar of all things dealing with Georgia and the Army of Northern Virginia. It would be rank ingratitude not to mention that his suggestions made *Spartan Band* a better book. I thank all three of these gentlemen for going above and beyond the call of duty.

My coauthor, Jimmy Edmonds, has more to do with the completion of this book than words can tell. He's a young man who came to Rome, Georgia, to get some research materials, and wound up igniting again my interest in finishing this history. Jimmy deserves a special vote of thanks. He is an excellent writer, researcher, and friend. Though I will likely never write a history again, I feel confident that I am leaving our Florida Confederates in capable hands. I look forward to seeing more from him very soon.

My extended family has been my rock in the storms of life. Vonda, my wife, has been completely supportive through all the years, even if she thinks my obsession with these long-dead Florida soldiers bizarre in the extreme. Her love and patience have made this whole odyssey a joyous experience. My "children," Luke and Amy Waters of Tallahassee and Lauren Rose Waters and Nikki

Sanchez of Rome, have feigned occasional interest in the project and never once treated me like the crazy uncle who should be chained to the attic wall.

My father, John T. Waters Sr. of Ocala and Rome, died while this book was in the publication phase. He first sparked my interest in Florida history, introduced me to Florida's guerilla hero, Capt. J. J. Dickison, and initially urged me to write this book. My mother, God rest her soul, thought I could do no wrong. John T. Waters Jr. (another brother and published author) has always been a steadfast supporter of this project. He also read the manuscript, offering cogent advice, and I suspect he will enjoy the final product more than all the others. Despite all the aggravation I inflicted upon my sister when she was young, Kim Waters of Bradenton, Florida, remains a staunch ally. To her I offer my profound apologies and a thousand thanks. Charlie and Mary Beth Williamson of Milton, Florida, and my in-laws, Rose and Leonard Fox of Rome, Georgia, have continued to offer love and support "through good and evil fortune."

I feel confident that I probably have left several deserving friends off this list of acknowledgments. To them, I beg your forgiveness; know that I love you. Finally, I offer a special thanks to the good folks at the Oak Hill Church of Christ, my spiritual family. My prayer is that we may we all meet again when we "cross over the river and rest in the shade of trees."

Zack Waters
Rome, Georgia

As Zack observes, this book would not have been possible without the help of a plethora of scholars, friends, and family along the way. I would like to thank my parents, Jim and Sue Edmonds, for their unfailing support and encouragement over the years, and my brother Chris who, for the most part, tolerates my lengthy monologues. To them and the rest of my family—whether Kearys, Nordlings, Edmondses, or Russells—I owe a debt of gratitude. My sixth-grade history teacher, Mrs. Kay George, deserves much praise as well. She instilled in me a love of history that shows no sign of dissipating.

Working with Zack has been both a pleasure and a privilege. He is uniquely a gentleman, scholar, and great friend. Joe Edmonds, ceaselessly loyal and true, departed for his eternal rest several years ago, but remains in my thoughts on almost a daily basis.

Lastly, and most importantly, I would like to thank a girl and a dachshund—the two loves of my life—for making life pleasant and unpredictable.

James Edmonds
Port Royal, South Carolina

Notes

Introduction

1. Irvin D. S. Winsboro, ed., *Florida's Civil War: Explorations into Conflict, Interpretations, and Memory* (Cocoa: Florida Historical Society Press, 2007), iii.

2. There are several excellent books on the era's history, including William Watson Davis, *The Civil War and Reconstruction in Florida* (Gainesville: University of Florida Press, 1964); John E. Johns, *Florida during the Civil War* (Gainesville: University of Florida Press, 1963); Lewis N. Wynne and Robert A. Taylor, *Florida in the Civil War* (Mt. Pleasant, SC: Arcadia, 2003); Robert A. Taylor, *Rebel Storehouse: Florida in the Confederate Economy* (Tuscaloosa: University of Alabama Press, 1995); Tracy Revels, *Grander in Her Daughters: Florida's Women during the Civil War* (Columbia: University of South Carolina Press, 2004).

3. These include Andrew Francis Lundstrom, "Perry's Brigade in the Army of Northern Virginia" (master's thesis, University of Florida, 1966); Richard S. Nichols, "Florida's Fighting Rebels: A Military History of Florida's Civil War Troops" (master's thesis, Florida State University, 1967); Jonathan C. Sheppard, "Everyday Soldiers: The Florida Brigade in the West, 1861–1862" (master's thesis, Florida State University, 2004); Shane Micah Turner, "Rearguard of the Confederacy: The Second Florida Infantry Regiment" (master's thesis, Florida State University, 2006).

4. J. J. Dickison, "Florida," vol. 11, *Confederate Military History* (New York: Blue & Gray, 1962); Francis P. Fleming, *Memoir of Captain C. Seton Fleming of the Second Florida Infantry, CSA* (Arlington, VA: Stonewall House, 1985). Several ex-Confederates suggested that Dickison was more interested in embellishing his legend than providing useful information on other units.

5. Don Hillhouse, *Heavy Artillery and Light Infantry: A History of the 1st Florida Special Battalion & 10th Infantry Regiment, CSA* (Jacksonville, FL: n.p., 1992); Gary Loderhose, *Far, Far from Home: The Ninth Florida Regiment in the Confederate Army* (Carmel, IN: Guild, 1999).

6. David W. Hartman and David J. Coles, eds., *Biographical Roster of Florida's Confederate and Union Soldiers, 1861–1865,* 6 vols. (Wilmington, NC: Broadfoot, 1995).

7. U.S. War Department, *The War of the Rebellion: A Compilation of the Official Records of the Union and Confederate Armies,* 127 vols. (Washington, DC: Government Printing Office, 1880–1901) (hereafter *OR*).

8. Bryan letter, July 22, 1863, Council Bryan Papers, M87-35, Florida State Archives, Tallahassee.

Chapter 1

1. W. D. Ballantine, "Floridians in the Fight," (Jacksonville) *Florida Times-Union,* July 16, 1895, 3. Florida governor H. L. Mitchell appointed Lang, Ballantine, and Moore to mark the battlefield. (Minor spelling errors in quotations have been corrected throughout this book to improve readability. Anything added, including capitalization and punctuation, is set off with brackets.)

2. Ibid.

3. Col. David Lang, "To the Editors of the *Enquirer,*" *Richmond Enquirer,* July 26, 1863.

4. *U.S. Census for 1860: Population* (Washington, DC: Government Printing Office, 1864), 598–99; Paul Taylor, *Discovering the Civil War in Florida: A Reader and Guide* (Sarasota, FL: Pineapple, 2001), 3.

5. Ronald W. Haase, *Classic Cracker: Florida Wood-Frame Vernacular Architecture* (Sarasota, FL: Pineapple, 1992), 25–26; Jonathan C. Sheppard, "'By the Noble Daring of Her Sons': The Florida Brigade of the Army of Tennessee" (PhD diss., Florida State University, 2008), 10–23; Johns, *Florida during the Civil War,* 2.

6. Sheppard, "'Noble Daring,'" 19–24; Canter Brown Jr., "The Civil War, 1861–1865," in *The New History of Florida* ed. Michael Gannon (Gainesville: University of Florida Press, 1996), 231.

7. Davis, *Civil War and Reconstruction,* 32–33; "Florida under Civil Strife," www.floridahistory.org; Erik Robinson, "Florida in 1845," in *Celebrating Florida: Works of Art from the Vickers Collection,* ed. Gary R. Libby (Gainesville: University of Florida Press, 1995), 15–19.

8. Sheppard, "'Noble Daring,'" 126–30; *Cedar Key Telegraph,* December 11, 1860; *St. Augustine Examiner,* December 22, 1860; Charlton W. Tebeau and Ruby Leach Carson, *Florida: From Indian Trail to Space Age—A History* (Delray Beach, FL: Southern Publishing, 1965), 1:173; Eloise Robinson Ott, *Ocali Country, Kingdom of the Sun: A History of Marion County, Florida* (Ocala, FL: Greene, 1966), 75.

9. Johns, *Florida during the Civil War,* 10; Samuel Proctor, ed., *Florida One Hundred Years Ago,* (Coral Gables: Florida Library and Historical Commission, 1960–1965), December 1960, 2; Joseph T. Glatthaar, *General Lee's Army: From Victory to Collapse* (New York: Free Press, 2008), 14.

10. Dickison, "Florida," 5–12; Proctor, *Florida One Hundred Years Ago,* January 1961, 1–2.

11. Tebeau and Carson, *Indian Trail to Space Age,* 172–73; Glatthaar, *Lee's Army,* 24. See,

generally, Herbert J. Doherty Jr., "Union Nationalism in Florida, *Florida Historical Quarterly* (hereafter *FHQ*) 29 (1950): 83–95.

12. Glatthaar, *Lee's Army*, 29–41; D. L. Geer, "Memories of the War," (Lake City) *Florida Index*, January 5, 1905. An old but valuable list of the various reasons given by Southerners for enlisting in the Confederate army can be found in Bell Irvin Wiley, *The Life of Johnny Reb: The Common Soldier in the Confederacy* (Baton Rouge: Louisiana State University Press, 1987), 15–20.

13. Robert Hawk, *Florida's Army: Militia/State Troops/National Guard, 1565–1985* (Englewood, FL: Pineapple, 1986), 77–81; George Cassel Bittle, "In Defense of Florida: The Organized Florida Militia from 1821–1920" (PhD diss., Florida State University, 1965), 221–35; George C. Bittle, "Florida Prepares for War, 1860–1861," *FHQ* 51 (1972): 143–52. See, generally, Everett W. Caudle, "To Defend or Pretend: The Social Role of Militia and Volunteer Units in the Antebellum South" (master's thesis: University of Florida, 1990).

14. James W. Covington, *The Billy Bowlegs War, 1855–1858, The Final Stand of the Seminoles against the Whites* (Chuluota, FL: Mickler House, 1982), 54–56.

15. Nichols, "Florida's Fighting Rebels," 1; *Session Laws of the State of Florida*, 10th sess. (Tallahassee: n.p., 1861), 16–24.

16. Dickison, "Florida," 19–20. "Army of the Heartland" is the designation Thomas L. Connelly used to describe the Army of Tennessee; see his *Army of the Heartland: The Army of Tennessee, 1861–1862* (Baton Rouge: Louisiana State University Press, 1967). Sheppard, "'Noble Daring,'" provides an excellent history of this unit and the other Florida troops in the West.

17. Dickison, "Florida," 143; Fleming, *C. Seton Fleming*, 25.

18. Fleming, *C. Seton Fleming*, 25; Johns, *Florida during the Civil War*, 21; Covington, *Billy Bowlegs War*, 71–80.

19. Dickison, "Florida," 143; Nichols, "Florida's Fighting Rebels," 14–15.

20. Fleming, *C. Seton Fleming*, 25–28; Robert K. Krick, *Lee's Colonels: Biographical Register of the Field Officers of the Army of Northern Virginia* (Dayton, OH: Morningside, 1991), 387, 326, 311–12; brief biographical sketch of Rogers in "Mrs. Livingston Rowe Schuyler, President General, UDC," *Confederate Veteran* (hereafter *CV*) 30 (1922): 4; E. Parker Scammon, "George T. Ward," *Catholic World* 54 324 (March 1892): 883; *OR*, 4, 1, 466–68; Dickison, "Florida," 143.

21. Johns, *Florida during the Civil War*, 21; *OR*, 1, 1, 466–68; Hartman and Coles, *Biographical Roster*, 1:138–259.

22. Glatthaar, *Lee's Army*, 17–28. Data taken from *Biographical Roster* and the authors' files resulted in date and place of birth for almost 500 Second Florida soldiers. This information was tabulated and compared to Glatthaar's conclusions. There were a few minor differences, but the results were generally very close. The number of foreign-born members of the Second is significantly higher than the percentage found in Ella Lonn's venerable classic, *Foreigners in the Confederacy* (Chapel Hill: University of North Carolina Press, 2002), 31 (table).

23. Ibid.

24. Ibid.

25. Fleming, *C. Seton Fleming*, 29–30. For a somewhat humorous account of the Floridians first weeks in Virginia, see J. J. Thompson letter, October 24, 1893, P. K. Yonge Library of Florida History, University of Florida, Gainesville.

26. Fleming, *C. Seton Fleming*, 30; Nichols, "Florida's Fighting Rebels," 20–21.

Chapter 2

1. Fleming, *C. Seton Fleming*, 31; *OR*, 9, 37.

2. Nichols, "Florida's Fighting Rebels," 22–24; "On to Richmond," (Fernandina) *Florida Mirror*, June 16, 1894, 1; "Co. 'A' in Camp," *Florida Mirror*, June 23, 1894, 1. (W. D. Ballantine is believed to be the author of this five-part memoir.) Strong Unionist sentiments existed in the mountains of east Tennessee, and the loyalists made numerous attempts to destroy the vital East Tennessee & Virginia Railroad bridges. Confederates strung up the guerillas they killed as a warning to other bridge burners.

3. Krick, *Lee's Colonels*, 44; UCV funeral announcement for W. D. Ballantine, Zack C. Waters Collection, Rome, GA; Dickison, "Florida," 207–8.

4. Stephen W. Sears, *To the Gates of Richmond: The Peninsula Campaign* (New York: Ticknor & Fields, 1992), 35–39; Gary W. Gallagher, "The Fall of 'Prince John' Magruder," *Civil War* 19 (August 1989): 10–11; John V. Quartein, "The Peninsula Campaign: From Hampton Roads to Seven Pines," *Hallowed Ground* 2 (Spring 1999): 8–13.

5. Fleming, *C. Seton Fleming*, 33; Dickison, "Florida," 143–44.

6. *OR*, 11, 1, 406, 482; "Col. Ward and the Florida Regiment at Yorktown," (Tallahassee) *Florida Sentinel*, April 29, 1862. See also Gilbert Wright, ed., "Some Letters to His Parents by a Floridian in the Confederate Army," *FHQ* 36 (1958): 356.

7. Ibid.

8. Gallagher, "Fall of 'Prince John,'" 11–12.

9. *OR*, 11, 1, 592–93, 602; Fleming, *C. Seton Fleming*, 34–35; J. Adrian Jackson, "Perry's Brigade of Florida's Fighting Rebels," *Apalachee* 9 (1970): 64–65; Carol Kettenburgh Dubbs, *Defend This Old Town: Williamsburg during the Civil War* (Baton Rouge: Louisiana State University Press, 2004), 115; Douglas Southall Freeman, *Lee's Lieutenants: A Study in Command* (New York: Charles Scribner's Sons, 1970), 1:179–88.

10. Dubbs, *Old Town*, 126.

11. Dickison, "Florida," 144–45; Fleming, *C. Seton Fleming*, 31–39.

12. Ibid. Dubbs, *Old Town*, 180, places casualties for Ward's demi-brigade at eighty killed, wounded, or captured.

13. Dickison, "Florida," 144–45; Fleming, *C. Seton Fleming*, 31–39; Dubbs, *Old Town*, 233. A grave marker for Ward is located in the churchyard of the Burton Episcopal Church in Colonial Williamsburg. Dubbs identifies the minister who presided over Ward's funeral service as Rev. Thomas Ambler.

14. Fleming, *C. Seton Fleming*, 41; Nichols, "Florida's Fighting Rebels," 70–71; Dickison, "Florida," 146.

15. Dickison, "Florida," 207–8; "Since the Blue and Gray," *Florida Mirror*, May 26, 1894, 1; Lawrence L. Hewitt, "Edward Aylesworth Perry," in *The Confederate General*, ed. William C. Davis (Washington, DC: National Historical Society, 1991), 5:20–21. For a

history (not always reliable) of the Perry family, see Genevieve Parkhill Lykes, *A Gift of Heritage* (n.p., 1969), 15–28.

16. Sears, *To the Gates of Richmond,* 111–24; Quartein, "The Peninsula Campaign," 12–13.

17. *OR,* 11, 1, 961–64; Fleming, *C. Seton Fleming,* 48–50.

18. Ibid.

19. The letter, from a member of Battery A, New York Artillery, is quoted in its entirety in Fleming, *C. Seton Fleming,* 49–50.

20. Unpublished manuscript entitled "Florida in the Civil War," no author, no date, Zack C. Waters Collection, Rome, GA. Information is taken from a scrapbook assembled by a female member of the Burroughs/Maxwell family from an anonymous source, and contains clippings and a wealth of other excellent information.

21. *OR,* 11, 1, 965; Fleming, *C. Seton Fleming,* 49–63.

22. John W. Bell, *Memoirs of Governor William Smith of Virginia: His Political, Military, and Personal History* (New York: Moss Engraving, 1891), 39.

23. Daniel Harvey Hill, "Lee Attacks North of the Chickahominy," in *Battles and Leaders of the Civil War,* ed. Robert U. Johnson and Clarence C. Buel (New York: Thomas Yoseloff, 1956), 2:352; Fleming, *C. Seton Fleming,* 48–50; *OR,* 11, 1, 963. At Seven Pines Capts. J. H. Pooser, C. S. Flagg, A. C. Butler, and T. A. Perry were killed. The other six captains, W. D. Ballantine (A), Lew Williams (B), W. R. Moore (C), M. G. C. Musgrove (D), W. E. Caslin (E), and M. J. Duncan (I), were wounded.

24. John S. Salmon, *The Official Virginia Civil War Battlefield Guide* (Mechanicsburg, PA: Stackpole, 2001), 95.

25. Sears, *To the Gates of Richmond,* 142–45; Robert E. L. Krick, "Robert E. Lee and the Seven Days," *Hallowed Ground* 2 (Spring 1999): 14.

26. "Virginia Correspondence," (Monticello, FL) *Family Friend,* November 9, 1861; Nichols, "Florida's Fighting Rebels," 24; Fred L. Robertson, ed., *Soldiers of Florida in the Seminole Indian, Civil, and Spanish-American Wars* (Macclenny, FL: Richard J. Ferry, 1983) 98–99 (hereafter *SOF*). The Howell Guards numbered about 100 men.

27. Krick, "Robert E. Lee and the Seven Days," 14–15; Nichols, "Florida's Fighting Rebels," 75.

28. Jeffry Wert, "Roger Atkinson Pryor," in *The Confederate General,* ed. William C. Davis (Washington, DC: National Historical Society, 1991), 5:64–65. See, generally, Sara A. Pryor, *Reminiscences of Peace and War* (New York: Grossett & Dunlap, 1905).

29. Krick, "Robert E. Lee and the Seven Days," 16–17; Sears, *To the Gates of Richmond,* 200–209; James I. Robertson Jr., *General A. P. Hill: The Story of a Confederate Warrior* (New York: Vintage, 1992), 71–75.

30. Robertson, *A. P. Hill,* 79–86; Krick, "Robert E. Lee and the Seven Days," 18; *OR,* 11, 2, 780.

31. *OR,* 11, 2, 780–81.

32. Fleming, *C. Seton Fleming,* 63; S. H. Wright to "My Dear Laura," July 5, 1862, S. H. Wright Letters, typescript, Research Library, Richmond National Battlefield, Richmond, VA.

33. *OR,* 11, 2, 980, 985; Dick [Richard Parkhill] to Mrs. Parkhill, June 28, 1862, folder

8, Parkhill Family Papers, Southern Historical Collection, Manuscripts Department, University of North Carolina, Chapel Hill.

34. Ibid.

35. Salmon, *Virginia Battlefield Guide,* 107–12; Sears, *To the Gates of Richmond,* 258–76.

36. Edward Porter Alexander, *Fighting for the Confederacy: The Personal Recollections of General Edward Porter Alexander,* ed. Gary W. Gallagher (Chapel Hill: University of North Carolina Press, 1989), 110.

37. Sears, *To the Gates of Richmond,* 277–307.

38. *OR,* 11, 2, 780–81; Terry L. Jones, *Lee's Tigers: The Louisiana Infantry in the Army of Northern Virginia* (Baton Rouge: Louisiana State University Press, 1987), 107.

39. Stephen R. Mallory to Gov. John Milton, July 5, 1862, Milton Letterbook, Florida State Archives, Tallahassee; *OR,* 11, 2, 760.

40. Freeman, *Lee's Lieutenants,* 1:603–4.

41. Nichols, "Florida's Fighting Rebels," 75–77; Dickison, "Florida," 148–49.

42. Ibid.

43. Ibid.

44. Hartman and Coles, *Biographical Roster,* 1:66, 2:460, 509; Krick, *Lee's Colonels,* 187, 227, 111.

45. Hartman and Coles, *Biographical Roster,* 2:460, 567, 569.

46. Nichols, "Florida's Fighting Rebels," 75–77; Dickison, "Florida," 148–49; Frank S. Jones, *History of Decatur County, Georgia* (Spartanburg, SC: n.p., 1980), 380–81.

47. Data on the unit came from Hartman and Coles, *Biographical Roster,* 2:460–577; Zack C. Waters Collection, Rome, GA; Robertson, *SOF.*

48. Krick, *Lee's Colonels,* 142–43, 308, 376; Zack C. Waters, "Tampa's Forgotten Defenders: The Confederate Commanders at Fort Brooke," *Sunland Tribune* 17 (1991): 7. Turner had journeyed to Tallahassee seeking a commission to raise a cavalry company, but Gov. Milton was holding Brig. Gen. John B. Grayson, commander of the Department of Middle and Western Florida, a virtual prisoner. According to Milton, Grayson was in the final stages of tuberculosis and "acted upon suggestion." Shortly thereafter, the chief executive received news that Federals had attacked St. Marks, and Milton headed south with all the troops he could muster. The report was a Turner ruse. When the governor returned to Tallahassee, he discovered Turner had visited Grayson, received his commission and supplies, and had scurried back to Tampa.

49. Krick, *Lee's Colonels,* 228–30; David Lang, "The Civil War Letters of Colonel David Lang," ed. Bertram H. Groene, *FHQ* 54 (1976): 340–66.

50. Krick, *Lee's Colonels,* 48–49; William Baya file, Zack C. Waters Collection, Rome, GA.

51. Geer, "Memories of the War," September 29, 1905, 1.

52. *OR,* 3, 5, 694–95; John E. Reiger, "Deprivation, Disaffection, and Desertion in Confederate Florida," in *Florida's Civil War,* ed. Winsboro, 69; Glatthaar, *Lee's Army,* 84–85.

53. Gary W. Gallagher, *The Confederate War* (Cambridge, MA: Harvard University Press, 1997), 32.

54. Hartman and Coles, *Biographical Roster,* 1:139–259; Zack Waters Collection, Rome, GA; and Robertson, *SOF,* were used in assessing the Second Florida 1862 desertions.

55. *OR,* 6, 402–3; Tebeau and Carson, *Indian Trail to Space Age,* 193; John E. Reiger,

"Florida After Secession: Abandonment by the Confederacy and Its Consequences," *FHQ* 50 (1971): 128–42.

56. Ibid.; John M. Sacher, "'A Very Disagreeable Business': Confederate Conscription in Louisiana," *Civil War History* 53 (June 2007): 142.

Chapter 3

1. Salmon, *Virginia Battlefield Guide,* 126.

2. Ibid., 125–26; John H. Hennessy, *Return to Bull Run: The Campaign and Battle of Second Manassas* (New York: Simon & Schuster, 1993), 1–24; John Hennessy, "Second Manassas," in *The Civil War Battlefield Guide,* ed. Frances H. Kennedy (Boston: Mariner, 1990), 74–77.

3. Salmon, *Virginia Battlefield Guide,* 132–50.

4. Hennessy, "Second Manassas," 74–77; Salmon, *Virginia Battlefield Guide,* 145–50; Freeman, *Lee's Lieutenants,* 2:81–119.

5. *OR,* 12, 2, 601–2; Fleming, *C. Seton Fleming,* 65–67.

6. Fleming, *C. Seton Fleming,* 66.

7. Hennessy, "Second Manassas," 77.

8. Stephen W. Sears, *Landscape Turned Red: The Battle of Antietam* (Boston: Ticknor & Fields, 1983), 10–15.

9. *OR,* 19, 1, 804; Sears, *Landscape Turned Red,* 72–73; Stephen W. Sears, "Antietam," in *The Civil War Battlefield Guide,* ed. Frances H. Kennedy (Boston: Mariner, 1990), 81–86.

10. Glatthaar, *Lee's Army,* 166.

11. Ibid.

12. Dennis E. Frye, "Stonewall Attacks! The Siege of Harpers Ferry," *Blue and Gray* 5 (September 1987): 10–62; Dennis Frye, "Harpers Ferry," in *The Civil War Battlefield Guide,* ed. Frances H. Kennedy (Boston: Mariner, 1990), 78–80; Robertson, *A. P. Hill,* 134–40.

13. Telephone conversation between Zack Waters and Dennis Frye, historian, Harpers Ferry National Historic Park, March 12, 2007, regarding placement of the Florida brigade; I. M. Auld, letter to "Dear Mother," September 22, 1862, Auld Letters, Putnam County Department of Archives and History, Palatka, FL.

14. Robertson, *A. P. Hill,* 138–41.

15. *OR,* 19, 1, 955. Jackson here classes the march as "severe"; Freeman, *Lee's Lieutenants,* 2:199–201; Auld, letter to "Dear Mother," September 22, 1862.

16. Freeman, *Lee's Lieutenants,* 2:203–10; Sears, *Landscape Turned Red,* 180–215.

17. Robert K. Krick, "'It Appeared As Though Mutual Extermination Would Put a Stop to the Awful Carnage:' Confederates in Sharpsburg's Bloody Lane," in *The Antietam Campaign,* ed. Gary W. Gallagher (Chapel Hill: University of North Carolina Press, 1999), 223–24. Much of the information presented about Antietam comes from Krick's study.

18. Sears, *Landscape Turned Red,* 236–40.

19. Krick, "Sharpsburg's Bloody Lane," 230–34; Sears, *Landscape Turned Red,* 235–40; Ezra A. Carman's Narrative, Library of Congress, Washington DC; "The Bloody Lane" section of Carman's Narrative, reprinted in "My Sons Were Faithful and They Fought," in *The Irish Brigade at Antietam: An Anthology,* ed. Joseph Bilby and Stephen O'Neill (Hightstown, NJ: Longstreet House, 1997) 51–58.

20. Krick, "Sharpsburg's Bloody Lane," 239–40.

21. Ibid.

22. David Lang to E. A. Carman, ca. 1898, David Lang Letterbooks, vol. 2, Florida State Archives, Tallahassee.

23. William D. Ballantine to Carman, February 23, 1895, Library of Congress, Washington, DC (photocopy in Zack C. Waters Collection, Rome, GA); see Antietam National Battlefield Park Web site "Army of Northern Virginia—Right Wing—Part 1," http://www.nps.gov/anti/historyculture/anv-right-wing1.htm.

24. Ballantine to Carman map; *OR*, 19, 1, 1037.

25. Krick, "Sharpsburg's Bloody Lane," 240.

26. Lang to Carman, cited above; Council A. Bryan, "Letter from the 5th Florida," (Tallahassee) *Florida Sentinel*, October 7, 1862; Benjamin Franklin Page, "A Letter from Antietam," *Magnolia Monthly* 2 (September 1964).

27. *OR*, 19, 1, 1048; Andrew Francis Lindstrom, "Perry's Brigade in the Army of Northern Virginia" (master's thesis, University of Florida, 1966), 56. Krick points out that Bennett suffered from being shell-shocked at the sunken road. After the war he wrote often, "but not always lucidly," about the Bloody Lane, and so great was the confusion in the sunken road that "it is hard to imagine how he could have recognized such an event." Krick, "Sharpsburg's Bloody Lane," 234–35, 244.

28. J. W. Mills's account in William W. Bennett, *A Narrative of the Great Revival Which Prevailed in the Southern States during the Late War between the States of the Federal Union* (Harrisonburg, VA: Hess, 1998) 200–201.

29. PWA, "A Gallant Floridian," Columbus, GA, newspaper, unknown journal and date, photocopy in Zack C. Waters Collection, Rome, GA.

30. Krick, "Sharpsburg's Bloody Lane," 246; Sears, *Landscape Turned Red*, 246.

31. Col. Robert F. Floyd to Gov, John Milton, September 22, 1862, Governor's Office Letterbook, ser. 32, vol. 6, 462, Florida State Archives, Tallahassee.

32. Sears, "Antietam," 82–85; Ronald H. Bailey, *The Bloodiest Day: The Battle of Antietam* (Alexandria, VA: Time-Life, 1984), 108–9.

33. Robertson, *A. P. Hill*, 142–47; Sears, *Landscape Turned Red*, 261–77.

34. Sears, "Antietam," 84–85; Bailey, *The Bloodiest Day*, 120–41.

35. Sharpsburg casualties are based on manuscript research by the authors. The Floridians' casualties amounted to 91 killed, 84 wounded, 107 missing: for a total of 282. The regimental losses are as follows: Second Florida—14 killed, 18 wounded, and 22 missing; Fifth Florida—52 killed, 42 wounded, and 57 missing; Eighth Florida—25 killed, 24 wounded, and 28 missing.

36. Freeman, *Lee's Lieutenants*, 2:265–66.

37. Dickison, "Florida," 146–47.

38. Krick, *Lee's Colonels*, 228–30, 187, 142–43; Lang letter to Carman, cited above.

Chapter 4

1. *OR*, 19, 2, 626–27; Jay Luvaas and Harold W. Nelson, eds., *The U.S. Army War College Guide to the Battles of Chancellorsville and Fredericksburg* (Carlisle, PA: South Mountain, 1988), vi.

2. Gary W. Gallagher, "The Net Result of the Campaign Was in Our Favor: Confederate Reaction to the Maryland Campaign," in *The Antietam Campaign,* ed. Gary W. Gallagher (Chapel Hill: University of North Carolina Press, 1999), 3–43.

3. Luvaas and Nelson, *The U.S. Army Guide,* vi–viii; *OR,* 19, 1, 87–89; George C. Rable, *Fredericksburg, Fredericksburg* (Chapel Hill: University of North Carolina Press, 2002), 42–57.

4. Luvaas and Nelson, *The U.S. Army Guide,* vii–x. For Southern reaction to McClennan's removal, see Freeman, *Lee's Lieutenants,* 2:312–13.

5. Luvaas and Nelson, *The U.S. Army Guide,* ix–x; Frank A. O'Reilly, "'One of the Greatest Feats of the War:' Military Milestone at Fredericksburg," *Journal of Fredericksburg History* 2 (1997): 1–2.

6. Ibid. See also Frank A. O'Reilly, *Stonewall Jackson at Fredericksburg* (Lynchburg, VA: H. E. Howard, 1993), 12.

7. *OR,* 21, 1, 603 and 619; Freeman, *Lee's Lieutenants,* 2:332–35; Rable, *Fredericksburg, Fredericksburg,* 160–61.

8. *OR,* 21, 1, 603; Rable, *Fredericksburg, Fredericksburg,* 165.

9. O'Reilly, "One of the Greatest Feats," 2; *OR,* 21, 603; David Lang to Hon. F. P. Fleming, August 31, 1901, F. P. Fleming Papers, Jacksonville Public Library, Jacksonville, FL.

10. *OR,* 21, 1, 603; Rable, *Fredericksburg, Fredericksburg,* 165–70; O'Reilly, "One of the Greatest Feats," 6.

11. Rable, *Fredericksburg, Fredericksburg,* 170. Dr. Rable, in his valuable study, mistakenly has Baya succeeding Lang in command of the larger Florida contingent.

12. Lang to Fleming, F. P. Fleming Papers.

13. *OR,* 21, 619; Rable, *Fredericksburg, Fredericksburg,* 165; O'Reilly, "One of the Greatest Feats," 6.

14. *OR,* 21, 1, 601–2; Lang to Fleming, F. P. Fleming Papers.

15. *OR,* 21, 1, 619; O'Reilly, "One of the Greatest Feats of the War," 6–7; Rable, *Fredericksburg, Fredericksburg,* 168–71.

16. *OR,* 21, 1, 601–2; O'Reilly, "One of the Greatest Feats of the War," 6–7; Lang, "Letters," 384.

17. Rable, *Fredericksburg, Fredericksburg,* 168; O'Reilly, "One of the Greatest Feats of the War," 6–10.

18. *OR,* 21, 603, 619.

19. *OR,* 21, 603; O'Reilly, "One of the Greatest Feats of the War," 18.

20. O'Reilly, "One of the Greatest Feats of the War," 18–20; *OR,* 21, 618.

21. Walter R. Moore to Elizabeth Peeples, March 8, 1865, CW Misc. Collection 3, U.S. Military History Institute, Carlisle, PA; Don Hillhouse, "Florida Flags," unpublished ms., Zack C. Waters Collection, Rome, GA.

22. Freeman, *Lee's Lieutenants,* 2:377–89.

23. Samuel A. Spencer to "Dear Joy," letter dated February 10, 1863, Atlanta Historical Society Collection, Atlanta, GA; John Walters, *Norfolk Blues: Civil War Diary of the Norfolk Light Artillery Blues* (Shippenburg, PA: White Mane, 1997), February 22, 1863 entry, 56.

24. Spencer letter; Junius Taylor, letter dated February 26, 1863, Pine Hill Plantation Papers, Strozier Library Special Collections, Florida State University, Tallahassee.

25. *Richmond Dispatch,* February 16, 1863, 2.

26. Hartman and Coles, *Biographical Roster,* 1:32, 61, 2:808; Krick, *Lee's Colonels,* 48, 92–93, 228–30. Krick avers that Lang received his colonelcy on October 2, 1862, while Hartman and Coles state, "He was promoted Colonel 4/30/63."

27. Geer, "Memories of the War," January 5 and April 6, 1905.

28. Taylor letter, February 26, 1863.

29. Edward J. Stackpole, *Chancellorsville: Lee's Greatest Battle* (Harrisburg, PA: Stackpole, 1958), 6–12; Stephen W. Sears, *Chancellorsville* (Boston: Mariner, 1996), 54–62, 505–6; Ezra J. Warner, *Generals in Blue: Lives of Union Commanders* (Baton Rouge: Louisiana State University Press, 1995), 233–35; Robert K. Krick, "Chancellorsville, 1–3 May 1863," in *The Civil War Battlefield Guide,* ed. Frances H. Kennedy (Boston: Mariner, 1990), 108–10.

30. Stackpole, *Chancellorsville,* 85–102.

31. Salmon, *Virginia Battlefield Guide,* 173–76; Stackpole, *Chancellorsville,* 87–98.

32. Sears, *Chancellorsville,* 193.

33. *OR,* 25, 1, 874–77; A. J. Peeler, letter published in unidentified Florida newspaper, Robert K. Krick Collection, Fredericksburg/Spotsylvania National Battlefield Park, Fredericksburg, VA.

34. Peeler letter; Stackpole, *Chancellorsville,* 189–92.

35. Peeler letter; Stackpole, *Chancellorsville,* 190–92.

36. Sears, *Chancellorsville,* 172–81.

37. Peeler letter; *OR,* 25, 1, 874–77.

38. Ibid.

39. Stackpole, *Chancellorsville,* 194–97; Sears, *Chancellorsville,* 230–34.

40. Lang, "Letters," May 16, 1863, letter; *OR,* 25, 1, 874–77.

41. *OR,* 25, 1, 825–26; Stackpole, *Chancellorsville,* 230–62; Krick, "Chancellorsville," 110.

42. Peeler letter; *OR,* 25, 1, 874–77.

43. J. H. B. letter, published May 21, 1863, *Savannah Daily Republican,* untitled clipping from Robert K. Krick Collection, Fredericksburg.

44. Stackpole, *Chancellorsville,* 277.

45. Peeler letter; *OR,* 25, 1, 874–77.

46. Ibid.; Auld, letter to "Dear Mother," May 8, 1863.

47. Hartman and Coles, *Biographical Roster,* 1:142, 161, 2:471. Lee lost his arm, and Moore received a wound in the throat.

48. Peeler letter; *OR,* 25, 1, 853 and 874–77.

49. Auld, letter to "Dear Mother," May 8, 1863; Stackpole, *Chancellorsville,* 301–4.

50. Sears, *Chancellorsville,* 367–400; Stackpole, *Chancellorsville,* 307–45.

51. Ibid.

52. "Floridians of Yesteryear," John H. Robarts to "Dear Brother," May 24, 1863, letter, *Florida Living Magazine,* 11 (April 1991); *OR,* 25, 1, 867, 869.

53. *OR,* 25, 1, 854; see also 806, for discrepancy; Nichols, "Florida's Fighting Rebels," 121.

54. Stackpole, *Chancellorsville,* 359–72.

55. Robertson, *A. P. Hill,* 193–94.

Chapter 5

1. Memorandum book, February 23, 1863, Jedediah Hotchkiss Papers, Library of Congress, Washington, DC; E. P. Alexander, *Military Memoirs of a Confederate Artillery Officer* (New York: Charles Scribner's Sons, 1907), 322; Mark Boatner III, *The Civil War Dictionary* (New York: David McKay, 1987), 411.

2. Edwin B. Coddington, *The Gettysburg Campaign: A Study in Command* (New York: Charles Scribner's Sons, 1964), 5–10.

3. Ibid.; A. Wilson Greene and Gary Gallagher, *The National Geographic Guide to the Civil War National Battlefield Parks* (Washington, DC: Random House, 1992), 80.

4. *OR*, 27, 2, 293; Robertson, *A. P. Hill*, 198–99.

5. *OR*, 29, 1, 30; Coddington, *The Gettysburg Campaign*, 52–53.

6. William P. Pigman diary, June 5, 1863, Savannah Historical Society, Savannah, GA; Roland E. Bowen, *From Balls Bluff to Gettysburg and Beyond: The Civil War Letters of Private Roland E. Bowen, 15th Massachusetts Infantry, 1861–1864*, ed. Gregory A. Coco (Gettysburg, PA: Thomas, 1994), 157; Terrence J. Winschel, "The Gettysburg Experience of James J. Kilpatrick," *Gettysburg* 8 (January 1993): 114; Wilbur Fisk, *Anti-Rebel: The Civil War Letters of Wilbur Fisk*, ed. Emil Rosenblatt (Croton-on-Hudson, NY: Emil Rosenblatt, 1983), 99; Wesley Brainerd, *Bridge Building in Wartime: Colonel Wesley Brainerd's Memoir of the 50th New York Engineers*, ed. Ed Malles (Knoxville: University of Tennessee Press, 1997), 152; see, generally, Noah Andre Trudeau, "False Start at Franklin's Crossing," *America's Civil War* (July 2001): 32–37, 86–88.

7. *OR*, 29, 1, 30.

8. Ibid., 27, 1, 31. For contrasting views regarding the wisdom of Hooker's proposed attack across the Rappahannock, see Coddington, *The Gettysburg Campaign*, 53; Walter H. Hebert, *Fighting Joe Hooker* (Indianapolis: Bobbs-Merrill, 1944), 233–34.

9. David Dunham diary, June 6–7, 1863, St. Augustine Historical Society, St. Augustine, FL.

10. Ibid., June 13, 1863.

11. *OR*, 27, 3, 69–73; Frank Foote, "Marching in Clover," *Philadelphia Weekly Times*, October 8, 1886.

12. Dunham diary, June 15–17, 1863; Winschel, "Kirkpatrick," 114.

13. J. B. Johnson, "A Limited Review of What One Man Saw at the Battle of Gettysburg," Gettysburg National Battlefield Park Collection, Gettysburg, PA (hereafter cited as Johnson narrative). James Barbour Johnson was born in Orange County, Virginia, and moved to Marion County, Florida, before the war to work as a cotton broker. See Robert E. L. Krick, *Staff Officers in Gray: A Biographical Register of the Staff Officers of the Army of Northern Virginia* (Chapel Hill: University of North Carolina Press, 2003), 172.

14. Winschel, "Kirkpatrick," 114; Dunham diary, June 15, 1863.

15. Winschel, "Kirkpatrick," 114; Dunham diary, June 17, 1863.

16. Winschel, "Kirkpatrick," 114; Dunham diary, June 15, 1863.

17. Ibid.; Foote, "Marching in Clover"; Pigman diary, June 16–23, 1863.

18. Francis P. Fleming, "Francis P. Fleming in the War for Southern Independence: Letters from the Front," ed. Edward C. Williamson, *FHQ* 28 (1949): 146.

19. Pigman diary, June 16–23, 1863.

20. Winschel, "Kirkpatrick," 115; Johnson narrative; Dunham diary, June 24, 1863; C. A. to "Dear Fitzgerald," *Macon Telegraph,* July 22, 1863.

21. Johnson narrative.

22. Winschel, "Kirkpatrick," 115.

23. D. to "J. M. Newby, Esq.," *Augusta Daily Chronicle and Sentinel,* July 29, 1863; Fleming, "Letters from the Front," 145–46.

24. Fleming, "Letters from the Front," 145–46.

25. Council Bryan letter, July 22, 1863, Council Bryan Papers, M87-35, Florida State Archives, Tallahassee; Winschel, "Kirkpatrick," 115; Coddington, *The Gettysburg Campaign,* 174, quoting Phillip Schaff, "The Gettysburg Week," *Scribner* 16 (July 1894): 25–26.

26. Winschel, "Kirkpatrick," 115–16; Dunham diary, June 27, 1863.

27. Bryan letter, July 22, 1863.

28. Dunham diary, June 27, 1863.

29. Fleming, "Letters from the Front," 146; Johnson narrative.

30. Pigman diary, July 1, 1863; Winschel, "Kirkpatrick, 116; Foote, "Marching in Clover."

31. *OR,* 27, 3, 369; Harry W. Pfanz, *Gettysburg: The Second Day* (Chapel Hill: University of North Carolina Press, 1987), 1–2.

32. Warner, *Generals in Blue,* 315–17; Charles A. Dana, *Recollections of the Civil War, with the Leaders in Washington and in the Field in the Sixties* (New York: D. Appleton, 1913), 190. For a more complimentary assessment of Meade's personality, see Coddington, *The Gettysburg Campaign,* 211–14.

33. Coddington, *The Gettysburg Campaign,* 196–97; see, generally, Freeman Cleaves, *Meade of Gettysburg* (Norman: University of Oklahoma Press, 1960).

34. Mary G. Whitehead, *From Grandmother's Trunk: A Family Portrayal* (Spartanburg, SC: Reprint Co., 1989), 110.

Chapter 6

1. Pfanz, *Second Day,* 21; Pigman diary, July 1, 1863.

2. Page, "A Letter from Antietam."

3. *OR,* 27, 2, 613; Pfanz, *Second Day,* 21.

4. Page, "A Letter from Antietam"; Johnson narrative.

5. Johnson narrative.

6. "The Battle of Gettysburg—Lee's Echelon Attack—The Battle of Gettysburg: Day 2," *http://library.thinkquest.org/17525/day2.htm.*

7. Harry W. Pfanz, "Gettysburg," in *The Civil War Battlefield Guide,* ed. Frances H. Kennedy (Boston: Mariner, 1990), 118; Pfanz, *Second Day,* 102–3.

8. Pfanz, "Gettysburg," 118; Pfanz, *Second Day,* 113–14; *OR,* 27, 2, 613–14.

9. David Lang to John B. Bachelder, October 16, 1893, M84-028, David Lang Letterbooks, vol. 2 (1893–1909), Florida State Archives, Tallahassee.

10. *OR,* 27, 2, 631.

11. Ibid.; Pfanz, *Second Day,* 384.

12. *OR,* 27, 2, 631; Johnson narrative.

13. Pfanz, *Second Day,* 368–74; Thomas L. Elmore, "The Florida Brigade at Gettysburg," *Gettysburg,* no. 15 (1996): 49–50.

14. "Where Honor Is Due," *Boston Sunday Herald,* July 23, 1899, 36; Maj. Robert L. Bodine, "From the 26th Regiment, PV," *Doylestown (PA) Democrat,* July 12, 1863; Henry N. Blake, *Three Years in the Army of the Potomac* (Boston: Lee & Shepard, 1865), 209–10.

15. Pfanz, *Second Day,* 372; Pigman diary, July 2, 1863; *OR,* 27, 2, 631.

16. *OR,* 27, 2, 631.

17. Regis de Trobriand, "Four Years in the Army of the Potomac," in *The Battle of Gettysburg,* by W. C. Storrick (Harrisburg, PA: McFarland, 1969), 55; Elmore, "Florida Brigade," 49–50; Sallie M. Smith, *My Marriage and Its Consequences* (Macon: Burke, Boykin, 1864), 74. Smith was the sister of A. J. Peeler. Only two copies of her book are known to exist.

18. Pfanz, *Second Day,* 386–87.

19. Ibid.; *OR,* 27, 2, 631; Coddington, *The Gettysburg Campaign,* 422–23.

20. *OR,* 27, 2, 632; Pfanz, *Second Day,* 377–80.

21. *OR,* 27, 2, 632.

22. Ibid.; "The Wentworth Diary," *United Daughters of the Confederacy* 53 (March 1990): 53.

23. *OR,* 27, 2, 632.

24. Hartman and Coles, *Biographical Roster,* 1:142, 151, 161, 208.

25. Ibid., 2:484, 496, 522, 534, 567.

26. Ibid., 1:51, 175; Anthony Staunton, comp., "Medal of Honor—Gettysburg," *http://www.gdg.org/Research/Authored%20items/medal.html.*

27. Fleming, "Letters from the Front," 147.

28. Robertson, *A. P. Hill,* 218–19; H. A. Herbert to E. P. Alexander letter, August 18, 1903, Gettysburg National Battlefield Park Collection, Gettysburg, PA; Pfanz, *Second Day,* 386–89.

29. Bodine, "From the 26th Regiment, PV"; Blake, *Three Years,* 211.

30. Glatthaar, *Lee's Army,* 279; Coddington, *The Gettysburg Campaign,* 454–64, 520; George R. Stewart, *Pickett's Charge: A Microhistory of the Final Attack at Gettysburg, July 3, 1863* (Boston: Houghton Mifflin, 1987), 1–4.

31. *OR,* 27, 2, 632.

32. Raymond J. Reid to Hal, September 4, 1863, Reid Family Papers, St. Augustine Historical Society, St. Augustine, FL; Lang, "Letters," 355; Elmore, "Florida Brigade," 52; Jim Studnicki, "Perry's Brigade: The Forgotten Floridians at Gettysburg," *www.nps.gov/archive/gett/gettour/sidebar/perry.htm.*

33. Lang to Bachelder letter.

34. Reid to Hal letter; Elmore, "Florida Brigade," 54; Johnson narrative.

35. Lang to E. A. Perry letter; see also Lang, "Letters," 354; *OR,* 27, 2, 613 and 632. For an interesting discussion of when Wilcox and Lang attacked, see Tony Trimble, "Paper Collars: Stannard's Brigade at Gettysburg, *Gettysburg* 2 (1990): 78–79.

36. *OR,* 27, 2, 632.

37. Pigman diary, July 3, 1863; "Wentworth Diary."

38. Elmore, "Florida Brigade," 54; Jeffry Wert, *Gettysburg, Day Three* (New York: Simon & Schuster, 2001), 240; "Wentworth Diary"; Reid to Hal letter.

39. Stewart, *Pickett's Charge*, 233; Trimble, "Paper Collars," 77.

40. Johnson narrative; Lang to Bachelder letter; David J. Coles and Zack C. Waters, "Forgotten Sacrifice: The Florida Brigade at the Battle of Gettysburg," *Apalachee* 11 (1996): 45; Wert, *Day Three*, 240–41; Earl J. Hess, *Pickett's Charge—The Last Attack at Gettysburg* (Chapel Hill: University of North Carolina Press, 2000), 299–301. Wilcox consistently claimed that Gen. Longstreet ordered the July 3 attack.

41. Lang to Bachelder letter; N. W. Eppes, Roll of Honor, vol. 340, 71, Eleanor Brockenbrough Library, Museum of the Confederacy, Richmond, VA; *OR*, 27, 2, 632.

42. *OR*, 27, 2, 632.

43. Ibid.

44. Don Hillhouse, "Three Flags," unpublished MS, Zack C. Waters Collection, Rome, GA; D. M. Pogue to Gov. Francis Fleming, April 9, 1906, Florida State Archives, Tallahassee.

45. Hillhouse, "Three Flags"; Fleming, *C. Seton Fleming*, 82; "Wentworth Diary"; Coles and Waters, "Forgotten Sacrifice," 44.

46. *OR*, 27, 2, 633.

47. Ibid.

48. Fleming, *C. Seton Fleming*, 79–80.

49. Pigman diary, July 3, 1863; Hartman and Coles, *Biographical Roster*, 1:51–52, 2:833–34; J. R. Hodges to Mrs. Z. T. Hodges, July 16, 1863, Joe A. Akerman Collection, Madison, FL. Part of the Hodges letter was published in Joe A. Akerman, *Florida Cowman: A History of Florida Cattle Ranching* (Kissimmee: Florida Cattleman's Association, 1976), 57.

50. Wert, *Day Three*, 242; Clifford Dowdey, *The Death of a Nation: The Story of Lee and His Men at Gettysburg* (New York: Knopf, 1958), 327.

51. "Florida's Roll of Honor," *Savannah Daily Morning News*, July 23, 1863; casualties are based upon manuscript research by the authors.

Chapter 7

1. *OR*, 27, 2, 633.

2. Coddington, *The Gettysburg Campaign*, 523–25; Hillary A. Herbert, "History of the Eighth Alabama Volunteer Regiment, CSA," *Alabama Historical Quarterly* 39 (1977): 128; Harry W. Pfanz, "The Gettysburg Campaign: After Pickett's Charge," *Gettysburg*, no. 1 (July 1989): 118. Also see, generally, Kent Masterson Brown, *Retreat from Gettysburg: Lee, Logistics, and the Pennsylvania Campaign* (Chapel Hill: University of North Carolina Press, 2005).

3. Herbert, "Eighth Alabama," 128; Coddington, *The Gettysburg Campaign*, 807–8n7 lists numerous sources detailing Confederate morale postbattle; Champ Clark, *Gettysburg: The Confederate High Tide* (Alexandria, VA: Time-Life, 1985), 147–50. For Confederate army and Southern civilian response to the defeat at Gettysburg, see Gary Gallagher, "Lee's

Army has Not Lost Any of Its Prestige," in *The Third Day at Gettysburg and Beyond* (Chapel Hill: University of North Carolina Press, 1998), 1–30.

4. Coddington, *The Gettysburg Campaign*, 537.

5. Pfanz, "After Pickett's Charge," 119.

6. Johnson narrative.

7. Robert Stiles, *Four Years under Marse Robert* (Dayton, OH: Morningside, 1977), 219; Gregory A. Coco, "A Wasted Valor: The Confederate Dead at Gettysburg," *Gettysburg*, no. 3 (July 1990): 93–108.

8. Augustus B. Dickert, *History of Kershaw's Brigade* (Dayton, OH: Morningside, 1976), 248–49; L. L. H., (Philadelphia) *Lutheran and Missionary*, July 16, 1863, quoted in Coco, "Wasted Valor," 95.

9. *OR*, 27, 2, 632; Winschel, "Kirkpatrick," 118; Johnson narrative.

10. Dickert, *Kershaw's Brigade*, 249; *OR*, 27, 1, 943–48.

11. Ballantine, "Floridians in the Fight"; "The Banishment of Miss Euphemia Goldsborough," unpublished MS, Gettysburg National Battlefield Collection Gettysburg, PA, which contains several letters of appreciation from Florida officers; Coddington, *The Gettysburg Campaign*, 809n18. For treatment of Southern surgeons left to care for the wounded, see Dickert, *Kershaw's Brigade*, 249.

12. Hartman and Coles, *Biographical Roster*, 1:227; Leon O. Prior, "Lewis Payne: Pawn of John Wilkes Booth," *FHQ* 43 (1964): 1–20.

13. Pfanz, "After Pickett's Charge," 121; Johnson narrative.

14. Johnson narrative.

15. Winschel, "Kirkpatrick," 118.

16. Johnson narrative.

17. Coddington, *The Gettysburg Campaign*, 542.

18. Ibid.; Alexander, *Military Memoirs of a Confederate*, 439.

19. *OR*, Atlas, plate XLII-5; Coddington, *The Gettysburg Campaign*, 565–66; Fleming, *C. Seton Fleming*, 83.

20. Johnson narrative; Winschel, "Kirkpatrick," 119.

21. Pfanz, "After Pickett's Charge," 123–24; *OR*, 27, 1, 91.

22. Alexander, *Fighting for the Confederacy*, 272; *OR*, 27, 2, 558–59.

23. Coddington, *The Gettysburg Campaign*, 571; Pfanz, "After Pickett's Charge," 124; Johnson narrative.

24. E. B. Long, "The Battle That Almost Was—Manassas Gap," *Civil War Times Illustrated* 11 (December 1972): 20–28.

25. Bryan letter, July 22, 1863; Alexander, *Fighting for the Confederacy*, 272; Fleming, *C. Seton Fleming*, 83.

26. Ibid.

27. Long, "The Battle That Almost Was," 20–28. The Georgia State Archives in Atlanta has a microfilm account of this action and a hand-drawn map of the battlefield by Capt. C. H. Andrews of the Third Georgia Infantry.

28. Bryan letter, July 22, 1863.

29. J. B. Johnson, "Perry's Brigade," *Savannah Republican*, August 14, 1863; William D. Henderson, *The Road to Bristoe Station: Campaigning with Lee and Meade, August 1–October*

20, 1863 (Lynchburg, VA: H. E. Howard, 1982), 18–23; Charles E. DeNoon, *Charlie's Letters: The Correspondence of Charles E. DeNoon,* ed. Richard T. Couture (n.p., 1982), 181–82. DeNoon's letter disputes Johnson's assertion that the Floridians did the only fighting at Culpepper Courthouse.

30. Johnson, "Perry's Brigade"; Henderson, *Road to Bristoe Station,* 22–23.

31. Bryan letter, July 22, 1863.

Chapter 8

1. Johnson narrative.

2. Ibid. For a scathing attack on Lee, see the *Charleston Mercury,* July 30, 1863, quoted in Freeman, *Lee's Lieutenants,* 3:168.

3. Johnson narrative.

4. Reprinted in *Richmond Enquirer,* July 25, 1863.

5. *Mobile Advertiser and Register,* July 23, 1863, reprinted in *Richmond Enquirer,* July 25, 1863.

6. Quoted in Fleming, *C. Seton Fleming,* 85–86.

7. Ibid., 83–85.

8. Keith S. Bohannon, "Ambrose Ransom Wright," in *The Confederate General,* ed. William C. Davis (Washington, DC: National Historical Society, 1991), 6:160–63; Joseph T. Derry, "Georgia," in *Confederate Military History* (New York: Blue & Gray, 1962), 6:456–58; *Tributes to the Memory of Gen'l A. R. Wright* (n.p., 1873), 3–33.

9. "Army Correspondence of the Augusta *Constitutionalist:* From Wright's Brigade," *Augusta Daily Constitutionalist,* July 23, 1863. Coddington classes Wright's letter "among the better Civil War romances [i.e., fiction]," and, in a masterpiece of understatement, notes "wide discrepancies between his account and those of other participants." Coddington, *The Gettysburg Campaign,* 422.

10. *Constitutionalist* letter. Wright makes no mention of fighting until his command reaches "the base of the range [Cemetery Ridge]." Pfanz, *Second Day,* 384–89. Regarding Wright's location on July 2, see Johnson narrative; Pvt. William B. Judkins, "Memoirs of a Soldier of the 22nd Georgia," Special Collections, Rome/Floyd County Library, Rome, GA; for a contemporary account stating Wright led his brigade, see C. A. to "Dear Fitzgerald," *Macon Telegraph,* July 22, 1863, which seemingly contradicts Johnson's and Judkins's assertions.

11. Johnson narrative; W. D. Burtchaell, "Veteran Defends Perry's Brigade," *Atlanta Journal,* March 30, 1901, 6, also mentions the "indignation committee."

12. Johnson narrative.

13. "Letter to the Editor of Georgia *Constitutionalist,* Hdqrs.," Wright's brigade, August 5, 1863, quoted in Frank Moore, ed., *Rebellion Record, Rumors, and Incidents* (New York: G. P. Putnam, 1861–68), 7:45.

14. C. H. Andrews, "Condensed History of the Campaigns of the Third Regiment of Georgia Volunteer Infantry in the Confederate States Army, 1861–1865," unpublished MS, Georgia Department of Archives and History, Atlanta (Andrews commanded Wright's brigade at Manassas Gap).

15. "Court Martial of Gen. A. R. Wright," *Augusta Daily Constitutionalist,* August 23, 1863.

16. Johnson narrative.

17. *OR,* 27, 2, 623.

18. "A Compliment," *Tallahassee Floridian,* November 3, 1863; Lang to Bachelder, October 16, 1893; Burtchaell, "Veteran Defends Perry's Brigade."

19. *Savannah Republican,* April 16, 1870; Douglas S. Freeman, *R. E. Lee: A Biography* (New York: Charles Scribner's Sons, 1949), 4:452, reports the incident at Jacksonville, but the author misinterprets the tribute as awe.

20. *OR,* 4, 2, 808–9 and 838–39; Boyd R. Murphree, "Rebel Sovereigns: The Civil War Leadership of Governors John Milton of Florida and Joseph E. Brown of Georgia, 1861–1865" (PhD diss., Florida State University, 2007), 30, 154.

21. *OR,* 4, 2, 839.

22. Ibid., 885–86; Fleming, *C. Seton Fleming,* 89–93.

23. Fleming, *C. Seton Fleming,* 89–93.

24. Salmon, *Virginia Battlefield Guide,* 218. For general accounts of the fight at Bristoe Station, see Robertson, *A. P. Hill,* 234–39; Freeman, *Lee's Lieutenants,* 3:239–47.

25. J. F. J. Caldwell, *The History of a Brigade of South Carolinians . . .* (Philadelphia: King & Baird, 1866), 115; Salmon, *Virginia Battlefield Guide,* 233–36.

26. "The Florida Brigade at Bristow Station," photocopy of unattributed news article, Zack C. Waters Collection, Rome, GA; J. B. Johnson, "From Lee's Army" (Florida brigade casualties at Bristoe Station), photocopy of unattributed news article, Zack C. Waters Collection, Rome, GA.

27. Johnson, "From Lee's Army."

28. Fleming, *C. Seton Fleming,* 93.

Chapter 9

1. Gordon Rhea, *The Battle of the Wilderness, May 5–6, 1864* (Baton Rouge: Louisiana State University Press, 1994), 8–10; John Cannan, *The Wilderness Campaign, May 1864* (Conshohocken, PA: Combined Books, 1993) 15; *OR,* 33, 1114.

2. James I. Robertson Jr., *Soldiers Blue and Gray* (Columbia: University of South Carolina Press, 1988), 187; Bennett, *A Narrative of the Great Revival,* 322–33; Lang, "Letters," 359; see, generally, John Shepard Jr., "Religion in the Army of Northern Virginia," *North Carolina Historical Review* 25 (1948): 341–76.

3. John F. Sale to aunt, April 22, 1864, John F. Sale Papers, Virginia State Library and Archives, Richmond (hereafter VSLA); letter from "A Fireside Defender," March 3, 1864, *Rome (GA) Tri-Weekly Courier.* "Fireside Defenders" was the nickname of Co. G, Twenty-second Georgia Infantry. See, generally, Gary W. Gallagher, "Our Hearts Are Full of Hope: The Army of Northern Virginia in the Spring of 1864," in *The Wilderness Campaign* (Chapel Hill: University of North Carolina Press, 1997), 36–65.

4. Fleming, *C. Seton Fleming,* 90–92.

5. "Casualties of Perry's Brigade, Fla, Vols. at the Battle of Wilderness, VA. May 5th, 6th, and 7th 1864," Council Bryan Papers, Florida State Archives, Tallahassee.

6. Salmon, *Virginia Battlefield Guide*, 267–68.

7. R. H. Anderson to Capt. Edward B. Robbins, May 14, 1879, Edward B. Robbins Papers, MsBB: 34, Massachusetts Military History Society, Boston University, Boston (hereafter R. H. Anderson letter).

8. Ibid.

9. For several years Mr. Alfred Young of Burtonville, Maryland, has been gathering data on ANV troop strengths and casualties. His information is based upon contemporary sources. Brigade strengths given above are based largely on his research. Alfred Young, letter to Zack Waters, November 4, 1995; all times in Civil War writings are approximations. See Arthur Candequist, "Did Anybody Really Know What Time It Was?" *Blue and Gray* 8 (August 1991): 32–34.

10. Dickert, *Kershaw's Brigade*, 344–45.

11. James E. Phillips memoir, VSLA.

12. E. A. Shiver, "Wright's Brigade in the Wilderness," *Atlanta Journal,* October 12, 1901.

13. C. H. Andrews, "History of the Third Georgia Regiment," chap. 42, 5, unpublished MS, C. H. Andrews Papers, Southern Historical Collection, Manuscripts Department, University of North Carolina, Chapel Hill.

14. Robert Garth Scott, *Into the Wilderness with the Army of the Potomac* (Bloomington: Indiana University Press, 1985), 184–85; Rhea, *Battle of the Wilderness,* 27–29.

15. Scott, *Into the Wilderness,* 7–9.

16. Robertson, *A. P. Hill,* 256–63; Henry Heth, *The Memoirs of Henry Heth,* ed. James L. Morrison (Westport, CT: Greenwood, 1974), 184.

17. Phillips memoir; E. A. Shiver, "A Rebel Yell for Gen. A. R. Wright," *Atlanta Journal,* September 7, 1901.

18. Shiver, "Wright's Brigade in the Wilderness."

19. Rhea, *Battle of the Wilderness,* 283–95.

20. Ibid., 295–308; Charles W. Field, "Campaign of 1864–65," *Southern Historical Society Papers* (hereafter *SHSP*), 14:546–47.

21. Ibid.

22. R. H. Anderson letter.

23. Scott, *Into the Wilderness,* 115; William F. Perry, "Reminiscences of the Campaign of 1864," *SHSP,* 7:49–63.

24. Rhea, *Battle of the Wilderness,* 336–39.

25. Perry, "Campaign of 1864," 57–58; Herbert, "Eighth Alabama," 138–39.

26. Ibid.

27. Perry, "Campaign of 1864," 57–58; Herbert, "Eighth Alabama," 138–39.

28. Frank Wilkeson, *Recollections of a Private Soldier in the Army of the Potomac* (New York: G. P. Putnam's Sons, 1887), 71–72.

29. Warren Wilkinson, *Mother, May You Never See the Sights I Have Seen: The Fifty-seventh Massachusetts Veteran Volunteers in the Last Year of the Civil War* (New York: Harper & Row, 1990), 73.

30. Alfred L. Scott, "Memoirs of Service in the Confederate Army," Virginia Historical

Society, Richmond (hereafter VHS); James Edmonds Saunders, *Early Settlers of Alabama—Part I* (New Orleans: L. Graham & Sons, 1899), 157.

31. S. W. Vance, "Heroes of the 8th Alabama," *CV* 7 (1879): 493; Herbert, "Eighth Alabama," 139.

32. Rhea, *Battle of the Wilderness,* 351–79.

33. Ibid.; Robert E. L. Krick, "Like a Duck on a June Bug: James Longstreet's Flank Attack, May 6, 1864," in *The Wilderness Campaign,* ed. Gary W. Gallagher (Chapel Hill: University of North Carolina Press, 1997), 236–67.

34. Scott, *Into the Wilderness,* 160.

35. George Skoch, "Burnside's Geography Class," *Civil War Times Illustrated* 33 (January/February 1995): 38–39; A. Wilson Greene, "The Bridge and Beyond," *Civil War Quarterly* 9 (June 1987): 65; Rhea, *Battle of the Wilderness,* 265–66; *OR,* 36, 1, 905; Morris Schaff, *The Battle of the Wilderness* (Boston: Houghton Mifflin, 1910), 225–27. Skoch reveals that a large percentage of IX Corps soldiers were completely untried in battle.

36. Perry, "Campaign of 1864," 61; William C. Oates, *The War between the Union and the Confederacy and Its Lost Opportunities* (New York: Neale, 1905), 350–51. The alignment does not conform to traditional accounts of the battle, but it seems the most likely scenario according to reliable accounts and sources. The authors thank Gordon Rhea for helping to make some sense of this confusing, little-documented engagement. A map in Rhea, *Battle of the Wilderness,* 381, shows Perrin attached to W. F. Perry's right, but on p. 400 Rhea suggests he joined Harris in the counterattack on Burnside.

37. Perry, "The Campaign of 1864," 61.

38. Ibid.

39. Ibid. Oates, *War between the Union and the Confederacy,* 350.

40. P. D. Bowles, "The Fourth Alabama Regiment in the Slaughter Pen on May 6, 1864," *Philadelphia Weekly Times,* October 4, 1884.

41. Ibid.

42. Geer, "Memories of the War," January 26, 1906.

43. "From Virginia," *Gainesville Cotton States,* June 4, 1864 (excerpt from a letter dated May 9, 1864, and signed "8th Fla Reg't").

44. Bowles, "Slaughter Pen."

45. Fleming, *C. Seton Fleming,* 94–95; Proctor, *Florida One Hundred Years Ago,* September 1962; "Casualties of Perry's Brigade," Council Bryan Papers, Florida State Archives, Tallahassee; Wilbur W. Gramling diary, 1864–65, Special Collections, Strozier Library, Florida State University, Tallahassee.

46. Fleming, *C. Seton Fleming,* 94–95; Proctor, *Florida One Hundred Years Ago,* September 1962.

47. Perry, "Campaign of 1864," 61–62.

48. Ibid.; Cannan, *The Wilderness Campaign, May 1864,* 183.

49. Perry, "Campaign of 1864," 61–62; Oates, *War between the Union and Confederacy,* 350.

50. Ibid.

51. Eugene Ott Jr., "The Civil War Diary of James J. Kirkpatrick, 16th Mississippi,

CSA" (master's thesis, Texas A&M University, 1984), diary, May 6, 1864; Nat Harris to William Mahone, August 2, 1866, William Mahone Papers, VSLA.

52. Ibid.; Perry, "Campaign of 1864," 61–64.

53. Rhea, *Battle of the Wilderness,* 390–403.

54. Shiver, "Wright's Brigade in the Wilderness."

55. George T. Stevens, *Three Years in the 6th Corps* (Albany: S. R. Gray, 1866), 319; Horace Porter, *Campaigning with Grant* (Bloomington, IN: Bonanza, 1961), 72–73.

56. Rhea, *Battle of the Wilderness,* 436, 440. Rhea concluded that both armies underestimated their losses, for obvious reasons.

57. Fleming, *C. Seton Fleming,* diary entry, May 6, 1864; newspaper clipping, Zack C. Waters Collection, Rome, GA; "Casualties of Perry's Brigade," Council Bryan Papers. The Fifth Florida suffered the heaviest losses of the brigade by far, with 11 killed, 61 wounded, and 74 missing, for a total of 146 casualties. The Second Florida lost 13 killed, 28 wounded, and 16 missing, or 57 casualties. Lang's Eighth Florida suffered 31 casualties, the fewest losses of the brigade, with 3 killed, 23 wounded, and 5 missing. Total losses for the Florida brigade at the Wilderness amounted to 27 killed, 112 wounded, and 95 missing, for a brigade total of 236.

Chapter 10

1. G. Moxley Sorrell, *Recollections of a Confederate Staff Officer* (New York: Domain, 1992), 210; John F. Sale diary, VSLA.

2. John O. Cassler, *Four Years in the Stonewall Brigade* (Dayton, OH: Morningside, 1971) 208; Bowles, "Slaughter Pen."

3. Shiver, "Wright's Brigade in the Wilderness"; Stevens, *Three Years in the 6th Corps,* 319.

4. Scott, *Into the Wilderness,* 178–82.

5. Phillips memoir, VSLA.

6. William D. Matter, *If It Takes All Summer: The Battle of Spotsylvania* (Chapel Hill: University of North Carolina Press, 1988), 4–5; Ulysses S. Grant, *The Personal Memoirs of Ulysses S. Grant* (New York: Charles L. Webster, 1885), 2:211.

7. Jacob Heater, "The Battle of the Wilderness," *CV* 14 (1906): 264; Matter, *If It Takes All Summer,* 14–15.

8. Freeman, *Lee's Lieutenants,* 3:374–75.

9. *OR,* 36, 2, 380–81 and 967; Robert E. Lee, *The Wartime Papers of Robert E. Lee,* ed. Clifford Dowdey and Louis H. Manarin (New York: Little, Brown, 1961), 725.

10. R. H. Anderson letter.

11. Ibid.; Freeman, *Lee's Lieutenants,* 3:373–87. A good account of the race to Spotsylvania can be found in Freeman and in Matter, *If It Takes All Summer,* 52–57.

12. Alexander, *Fighting for the Confederacy,* 372; Freeman, *Lee's Lieutenants,* 3:445–46, asserts Ewell laid out the salient section of the line after dark, and it was inspected the next morning by Martin L. Smith and approved.

13. Ott, "Diary of Kirkpatrick," May 8, 1864.

14. George Clark, *A Glance Backward; or, Some Events in the Past History of My Life* (Houston: Rein & Sons, 1914), 49; Fleming, *C. Seton Fleming*, May 8, 1864, diary entry.

15. Jubal Early, *A Memoir of the Last Year of the War for the Independence of the Confederate States of America* (News Orleans: Lovell & Gibson, 1867), 18–19.

16. Ibid.; John Horn, "A History of the 12th Virginia Regiment," unpublished MS, Zack C. Waters Collection, Rome, GA; Phillips memoir, VSLA.

17. Early, *Last Year of the War*, 20–21; Matter, *If It Takes All Summer*, 109.

18. Gordon Rhea, *The Battles for Spotsylvania Court House and the Road to Yellow Tavern, May 7–12, 1864* (Baton Rouge: Louisiana State University Press, 1997), 112–14.

19. Ibid., 122.

20. Ibid., 114, 123–30.

21. Ibid.; Ott, "Diary of Kirkpatrick," May 10, 1864; Fleming, *C. Seton Fleming*, May 10, 1864, diary entry.

22. E. A. Shiver, "Wright's Brigade at Spotsylvania Court House," *Atlanta Journal*, October 16, 1901; JDH, "Death Angle," undated newspaper clipping, Mississippi Department of Archives and History, Jackson; David Holt, *A Mississippi Rebel in the Army of Northern Virginia: The Civil War Memoirs of Private David Holt*, ed. Michael B. Ballard and Thomas D. Cockrell (Baton Rouge: Louisiana State University Press, 1995), 252–53.

23. Several excellent accounts are available, including Matter, *If It Takes All Summer*, and Rhea, *Spotsylvania Court House*. For a short, well-written account, we suggest Robert K. Krick, "An Insurmountable Barrier between the Army and Ruin; The Confederate Experience at Spotsylvania's Bloody Angle," in *The Spotsylvania Campaign*, ed. Gary W. Gallagher (Chapel Hill: University of North Carolina Press, 1998), 80–126.

24. Ibid.

25. Fleming, *C. Seton Fleming*, May 12, 1864, diary entry.

26. Rhea, *Spotsylvania Court House*, 294–302.

27. Fleming, *C. Seton Fleming*, May 12, 1864, diary entry.

28. Ibid.; Rhea, *Spotsylvania Court House*, 306–7.

29. Robertson, *A. P. Hill*, 273–77.

30. Salmon, *Virginia Battlefield Guide*, 284–85. For a general account, see J. Michael Miller, "Along the North Anna," *Civil War Time Illustrated* (November 1987): 27–31, 45–49.

31. Ibid.

32. Ibid.; Geer, "Memories of the War," February 2, 1906; Council Bryan, letter to wife, May 25, 1864; Stephen Weld, *War Diary and Letters of Stephen Minot Weld, 1861–1865* (Boston: Massachusetts Historical Society, 1979), 297.

33. Council Bryan, letter to wife, May 25, 1864.

34. Robertson, *A. P. Hill*, 277.

35. Freeman, *Lee's Lieutenants*, 3:497–504, describes the reinforcements to Lee's army in May 1864. The new Florida troops receive only the slightest mention.

36. Fleming, *C. Seton Fleming*, May 28, 1864, diary entry; Hillhouse, *Light Infantry*, 138 (appendix contains entire text of Dorman's *Fifty Years Ago; Reminiscences of 61–65*, 133–50).

37. *OR*, 36, 2, 1013; H. M. Hamil, "A Boy's First Fight," *CV* 12 (1904): 540.

38. Dickison, "Florida," 157; Hartman and Coles, *Biographical Roster*, 3:876–985; Robertson, *SOF*, 206–19.

39. J. M. Martin file, Zack C. Waters Collection, Rome, GA; Zack C. Waters, "Florida's Confederate Guerillas: John W. Pearson and the Oklawaha Rangers," *FHQ* 70 (1991): 133–49.

40. Bittle, "In Defense of Florida," 308; Zack C. Waters, "All That Brave Men Could Do: Joseph Finegan's Florida Brigade at Cold Harbor," *Civil War Regiments* 3, no. 4 (1994): 3–5.

41. Figures regarding the Ninth Florida Regiment were taken from Hartman and Coles, *Biographical Roster*, 3:875–985, and the authors' files.

42. Hartman and Coles, *Biographical Roster*, 3:986–1083; Waters, "All That Brave Men Could Do," 3–5; Don Hillhouse, "From Olustee to Appomattox: The First Florida Special Battalion," *Civil War Regiments* 3, no. 1 (1993): 64–77.

43. Hillhouse, *Light Infantry*, 127–29; Hartman and Coles, *Biographical Roster*, 3:1053.

44. Hartman and Coles, *Biographical Roster*, 3:986–1066; Robertson, *SOF*; and authors' files. Hillhouse's *Light Infantry*, a rare volume, contains the best information on this unit.

45. Hillhouse, *Light Infantry*, 94–97.

46. Hartman and Coles, *Biographical Roster*, 3:1163–1233.

47. Ibid., 1:169; Richard J. Sommers, "Theodore Washington Brevard," in *The Confederate General*, ed. William C. Davis (Washington, DC: National Historical Society, 1991), 1:128–29.

48. Hartman and Coles, *Biographical Roster*, 3:1084–1162; Robertson, *SOF*; and authors' files. The records of the Fourth Battalion are included in the Eleventh Florida Regiment section.

49. Hartman and Coles, *Biographical Roster*, 1:189; J. F. McClellan file, Zack C. Waters Collection, Rome, GA; Hillhouse, *Light Infantry*, 94–97.

50. Glatthaar, *Lee's Army*, 200–207. Information regarding the Second Florida Battalion and Fourth Florida Battalion is derived from Hartman and Coles, *Biographical Roster*; Robertson, *SOF*; and authors' files.

51. Waters, "All That Brave Men Could Do," 5–7; William C. Davis, "Joseph Finegan," in Davis, *The Confederate General*, 2:126; Ed Gleeson, *Erin Go Gray! An Irish Trilogy* (Carmel, IN: Guild, 1998) provides an excellent overview of Finegan's military career.

52. Geer, "Memories of the War," February 2, 1906; Hamil, "A Boy's First Fight," 540.

Chapter 11

1. Ernest B. Furgurson, *Not War but Murder: Cold Harbor, 1864* (New York: Knopf, 2000), 60.

2. Ibid., 58–64 for a general account of Totopotomoy Creek; A. F. G. to "Dear Friend Rogero," June 7, 1864, MS box 79, P. K. Yonge Library of Florida History, University of Florida, Gainesville.

3. Waters, "Florida's Confederate Guerillas," 133–49.

4. Furgurson, *Not War but Murder*, 77–78.

5. Ibid., 75–77.

6. Hillhouse, *Light Infantry*, 138.

7. Andrew A. Humphreys, *The Virginia Campaign, 1864 and 1865: The Army of the Potomac and the Army of the James* (New York: Da Capo, 1995), 171; Furgurson, *Not War but Murder*, 78–84.

8. Furgurson, *Not War but Murder*, 82–84.

9. Jeffry Wert, "One Great Regret: Cold Harbor," *Civil War Times Illustrated* 17 (February 1979): 28; Freeman, *Lee*, 3:375.

10. Stiles, *Four Years under Marse Robert*, 274; Dickert, *Kershaw's Brigade*, 369–70; *OR*, 36, 3, 858, and 36, 1, 1049; Wert, "Cold Harbor," 28–29; Gordon C. Rhea, *Cold Harbor: Grant and Lee, May 26–June 3, 1864* (Baton Rouge: Louisiana State University Press, 2002), 202.

11. Freeman, *Lee*, 3:379; Furgurson, *Not War but Murder*, 101–9; Rhea, *Cold Harbor*, 243.

12. Furgurson, *Not War but Murder*, 121–23; *OR* 36, 3, 469, 482; Joseph P. Cullen, "Cold Harbor," *Civil War Times Illustrated* (November 1963): 13.

13. Cullen, "Cold Harbor," 13; Stiles, *Four Years under Marse Robert*, 289.

14. Clifford Dowdey, *Lee's Last Campaign: The Story of Lee and His Men against Grant—1864* (Wilmington, NC: Broadfoot, 1988), 284.

15. Salmon, *Virginia Battlefield Guide*, 295.

16. Furgurson, *Not War but Murder*, 137–38.

17. Hillhouse, *Light Infantry*, 138.

18. Rhea, *Cold Harbor*, 318–95; Noah Andre Trudeau, *Bloody Roads South: The Wilderness to Cold Harbor, May–June 1864* (Boston: Little, Brown, 1989), 281–99.

19. Rhea, *Cold Harbor*, 312.

20. Lang, "Letters," June 7, 1864, 364; Lt. Henry R. Swan to "Dear Abbie," June 4, 1864, in "And Some Letters from the Second Runner-Up," *Civil War Times Illustrated* 11, no. 4 (1972): 45; Furgurson, *Not War but Murder*, 177–78, discusses reports of Union drunkenness.

21. Salmon, *Virginia Battlefield Guide*, 296.

22. A. L. Long, *Memoirs of Robert E. Lee: His Military and Personal History* (New York: J. M. Stoddart, 1887), 347–48; Krick, *Lee's Colonels*, 299–300. Echols relinquished command due to "neuralgia of the heart." Jeffery Wert, "John Echols," in *The Confederate General*, ed. William C. Davis (Washington, DC: National Historical Society, 1991), 2:93; *OR*, 36, 1, 345.

23. T. C. Morton, "Gave His Life for His Flag," *CV* 12 (1904): 71; Breckinridge to J. Thomas Scharf, January 6, 1874, quoted in William C. Davis, *Breckinridge: Statesman, Soldier, Symbol* (Baton Rouge: Louisiana State University, 1974), 437.

24. Bryan to "My Dear Wife," June 3, 1864, Council Bryan Papers; Charles G. Elliott, "Martin's Brigade of Hoke's Division," *SHSP* 23 (1895): 193; Geer, "Memories of the War," February 2, 1906; Val Husley, "'Men of Virginia—Men of Kanawha—to Arms!' A History of the Twenty-second Virginia Volunteer Infantry Regiment, CSA," *West Virginia History* 35 (April 1974): 233.

25. Hamil, "A Boy's First Fight," 540; Hillhouse, *Light Infantry*, 139–40.

26. Bryan to "My Dear Wife," June 3, 1864. In the past, author Waters has downplayed

the significance of the Second Maryland in retaking the works at Cold Harbor. Further research and discussions with Gordon Rhea reveal that the Marylanders provided equally distinguished service as the Floridians.

27. *OR,* 36, 1, 345; A. F. G. to "Dear Friend Rogero."

28. J.F.T., "Some Florida Heroes," *CV* 11 (1903): 363. The author of this valuable account was almost certainly Capt. James F. Tucker, Co. D, Ninth Florida Infantry.

29. Ibid.

30. Ibid.

31. Ibid.

32. H. W. Long, "Reminiscence of the Battle of Cold Harbor," unpublished MS, United Daughters of the Confederacy Scrapbooks, vol. 1, Florida State Library, Tallahassee. Harrison was the son-in-law of Lt. Col. Pearson.

33. J.F.T., "Some Florida Heroes," 364.

34. "A War Incident," unidentified newspaper clipping, Dunham Family Papers, St. Augustine Historical Society, St. Augustine, FL.

35. J.F.T., "Some Florida Heroes," 364; Waters, "All That Brave Men Could Do," 21–22.

36. J.F.T., "Some Florida Heroes," 364.

37. Ibid.; Fleming, *C. Seton Fleming,* 100–101.

38. J.F.T., "Some Florida Heroes," 364; Long, "Reminiscence of Cold Harbor."

39. Long, "Reminiscence of Cold Harbor."

40. Geer, "Memories of the War," February 2, 1906.

41. Hamil, "A Boy's First Fight," 540.

42. Aaron Geiger to "Dear Wife," June 17, 1864, History/Civil War to 1876 (clipping file), Florida Collection, Florida State Archives, Tallahassee.

43. Dr. Thomas M. Palmer of Monticello was surgeon for the Second Florida Infantry before becoming supervisor of the Florida Hospital in Richmond. Samuel Proctor, "Mary Martha Reid—Florence Nightingale of Florida," in Proctor, *Florida One Hundred Years Ago,* September 1962; J.F.T., "Some Florida Heroes," 365.

44. James F. Tucker and Early Allen biographical files, Zack C. Waters Collection, Rome, GA.

45. Furgurson, *Not War but Murder,* 202–15. Furgurson's opening description of the arrival of buzzards from as far away as Florida at the Cold Harbor battlefield is one of the most chilling scenes in Civil War writing.

Chapter 12

1. Hillhouse, *Light Infantry,* 92–98; Nichols, "Florida's Fighting Rebels," 170–71; *OR,* 36, 3, 883, 843.

2. Hillhouse, *Light Infantry,* 95–97; *OR,* 36, 3, 843.

3. Nichols, "Florida's Fighting Rebels," 171; Hillhouse, *Light Infantry,* 95; Hartman and Coles, *Biographical Roster,* 3:986–1083; Robertson, *SOF,* 206–19.

4. Hillhouse, *Light Infantry,* 93; Charles Hopkins, Compiled Service Records, National Archives, Washington, DC; Krick, *Lee's Colonels,* 198, 337, 390. For more on Westcott, see Waters, "Tampa's Forgotten Defenders," 3–12.

5. Nichols, "Florida's Fighting Rebels," 171; Hartman and Coles, *Biographical Roster,* 3:1084–1162; Robertson, *SOF,* 219–36. The records of the Eleventh Florida Regiment are very sketchy.

6. Hillhouse, *Light Infantry,* 97; Hopkins, Compiled Service Records.

7. Krick, *Lee's Colonels,* 152, 247; Sommers, "Brevard," 1:128–29; J. F. McClellan file, Zack C. Waters Collection, Rome, GA.

8. Hillhouse, *Light Infantry,* 83–84, 142; Council Bryan to "My Dear Wife," June 7, 1864; Scott, "Memoirs of Service," VHS, discusses the animosity expressed by Perry's troops about the arrival of Finegan preventing Lang's promotion.

9. Council Bryan to "My Dear Wife," June 10, 1864; Hillhouse, *Light Infantry,* 83–84.

10. J. B. Jones, *A Rebel War Clerk's Diary* (Philadelphia: Lippincott, 1866), 2:226.

11. Noah Andre Trudeau, *The Last Citadel: Petersburg, Virginia, June 1864–April 1865* (Baton Rouge: Louisiana State University Press, 1991), 16–17.

12. Ibid., 6–1; Robertson, *A. P. Hill,* 282.

13. Trudeau, *The Last Citadel,* 23–55, provides a good overview of this phase of the battle. Stiles, *Four Years under Marse Robert,* 308.

14. Trudeau, *The Last Citadel,* 23–55.

15. Ibid.

16. Loderhose, *Far, Far from Home,* 53; Robertson, *A. P. Hill,* 283.

17. William J. Jones, *Life and Letters of Robert E. Lee, Soldier and Man* (Washington, DC: Neale, 1906), 40.

18. Freeman, *Lee's Lieutenants,* 3:xxxviii.

19. Sorrell, *Confederate Staff Officer,* 232; Freeman, *Lee's Lieutenants,* 1:567–68; Shiver, "A Rebel Yell for Gen. A. R. Wright"; LaFayette McLaws to Capt. A. J. McBride, July 3, 1895, Robert K. Krick Collection, Fredericksburg/Spotsylvania National Battlefield Park, Fredericksburg, VA.

20. Sorrell, *Confederate Staff Officer,* 232–33; Freeman, *Lee's Lieutenants,* 3:552–53; Robertson, *A.P. Hill,* 285.

21. John Mason, "Three Years in the Army; or, The Life and Adventures of a Rebel Soldier," typescript, Robert K. Krick Collection, Fredericksburg/Spotsylvania National Battlefield Park, Fredericksburg, VA.

22. Salmon, *Virginia Battlefield Guide,* 406–8.

23. Trudeau, *The Last Citadel,* 64–80; Bruce Catton, *A Stillness at Appomattox* (New York: Doubleday, 1953), 412.

24. Trudeau, *The Last Citadel,* 64–80; David Faris Cross, *A Melancholy Affair at the Weldon Railroad: The Vermont Brigade, June 23, 1864* (Shippensburg, PA: White Mane, 2003), 8–9; *OR,* 40, 1, 218–30. Dr. Cross spent many years researching the battle of the Gurley Farm (June 23), and much of the information below comes from his book.

25. Cross, *A Melancholy Affair,* 20–27; OR, 40, 2, 354; George G. Benedict, *Vermont in the Civil War: A History of the Part Taken by the Vermont Soldiers and Sailors in the War for the Union, 1861–1865* (Burlington, VT: Free Press Association, 1886), 2:358.

26. Cross, *A Melancholy Affair,* 26–45; William Mahone, letter to George G. Benedict, October 2, 1887, quoted in Benedict, *Vermont in the Civil War,* 2:362–63, 359–61 ("hold at all hazards"); *OR,* 40, 2, 354.

27. Mahone letter, in Benedict, *Vermont in the Civil War*, 2:362–63; letter fragment from Lt. Col. William Baya to E. P. Alexander, Edward Porter Alexander Papers, Southern Historical Collection, Manuscripts Department, University of North Carolina, Chapel Hill, specifically names David Lang as commander at Gurley Farm.

28. Auld, letter to "Dear Mother," June 29, 1864. Various figures were given for the Vermonters captured, but we accept the number provided in Cross, *A Melancholy Affair*, 80–91.

29. Cross, *A Melancholy Affair*, 46–51.

30. *Richmond Daily Dispatch*, June 27, 1864, quoting the *Petersburg Express*, June 25, 1864; *OR*, 40, 2, 375–76, and 404; Loderhose, *Far, Far from Home*, 103, quoting from W. A. Hunter letter dated June 25, 1864.

31. *OR*, 40, 1, 620–33 (the map in Wilson's after-action report is particularly helpful); W. Gordon McCabe, "The Defense of Petersburg," *SHSP* 2 (December 1876): 274–75; Trudeau, *The Last Citadel*, 87–90.

32. Salmon, *Virginia Battlefield Guide*, 397–98.

33. Ibid.; "Fight Near Reams Station," letter from a private dated July 23, 1864, newspaper clipping (*Petersburg Daily Express*—date of publication unknown), Zack C. Waters Collection, Rome, GA; Hillhouse, *Light Infantry*, 145–48.

34. Hillhouse, *Light Infantry*, 145–48; "Fight Near Reams Station"; Gleeson, *Erin Go Gray*, 28.

35. Newton Jasper Brooks memoir, in *Reminiscences of the Boys in Gray, 1861–1865*, ed. Mamie Yeary (Dayton, OH: Morningside, 1986), 84.

36. *OR*, 40, 1, 623; "Fight Near Reams Station."

37. "Fight Near Reams Station."

38. Ibid.; *OR*, 40, 1, 623–24; Trudeau, *The Last Citadel*, 189–90.

39. Hillhouse, *Light Infantry*, 146–48.

40. McCabe, "The Defense of Petersburg," 274–77; Trudeau, *The Last Citadel*, 90; Hillhouse, *Light Infantry*, 147; Roger Hannaford, "The Wilson Raid, June 1864: A Trooper's Reminiscences," ed. Stephen Z. Starr, *Civil War History* 21 (September 1975): 236.

41. McCabe, "The Defense of Petersburg," 277, contains a partial list of the plunder; Trudeau, *The Last Citadel*, 90, gives a brief description of the trials of the captured "contraband." See also Clark, *A Glance Backward*, 56–57.

42. Richard H. Hephner, "Where Youth and Laughter Go: The Experiences of Trench Warfare from Petersburg to the Western Front" (master's thesis, Virginia Polytechnic Institute and State University, 1997), 11–12.

43. J. Tracy Power, "From the Wilderness to Appomattox: Life in Lee's Army of Northern Virginia, May 1864–April 1865 (PhD diss., University of South Carolina, 1993); John H. Chamberlayne, *Ham Chamberlayne, Virginian: Letters and Papers of an Artillery Officer in the War of Southern Independence* (Richmond, VA: Dietz, 1932), letter from Chamberlayne to his mother, July 11, 1864, 242–43.

44. Loderhose, *Far, Far from Home*, 66, quoting W. A. Hunter, letters to his wife dated July 10, July 14, and July 17, 1864.

45. Trudeau, *The Last Citadel*, 91–92.

46. Hillhouse, *Light Infantry*, 97–98, 144.

47. Loderhose, *Far, Far from Home*, 67; Grady to wife, July 12, 1864, Henry Woodfin

Grady Papers, Emory University, Atlanta, quoted in Power, "From the Wilderness to Appomattox," 231.

48. William H. Smith diary, August 11, 1864, Zack C. Waters Collection, Rome, GA.

49. Geer, "Memories of the War," March 2, 1906.

50. Glatthaar, *Lee's Army*, 208–19.

51. Glatthaar, *Lee's Army*, 208–19; Robert A. Taylor, "Rebel Beef: Florida Cattle and the Confederate Army, 1862–1864," *FHQ* 67 (1988): 15–31. See also, generally, Taylor, *Rebel Storehouse* and Richard D. Goff, *Confederate Supply* (Durham, NC: Duke University Press, 1969).

52. Taylor, "Rebel Beef," 15–31.

53. Geer, "Memories of the War," February 16, 1906. Several other units of Mahone's brigade, particularly the Third Georgia, also claimed "credit" for stealing Mahone's milk cow. Adding veracity to Geer's story is a letter by W. A. Hunter of the Ninth Florida quoted in Loderhose, *Far, Far from Home*, 64.

54. Trudeau, *The Last Citadel*, 98–127, and Michael A. Cavanaugh and William Marvel, *The Petersburg Campaign: The Battle of the Crater; "The Horrid Pit," June 25–August 6, 1864* (Lynchburg, VA: H. E. Howard, 1989), 1–27, both give good information on the Crater engagement.

55. Trudeau, *The Last Citadel*, 109; Geer, "Memories of the War," February 9, 1906.

56. Cavanaugh and Marvel, *"The Horrid Pit,"* 52–53; Trudeau, *The Last Citadel*, 120–21.

57. Cavanaugh and Marvel, *"The Horrid Pit,"* 97–108; John Cannan, *The Crater: Burnside's Assault on the Confederate Trenches, June 30, 1864* (Cambridge, MA: Da Capo, 2002), 137–49; Trudeau, *The Last Citadel*, 98–127; Hillhouse, *Light Infantry*, 99–101; Richard J. Sommers, "Victor Jean Baptiste Girardey," in *The Confederate General*, ed. William C. Davis (Washington, DC: National Historical Society, 1991), 2:192–93.

58. Cavanaugh and Marvel, *"The Horrid Pit,"* 97–98.

59. Ibid., 98–101.

60. Salmon, *Virginia Battlefield Guide*, 421; Trudeau, *The Last Citadel*, 127.

61. Hillhouse, *Light Infantry*, 100–101; Loderhose, *Far, Far from Home*, 79–80; Geer, "Memories of the War," February 9, 1906.

62. Cavanaugh and Marvel, *"The Horrid Pit,"* 54–55; Loderhose, *Far, Far from Home*, 128; Freeman, *Lee*, 3:468; Hillhouse, *Light Infantry*, 100, 128. Harris's Mississippi brigade also remained in the trenches, but has escaped similar innuendoes of incompetence or cowardice.

63. John Horn, *The Destruction of the Weldon Railroad: Deep Bottom, Globe Tavern, and Reams Station, August 14–25, 1864* (Lynchburg, VA: H. E. Howard, 1991), provides an excellent overview of this campaign; Trudeau, *The Last Citadel*, 142–58.

64. Horn, *Weldon Railroad*, 54–68; Theodore Lyman, *Meade's Headquarters, 1863–1865: Letters of Colonel Theodore Lyman from the Wilderness to Appomattox* (Boston: Atlantic Monthly, 1922), 217.

65. Horn, *Weldon Railroad*, 69–89; Trudeau, *The Last Citadel*, 164–70.

66. Horn, *Weldon Railroad*, 90–95; *OR*, 42, 1, 488

67. Horn, *Weldon Railroad*, 90–95; Robertson, *A. P. Hill*, 297, suggests Weisiger's Virginians were present for the fight, apparently mistaking William H. Stewart's account of the

fight on the 19th for the combat on August 21. William H. Stewart, *A Pair of Blankets: War-time History in Letters* (Wilmington, NC: Broadfoot, 1990), 174–75.

68. Loderhose, *Far, Far from Home,* 87–90; Horn, *Weldon Railroad,* 90–99; Herbert, "Eighth Alabama," 172–75 (letter from Capt. W. L. Fagan to "Dear Sister," dated August 22, 1864); Hillhouse, *Light Infantry,* 103–4; Gleeson, *Erin Go Gray,* 31–33. Estimates of the time of the attack of Mahone's division range from 9:00 a.m. to noon.

69. Gleeson, *Erin Go Gray,* 31–34.

70. Loderhose, *Far, Far from Home,* 87–89.

71. Trudeau, *The Last Citadel,* 172–73.

72. Horn, *Weldon Railroad,* 91–113; Hillhouse, *Light Infantry,* 104, 265n41; Herbert, "Eighth Alabama," 173–75; Krick, *Staff Officers in Gray,* 272; Dickison, "Florida," 162–63.

73. Herbert, "Eighth Alabama," 174; Salmon, *Virginia Battlefield Guide,* 426, put Federal losses at 4,455 and Southern casualties at about 1,600.

74. Glatthaar, *Lee's Army,* 408–20, provides a good overview of Confederate desertion in 1864–65.

75. Loderhose, *Far, Far from Home,* 59–76; Hillhouse, *Light Infantry,* 114–18.

76. Blackford to wife, July 17, 1864, quoted in Power, "From the Wilderness to Appomattox," 256.

77. Loderhose, *Far, Far from Home,* 64–65; *OR,* 40, 3, 127, and 46, 2, 1145; Geer, "Memories of the War," March 2, 1906.

78. Hillhouse, *Light Infantry,* 116; Loderhose, *Far, Far from Home,* 67.

79. *OR,* 40, 3, 1188; Loderhose, *Far, Far from Home,* 61–62; Hillhouse, *Light Infantry,* 102–3; Inspection Report 6-P-17, August 16, 1864, National Archives, Washington, DC; Walters, *Norfolk Blues,* 56.

80. *OR,* 40, 3, 1188.

81. Glatthaar, *Lee's Army,* 411–12.

82. Loderhose, *Far, Far from Home,* 68–69.

83. Gilbert A. Hays, *Under the Red Patch* (Pittsburgh: Sixty-third Pennsylvania Volunteer Regimental Association, 1908), 271; similar report in Ruth L. Silliker, ed., *The Rebel Yell and the Yankee Hurrah: The Civil War Journal of a Maine Volunteer* (Camden, ME: Down East, 1985), 192.

84. Hillhouse, *Light Infantry,* 105–6; Loderhose, *Far, Far from Home,* 73–74; Robertson, *SOF,* 208. Hillhouse includes a biographical sketch of Richard at 129–30.

85. Hillhouse, *Light Infantry,* 109–10, 114; *OR,* 42, 3, 613, 621, and 46, 2, 1143–49.

86. Loderhose, *Far, Far from Home,* 64; Gleeson, *Erin Go Gray,* 31–33; *OR,* 46, 2, 1143–49.

87. Hartman and Coles, *Biographical Roster,* 2:811–12.

88. Glatthaar, *Lee's Army,* 411; Reiger, "Deprivation, Disaffection, and Desertion, 298; Hillhouse, *Light Infantry,* 200.

89. Statistics regarding desertion are from Hartman and Coles, *Biographical Roster,* vols. 1–3; Robertson, *SOF;* and Zack C. Waters Collection, Rome, GA.

90. Hartman and Coles, *Biographical Roster,* 3:951, 1103, 1011, 1153; Peter Boyer Perry file, Zack C. Waters Collection, Rome, GA.

91. Hillhouse, *Light Infantry,* 108–9. The battle of Burgess' Mill is also called the first

battle of Hatcher's Run and the battle of Boydton Plank Road. See also Trudeau, *The Last Citadel*, 218–54.

92. "Village View—'Apple Jack' Raid—Emporia, Virginia," www.waymarking.com.

93. Herbert, "Eighth Alabama," 178; C. O. Bailey, letter to "Dear Father," December ——, 1864, James Bailey Letters, P. K. Yonge Library of Florida History, University of Florida; Trudeau, *The Last Citadel*, 266–85.

94. C. O. Bailey letter; Trudeau, *The Last Citadel*, 283.

95. "Village View—'Apple Jack' Raid."

96. Caption and Records of Events, 10th Florida Regiment, *OR*, 42, 3, 613, 621, and 774; Hillhouse, *Light Infantry*, 112.

Chapter 13

1. William C. Leak to his wife and children, January 30, 1865, Petersburg National Battlefield, Petersburg, VA, quoted in Power, "From the Wilderness to Appomattox," 474–75; Jerry Korn, *Pursuit to Appomattox: The Last Battles* (Alexandria, VA: Time-Life, 1987), 16.

2. Hillhouse, *Light Infantry*, 114; *OR*, 46, 2, 1143–49.

3. Hillhouse, *Light Infantry*, 102; Geer, "Memories of the War," March 16, 1906. See also, generally, Power, "From Wilderness to Appomattox," 466–69.

4. *Richmond Daily Dispatch*, February 10, 1865; Power, "From the Wilderness to Appomattox," 499–510.

5. Hartman and Coles, *Biographical Roster*, 2:564; Glatthaar, *Lee's Army*, 452–54; Power, "From the Wilderness to Appomattox," 499–510, gives a balanced account of the army's response to this desperate measure.

6. Edwin C. Bearss, "The Battle of Hatcher's Run, February 5–7, 1865," 1–42, unpublished MS, Petersburg National Battlefield Park, Petersburg, VA; Trudeau, *The Last Citadel*, 312–25; *OR*, 46, 2, 367–81; Humphreys, *The Virginia Campaign*, 310–12.

7. Ibid.

8. Gleeson, *Erin Go Gray*, 35; *OR*, 46, 2, 1206; Trudeau, *The Last Citadel*, 318; John Horn, *The Petersburg Campaign, June 1864–April 1865* (Conshohocken, PA: Combined Books, 1993), 199–207.

9. Gleeson, *Erin Go Gray*, 35.

10. Ibid., 35–36; Trudeau, *The Last Citadel*, 318–19.

11. "The Battle of Hatcher's Run," *Atlanta Weekly Intelligencer*, April 12, 1865.

12. Ibid.

13. Gleeson, *Erin Go Gray*, 36–37.

14. Hillhouse, *Light Infantry*, 115, citing R. F. Davis, Florida Pension Application, A05905.

15. Michael A. Cavanaugh, *Sixth Virginia Infantry* (Lynchburg, VA: H. E. Howard, 1988), 58; Stewart, *A Pair of Blankets*, 190; Herbert, "Eighth Alabama," 178; Gleeson, *Erin Go Gray*, 37.

16. Gleeson, *Erin Go Gray*, 37–38

17. Ibid.; Lang, "Letters," 364–66; *Richmond Enquirer*, March 2, 1865.

18. Trudeau, *The Last Citadel*, 321–22.

19. Ibid.

20. Ibid., 322; Hillhouse, *Light Infantry*, 115; Freeman, *Lee's Lieutenants*, 3:629; Brevard letter to "My Dear Mother," dated February 27, 1865, posted on http://fpc.dos.state.fl.us/memory/Collections//CallBrevard papers. Gabriel Floyd had previously served as an enlisted man in Florida with the hard-riding Second Florida Cavalry.

21. Loderhose, *Far, Far from Home*, 100–101; *OR*, 46, 2, 1128, and 46, 3, 1327; Gleeson, *Erin Go Gray*, 40; *Richmond Whig*, February 15, 1865, 2.

22. *OR* 46, 2, 1128, and 46, 3, 1327.

23. Sommers, "Brevard," 128–29; William Mahone to Walter Taylor, March 10, 1865, Confederate States Army, Theodore Brevard file, reel 32, Compiled Service Records of Confederate General and Staff Officers and Non-regimental Enlisted Men, M-331, RG 109, National Archives, Washington, DC; William Marvel, *Lee's Last Retreat: The Flight to Appomattox* (Chapel Hill: University of North Carolina Press, 2002), 260n62.

24. Sommers, "Brevard"; Washington Waters papers, Florida State Archives, Tallahassee; Lang, "Letters."

25. Ibid.

26. Power, "From the Wilderness to Appomattox," 515–20; Brevard letter, February 27, 1865.

27. Stiles, *Four Years under Marse Robert*, 311.

28. Edmund DeWitt Patterson, *Yankee Rebel: The Civil War Journal of Edmund DeWitt Patterson* (Chapel Hill: University of North Carolina Press, 1966), 205–6.

29. Trudeau, *The Last Citadel*, 330–54; Horn, *Petersburg Campaign*, 209–16. If the Southern casualties at Fort Stedman amounted to 4,000, the desperate gamble cost Lee fully one-tenth of the Virginia army's total strength.

30. William Mahone, "On the Road to Appomattox," ed. William C. Davis, *Civil War Times Illustrated* 9 (January 1971): 7; Freeman, *Lee's Lieutenants*, 3:682–83; Geer, "Memories of the War," March 2, 1906. Mahone's valuable account will form the basis for much of the section for the retreat to Appomattox.

31. Mahone, "Road to Appomattox," 7; Geer, "Memories of the War," March 2, 1906.

32. Mahone, "Road to Appomattox," 7–8.

33. Ibid., 8.

34. Ibid.

35. Ibid., 8–9; Marvel, *Lee's Last Retreat*, 78–81, 257nn27, 30. T. W. Brevard to "Madame [Ann Mary Coleman]," June 27, 1865, Manuscript Department, William R. Perkins Library, Duke University, Durham, NC, in which Brevard refers to himself as "a Colonel from Florida."

36. Dickison, "Florida," 159–63; Stephen Z. Starr, *The Union Cavalry in the Civil War: The War in the East from Gettysburg to Appomattox, 1863–1865*, vol. 2 (Baton Rouge: Louisiana State University Press, 1981), 469; Noah Andre Trudeau, *Out of the Storm: The End of the Civil War, April–June, 1865* (Boston: Little, Brown, 1994), 109–14.

37. Starr, *Union Cavalry*, 469. The traditional view seems to be that the Florida wagon guards surrendered without a fight, but Hannaford's account appears to shed a different light on the matter. See Marvel, *Lee's Last Retreat*, 78–81, for the traditional view.

38. Geer, "Memories of the War," March 2, 1906.

39. Mahone, "Road to Appomattox," 9.

40. Ibid., 42–43; Salmon, *Virginia Battlefield Guide*, 484–87; Trudeau, *Out of the Storm*, 121–22.

41. Ibid.

42. Ibid.

43. Ibid.

44. Mahone, "Road to Appomattox," 43; Trudeau, *Out of the Storm*, 122–24. Davis's note regarding Mahone's reaction to the capture of his supply wagon quotes William T. Poague, *Gunner with Stonewall* (Jackson, TN: McCowat-Mercer, 1957), 118.

45. Mahone, "Road to Appomattox," 43.

46. Salmon, *Virginia Battlefield Guide*, 489.

47. Numerous sources are available that detail almost pen stroke by pen stroke this momentous event. We relied primarily on Trudeau, *Out of the Storm*, 125–52; Salmon, *Virginia Battlefield Guide*, 487–96; and, of course, Freeman, *Lee's Lieutenants*, 3:712–52.

48. Herbert, "Eighth Alabama," 186; Hillhouse, *Light Infantry*, 122.

49. Hillhouse, *Light Infantry*, 122–23; Loderhose, *Far, Far from Home*, 104.

50. Ibid.

51. Geer, "Memories of the War," March 16, 1906.

52. Waters, "All That Brave Men Could Do," 23; R. A. Brock, *The Appomattox Roster* (New York: Antiquarian, 1962), 302–13.

53. Hillhouse, *Light Infantry*, 123.

54. Geer, "Memories of the War," March 16, 1906.

55. Susan Bradford Eppes, *Through Some Eventful Years* (Gainesville: University of Florida Press, 1968), 275.

Chapter 14

1. Hartman and Coles, *Biographical Roster*, 1:227; Prior, "Lewis Paine: Pawn of John Wilkes Booth," 1–20.

2. Prior, "Lewis Paine," 13–20.

3. Ibid.; www.infoplease.com/c6/history/A0860645.html; www.floridahistory.org/floridians/civilw.html.

4. Tebeau and Carson, *Indian Trail to Space Age*, 217–20; George C. Rable, *But There Was No Peace: The Role of Violence in the Politics of Reconstruction* (Athens: University of Georgia Press, 1984), xi.

5. Eric Foner, *Reconstruction: America's Unfinished Revolution, 1863–1877* (New York: Harper & Row, 1988), 73–74, 176–227; "Finegan" quote in Robert Selph Henry, *The Story of Reconstruction* (New York: Konecky & Konecky, 1999), 5, 114; and see, generally, Jerrell H. Shofner, *Nor Is It Over Yet: Florida in the Era of Reconstruction—1863–1877* (Gainesville: University of Florida Press, 1974).

6. Foner, *Reconstruction*, 228–80; Tebeau and Carson, *Indian Trail to Space Age*, 220–26; Rable, *But There Was No Peace*, 9.

7. Shofner, *Nor Is It Over*, 162, 229–30.

8. Ralph L. Peek, "Lawlessness in Florida, 1868–1871," *FHQ* 40 (1961): 172–80; Hartman and Coles, *Biographical Roster*, 2:460. The number of casualties in the Jackson County

War more than doubled the Union and Confederate losses suffered at the 1864 battle of Marianna (the county seat of Jackson County).

9. Shofner, *Nor Is It Over,* 162, 229–30; Hartman and Coles, *Biographical Roster,* 2:833–34, 851; www.freepages.history.rootsweb.com/~oldpinecastle/aftermath.html.

10. Shofner, *Nor Is It Over,* 314–39; Henry, *Reconstruction,* 592. Shofner concludes that Tilden likely won the vote in Florida and should have been elected president.

11. Obituary of Dr. Richmond N. Gardner, *Tallahassee Floridian,* February 8, 1876.

12. Robertson, *SOF,* 329; UCV funeral notice, photocopy in Zack C. Waters Collection, Rome, GA.

13. Sigsbee C. Prince, "Edward A. Perry: Yankee General of the Florida Brigade," *FHQ* 29 (1951): 201–5; Dickison, "Florida," 207–8.

14. Correspondence between Daniel Hagin and Jimmy Edmonds. The authors thank Wentworth family relative Mr. Daniel Hagin for information on James's postwar career.

15. Obituary of Col. Walter R. Moore, undated minutes of R. E. Lee Camp, no. 58, UCV; copy on file at Gettysburg National Battlefield Park Collection, Gettysburg, PA.

16. Hartman and Coles, *Biographical Roster,* 2:808; William Baya biographical file, Zack C. Waters Collection, Rome, GA.

17. Hartman and Coles, *Biographical Roster,* 2:484; Bryan to "My Dear Wife," June 3, 1864, Council Bryan Papers. The Council A. Bryan Papers in the Florida State Archives can be found under collection number M87-035, and include documents that cover his life from 1862 to 1902. The papers mainly focus on Bryan's war service, including a series of war letters to his wife, Cornelia Archer Bryan, from 1862 to 1864, which are widely used throughout this study. The collection also includes an invaluable casualty list for the Florida brigade during the Wilderness campaign.

18. W. D. Ballantine file, Zack C. Waters Collection, Rome, GA; photocopy of Headquarters Florida Division U.C.V., Special Order No. 2, dated March 5, 1907, Jacksonville.

19. "In Memoriam: Francis Phillip Fleming, *FHQ* 2 (1909): 3–8; "Obituary of Hon. Francis P. Fleming," *CV* 17 (1909): 247.

20. Robertson, *SOF,* 336; Lang, "Letters," 341–42; 1870 U.S. Census, Subdivision 9, Suwannee County, FL, Post Office, Wellborn (microfilm roll M593_1330), 681; 1880 Census, Precinct 4, Levy County (microfilm roll T9_130), 428D; "Who's Who and What to See in Florida" (1935), 161–62 (available online at Florida Heritage Collection, http://susdl.fcla.edu/fh). Material at the Florida State Archives concerning David Lang's life and career are located in several collections: M84-28 consists of two letterbooks—volume 1 (1886–89) and volume 2 (1893–1909); M88-18 contains fourteen letters that Lang wrote from 1862 to 1864 to his cousin Elizabeth Atkinson of Marietta, Georgia; M94-6 consists of letters written by Lang that range from 1864 to 1889, and family photographs.

21. This summary of Hilliard's life is derived from original papers in the possession of the authors, courtesy of Mrs. Ruby Munroe Walters of Ocala, Florida. In her late nineties, Mrs. Walters is the sole surviving granddaughter of Ed Hilliard. Part of the account was written when he was still alive. The authors thank Karen Holzhauser, Hilliard's great-great-granddaughter, for typing out a copy of the lengthy document.

22. Fleming, *C. Seton Fleming,* 93.

23. Ibid., 84–85.

Bibliography

Manuscript Collections

Atlanta Historical Society Collection, Atlanta, GA

Samuel A. Spencer letter

Duke University, William R. Perkins Library, Manuscript Department, Durham, NC

T. W. Brevard to Ann Mary Coleman letter

Florida State Archives, Tallahassee, FL

Council Bryan Papers
History/Civil War to 1876 (clipping file)
David Lang Letterbooks
Gov. John Milton Letterbooks

Florida State Library, Tallahassee, FL

United Daughters of the Confederacy Scrapbooks, 12 vols.

Florida State University, Strozier Library, Special Collections, Tallahassee, FL

Wilbur W. Gramling diary
Pine Hill Plantation Papers

Georgia Department of Archives and History, Atlanta, GA

Third Georgia Infantry microfilm

Gettysburg National Battlefield Park Collection, Gettysburg, PA

"The Banishment of Miss Euphemia Goldsborough," unpublished MS
H. E. Herbert to E. P. Alexander letter

J. B. Johnson, "A Limited Review of What One Man Saw at the Battle of Gettysburg," unpublished MS
Minutes of R. E. Lee Camp, no. 58 (Walter R. Moore obituary)

Jacksonville Public Library, Jacksonville, FL

Francis P. Fleming Papers

Robert K. Krick Collection, Fredericksburg/Spotsylvania National Battlefield Park, Fredericksburg, VA

John Mason, "Three Years in the Army; or, The Life and Adventures of a Rebel Soldier"
Lafayette McLaws letter
Anderson J. Peeler letter to newspaper (Chancellorsville), typescript

Library of Congress, Washington, DC

Ezra A. Carman Papers
Jedediah Hotchkiss Papers

Massachusetts Military History Society, Boston University, Boston, MA

Edward B. Robbins Papers (R. H. Anderson letter)

Mississippi Department of Archives and History, Jackson, MS

JDH, "Death Angle," undated newspaper clipping

Museum of the Confederacy, Eleanor Brockenbrough Library, Richmond, VA

N. W. Eppes, Roll of Honor, vol. 340.71

National Archives, Washington, DC

Charles Hopkins, Compiled Service Records
RG 109, Compiled Service Records of Confederate General and Staff Officers and Non-regimental Enlisted Men, microcopy M331
Compiled Service Records of Confederate Soldiers Who Served in Organizations from the State of Florida, microcopy M251
Office of the Adjutant and Inspector General: Army of Northern Virginia Inspection Reports

Petersburg National Battlefield Park, Petersburg, VA

Edwin C. Bearss, "The Battle of Hatcher's Run, February 5–7, 1865," unpublished MS

Putnam County Department of Archives and History, Palatka, FL

Isaac M. Auld Letters and Papers

Richmond National Battlefield Park, Richmond, VA

S. H. Wright Letters

Rome/Floyd County Library, Special Collections, Rome, GA

William B. Judkins, "Memoirs of a Soldier of the 22nd Georgia"

Savannah Historical Society, Savannah, GA

William P. Pigman diary

Southern Historical Collection, Manuscripts Department, University of North Carolina, Chapel Hill, NC

Edward Porter Alexander Papers
C. H. Andrews Papers, "History of the Third Georgia Regiment," unpublished MS
C. O. Bailey Papers
Parkhill Family Papers

St. Augustine Historical Society, St. Augustine, FL

Dunham Family Papers
Reid Family Papers

University of Florida, P. K. Yonge Library of Florida History, Gainesville, FL

A.F.G. letter, MS 79
J. J. Thompson letter
C. O. Bailey Letters

U.S. Military History Institute, Carlisle, PA

Civil War Miscellaneous Collection

Virginia Historical Society, Richmond, VA

Alfred L. Scott, "Memoirs of Service in the Confederate Army," unpublished MS

Virginia State Library and Archives, Richmond, VA

William Mahone Papers
James E. Phillips memoir
John F. Sale Papers

Ruby Munroe Walters Collection, Ocala, FL

Edward Hilliard Papers

Zack C. Waters Collection, Rome, GA

Early Allen file
W. D. Ballantine file
William Baya file
"Fight Near Reams Station," unattributed newspaper clipping
Finegan funeral notice

"Florida in the Civil War," typescript, unpublished MS
Don Hillhouse, "Three Flags," unpublished MS
John Horn, "A History of the 12th Virginia Regiment," unpublished MS
J. M. Martin file
J. F. McClellan file
"Perry's Brigade at Bristow Station," unattributed newspaper clipping
Peter Boyer Perry file
William H. Smith diary (1864 only)
Alfred Young letter

Newspapers

Atlanta (GA) Journal
Atlanta (GA) Weekly Intelligencer
Augusta (GA) Daily Chronicle and Sentinel
Augusta (GA) Daily Constitutionalist
Boston (MA) Sunday Herald
Cedar Key (FL) Telegraph
(Micanopy, FL) *Cotton States*
Doylestown (PA) Democrat
(Monticello, FL) *Family Friend*
(Lake City) *Florida Index*
(Fernandina) *Florida Mirror*
(Tallahassee) *Florida Sentinel*
(Jacksonville) *Florida Times-Union*
(Philadelphia, PA) *Lutheran and Missionary*
Macon (GA) Telegraph
Mobile (AL) Advertiser and Register
Philadelphia (PA) Weekly Tribune
Richmond (VA) Daily Dispatch
Richmond Enquirer
Rome (GA) Tri-Weekly Courier
Savannah (GA) Daily Republican
Savannah (GA) Republican
St. Augustine (FL) Examiner
Tallahassee Floridian

Primary Sources

Alexander, Edward Porter. *Fighting for the Confederacy: The Personal Recollections of General Edward Porter Alexander.* Edited by Gary W. Gallagher. Chapel Hill: University of North Carolina Press, 1989.
———. *Military Memoirs of a Confederate Artillery Officer.* New York: Charles Scribner's Sons, 1907.

"And Some Letters from the Second Runner-Up." *Civil War Times Illustrated* 11, no. 4 (1972): 43–45.

Bell, John W. *Memoirs of Governor William Smith of Virginia: His Political, Military, and Personal History.* New York: Moss Engraving, 1891.

Benedict, George G. *Vermont in the Civil War: A History of the Part Taken by Vermont Soldiers and Sailors in the War for the Union, 1861–1865.* 2 vols. Burlington, VT: Free Press Association, 1886.

Bennett, William W. *A Narrative of the Great Revival Which Prevailed in the Southern States during the Late War between the States of the Federal Union.* Harrisonburg, VA: Hess, 1989.

Blake, Henry N. *Three Years in the Army of the Potomac.* Boston: Lee & Shepard, 1865.

Bowen, Roland E. *From Balls Bluff to Gettysburg and Beyond: The Civil War Letters of Private Roland E. Bowen, 15th Massachusetts Infantry, 1861–1864.* Edited by Gregory A. Coco. Gettysburg, PA: Thomas, 1994.

Brainerd, Wesley. *Bridge Building in Wartime: Colonel Wesley Brainerd's Memoir of the 50th New York Engineers.* Edited by Ed Malles. Knoxville: University of Tennessee Press, 1997.

Cassler, John O. *Four Years in the Stonewall Brigade.* Dayton, OH: Morningside, 1971.

Chamberlayne, John H. *Ham Chamberlayne, Virginian: Letters and Papers of an Artillery Officer in the War of Southern Independence.* Richmond, VA: Dietz, 1932.

Clark, George. *A Glance Backward; or, Some Events in the Past History of My Life.* Houston: Rein & Sons, 1914.

Dana, Charles A. *Recollections of the Civil War, with the Leaders in Washington and in the Field in the Sixties.* New York: D. Appleton, 1913.

DeNoon, Charles E. *Charlie's Letters: The Correspondence of Charles E. DeNoon.* Edited by Richard T. Couture. N.p., 1982.

De Trobriand, Regis. "Four Years in the Army of the Potomac." In *The Battle of Gettysburg,* by W. C. Storrick. Harrisburg, PA: McFarland, 1969.

Dickert, Augustus B. *History of Kershaw's Brigade.* Dayton, OH: Morningside, 1976.

Early, Jubal. *A Memoir of the Last Year of the War for the Independence of the Confederate States of America.* New Orleans: Lovell & Gibson, 1867.

Elliott, Charles G. "Martin's Brigade of Hoke's Division." *Southern Historical Society Papers* 23 (1895): 189–98.

Eppes, Susan Bradford. *Through Some Eventful Years.* Gainesville: University of Florida Press, 1968.

Fisk, Wilbur. *Anti-Rebel: The Civil War Letters of Wilbur Fisk.* Edited by Emil Rosenblatt. Croton-on-Hudson, NY: Emil Rosenblatt, 1983.

Fleming, Francis P. "Francis P. Fleming in the War for Southern Independence: Letters from the Front." Edited by Edward C. Williamson. *Florida Historical Quarterly* 28 (1949): 143–55.

——. *Memoir of Captain C. Seton Fleming of the Second Florida Infantry, CSA.* Arlington, VA: Stonewall House, 1985.

"Floridians of Yesteryear." *Florida Living* 11 (April 1991): 10–11.

Grant, Ulysses S. *The Personal Memoirs of Ulysses S. Grant.* 2 vols. New York: Charles L. Webster, 1885.

Hamil, H. M. "A Boy's First Fight." *Confederate Veteran* 12 (1904): 540–41.

Hannaford, Roger. "The Wilson Raid, June 1864: A Trooper's Reminiscences." Edited by Stephen Z. Starr. *Civil War History* 21 (September 1975): 218–41.

Hays, Gilbert A. *Under the Red Patch*. Pittsburgh: Sixty-third Pennsylvania Volunteer Regimental Association, 1908.

Heater, Jacob. "The Battle of the Wilderness." *Confederate Veteran* 14 (1906): 262–64.

Herbert, Hilary A. "History of the Eighth Alabama Volunteer Regiment, CSA." *Alabama Historical Quarterly* 39 (1977): 5–200.

Heth, Henry. *The Memoirs of Henry Heth*. Edited by James L. Morrison. Westport, CT: Greenwood, 1974.

Hill, Daniel Harvey. "Lee Attacks North of the Chickahominy." In *Battles and Leaders of the Civil War*, edited by Robert U. Johnson and Clarence C. Buel, 2:347–62. New York: Thomas Yoseloff, 1956.

Holt, David. *A Mississippi Rebel in the Army of Northern Virginia: The Civil War Memoirs of Private David Holt*. Edited by Michael B. Ballard and Thomas D. Cockrell. Baton Rouge: Louisiana State University Press, 1995.

Humphreys, Andrew A. *The Virginia Campaign, 1864 and 1865: The Army of the Potomac and the Army of the James*. New York: Da Capo, 1995.

J.F.T. [James F. Tucker]. "Some Florida Heroes." *Confederate Veteran* 11 (1903): 363–65.

Johnson, Robert U., and Clarence C. Buel, eds. *Battles and Leaders of the Civil War*. 4 vols. New York: Thomas Yoseloff, 1956.

Jones, J. B. *A Rebel War Clerk's Diary*. 2 vols. Philadelphia: Lippincott, 1866.

Jones, William. *Army of Northern Virginia Memorial Volume*. Whitefish, MT: Kessinger, 2007.

Jones, William J. *Life and Letters of Robert E. Lee, Soldier and Man*. Washington, DC: Neale, 1906.

Lang, David. "The Civil War Letters of Colonel David Lang." Edited by Bertram H. Groene. *Florida Historical Quarterly* 54 (1976): 340–66.

Law, Evander E. "From the Wilderness to Cold Harbor." In *Battles and Leaders of the Civil War*, edited by Robert U. Johnson and Clarence C. Buel, 4:118–44. New York: Thomas Yoseloff, 1956.

Lee, Robert E. *The Wartime Papers of Robert E. Lee*. Edited by Clifford Dowdey and Louis H. Manarin. New York: Little, Brown, 1961.

Lyman, Theodore. *Meade's Headquarters, 1863–1865: Letters of Colonel Theodore Lyman from the Wilderness to Appomattox*. Boston: Atlantic Monthly, 1922.

Mahone, William. "On the Road to Appomattox." Edited by William C. Davis. *Civil War Times Illustrated* 9 (January 1971): 4–11, 42–47.

McCabe, W. Gordon. "The Defense of Petersburg." *Southern Historical Society Papers* 2 (December 1876): 257–306.

Moore, Frank, ed. *Rebellion Record, Rumors, and Incidents*. 12 vols. New York: G. P. Putnam, 1861–68.

Morton, T. C. "Gave His Life for His Flag." *Confederate Veteran* 12 (1904): 70.

Oates, William C. *The War between the Union and the Confederacy and Its Lost Opportunities*. New York: Neale, 1905.

Ott, Eugene, Jr. "The Civil War Diary of James J. Kirkpatrick, 16th Mississippi, CSA." Master's thesis, Texas A&M University, 1984.

Page, Benjamin Franklin. "A Letter from Antietam." *Magnolia Monthly* 2 (September 1964): no pagination.

Patterson, Edmund DeWitt. *Yankee Rebel: The Civil War Journal of Edmund DeWitt Patterson.* Chapel Hill: University of North Carolina Press, 1966.

Perry, William F. "Reminiscences of the Campaign of 1864." *Southern Historical Society Papers* 7 (February 1879): 118–24.

Poague, William T. *Gunner with Stonewall.* Jackson, TN: McCowat-Mercer, 1957.

Porter, Horace. *Campaigning with Grant.* Bloomington, IN: Bonanza, 1961.

Pryor, Sara A. *Reminiscences of Peace and War.* New York: Grosset & Dunlap, 1905.

Report of the Joint Committee on the Conduct of the War at the Second Session of the Thirty-eighth Congress. Washington, DC: Government Printing Office, 1865.

Saunders, James Edmonds. *Early Settlers of Alabama—Part I.* New Orleans: L. Graham & Sons, 1899.

Scammon, E. Parker. "George T. Ward." *Catholic World* 54 (March 1892): 883.

Session Laws of the State of Florida. 10th sess. Tallahassee: n.p., 1861.

Silliker, Ruth L., ed. *The Rebel Yell and the Yankee Hurrah: The Civil War Journal of a Maine Volunteer.* Camden, ME: Down East, 1985.

Smith, Sallie M. *My Marriage and Its Consequences.* Macon, GA: Burke, Boykin, 1864.

Sorrell, G. Moxley. *Recollections of a Confederate Staff Officer.* New York: Domain, 1992.

Stevens, George T. *Three Years in the 6th Corps.* Albany: S. R. Gray, 1866.

Stewart, William H. *A Pair of Blankets: War-time History in Letters.* Wilmington, NC: Broadfoot, 1990.

Stiles, Robert. *Four Years under Marse Robert.* Dayton, OH: Morningside, 1977.

The Story of the Twenty-first Regiment of Connecticut Volunteer Infantry, during the Civil War, 1861–1865. Middletown, CT: Stewart, 1900.

Tributes to the Memory of Gen'l A. R. Wright. N.p., 1873.

"T. W. Brevard Letters." http://fpc.dos.state.fl.us/memory/collections/CallBrevardpapers.

U.S. War Department. *The War of the Rebellion: A Compilation of the Official Records of the Union and Confederate Armies.* 127 vols. Washington, DC: Government Printing Office, 1880–1901.

Vance, S. W. "Heroes of the 8th Alabama." *Confederate Veteran* 7 (1899): 492–93.

Walters, John. *Norfolk Blues: Civil War Diary of the Norfolk Light Artillery Blues.* Edited by Ken Wiley. Shippenburg, PA: White Mane, 1997.

Weld, Stephen. *War Diary and Letters of Stephen Minot Weld, 1861–1865.* Boston: Massachusetts Historical Society, 1979.

"The Wentworth Diary." *United Daughters of the Confederacy* 53 (March 1990): 22–28.

Wilkeson, Frank. *Recollections of a Private Soldier in the Army of the Potomac.* New York: G. P. Putman's Sons, 1887.

Wright, Gilbert, ed. "Some Letters to His Parents by a Floridian in the Confederate Army." *Florida Historical Quarterly* 36 (1958): 353–72.

Yeary, Mamie, ed. *Reminiscences of the Boys in Gray, 1861–1865.* Dayton, OH: Morningside, 1986.

Secondary Sources

Akerman, J. Mark. "'They Charged the Enemy Like a Whirlwind:' Lee's Florida Brigade," *Confederate Veteran*, n.s. (1992): 28–39.

Akerman, Joe A. *Florida Cowman: A History of Florida Cattle Ranching.* Kissimmee: Florida Cattleman's Association, 1976.

Antietam National Battlefield Park. "Army of Northern Virginia—Right Wing—Part 1." http://www.nps.gov/anti/historyculture/anv-right-wing1.htm.

Bailey, Ronald H. *The Bloodiest Day: The Battle of Antietam.* Alexandria, VA: Time-Life, 1984.

"The Barber-Mizell Feud." www.freepages.history.rootsweb.com/~oldpinecastle/.

Bilby, Joseph, and Stephen O'Neill, eds. *The Irish Brigade at Antietam: An Anthology.* Hightstown, NJ: Longstreet House, 1997.

Bittle, George C. "Florida Prepares for War, 1860–1861." *Florida Historical Quarterly* 51 (1972): 143–52.

———. "In Defense of Florida: The Organized Florida Militia from 1821–1920." PhD diss., Florida State University, 1965.

Boatner, Mark, III. *The Civil War Dictionary.* New York: David McKay, 1987.

Bohannon, Keith S. "Ambrose Ransom Wright." In *The Confederate General,* edited by William C. Davis, 6:160–63. Washington, DC: National Historical Society, 1991.

Brock, R. A. *The Appomattox Roster.* New York: Antiquarian, 1962.

Brown, Canter, Jr. "The Civil War, 1861–1865." In *The New History of Florida,* edited by Michael Gannon, 231–48. Gainesville: University of Florida Press, 1996.

Brown, Kent Masterson. *Retreat from Gettysburg: Lee, Logistics, and the Pennsylvania Campaign.* Chapel Hill: University of North Carolina Press, 2005.

Burton, Brian K. *Extraordinary Circumstances: The Seven Days Battles.* Bloomington: Indiana University Press, 2001.

Candequist, Arthur. "Did Anybody Really Know What Time It Was?" *Blue and Gray* 8 (August 1991): 32–34.

Cannan, John. *The Crater: Burnside's Assault on the Confederate Trenches, June 30, 1864.* Cambridge, MA: Da Capo, 2002.

———. *The Wilderness Campaign, May 1864.* Conshohocken, PA: Combined Books, 1993.

Caudle, Everett W. "To Defend or Pretend: The Social Role of the Militia and Volunteer Units in the Antebellum South." Master's thesis, University of Florida, 1990.

Cavanaugh, Michael A., and William Marvel. *The Petersburg Campaign: The Battle of the Crater; "The Horrid Pit," June 25–August 6, 1864.* Lynchburg, VA: H. E. Howard, 1989.

Clark, Champ. *Gettysburg: The Confederate High Tide.* Alexandra, VA: Time-Life, 1985.

Cleaves, Freeman. *Meade of Gettysburg.* Norman: University of Oklahoma Press, 1960.

Coco, Gregory. "A Wasted Valor: The Confederate Dead at Gettysburg." *Gettysburg,* no. 3 (July 1990): 95–108.

Coddington, Edwin B. *The Gettysburg Campaign: A Study in Command.* New York: Charles Scribner's Sons, 1964.

Coles, David J., and Zack C. Waters. "Forgotten Sacrifice: The Florida Brigade at the Battle of Gettysburg." *Apalachee* 11 (1996): 36–49.

Connelly, Thomas L. *Army of the Heartland: The Army of Tennessee, 1861–1862.* Baton Rouge: Louisiana State University Press, 1967.

Covington, James W. *The Billy Bowlegs War, 1855–1858: The Final Stand of the Seminoles against the Whites.* Chuluota, FL: Mickler House, 1982.

Cross, David Faris. *A Melancholy Affair at the Weldon Railroad: The Vermont Brigade, June 23, 1864.* Shippenburg, PA: White Mane, 2003.

Cullen, Joseph P. "Cold Harbor." *Civil War Times Illustrated* (November 1963): 11–17.

Davis, William C. *Breckinridge: Statesman, Soldier, Symbol.* Baton Rouge: Louisiana State University Press, 1974.

———, ed. *The Confederate General.* 6 vols. Washington, DC: National Historical Society, 1991.

———. "Joseph Finegan." In *The Confederate General,* edited by William C. Davis, 2:126–27. Washington, DC: National Historical Society, 1991.

Davis, William Watson. *The Civil War and Reconstruction in Florida.* Gainesville: University of Florida Press, 1964.

Derry, Joseph T. "Georgia." In *Confederate Military History.* New York: Blue & Gray, 1962.

Dickison, J. J. "Florida." In *Confederate Military History.* New York: Blue & Gray, 1962.

Doherty, Herbert J., Jr. "Union Nationalism in Florida." *Florida Historical Quarterly* 29 (1950): 83–95.

Dowdey, Clifford. *The Death of a Nation: The Story of Lee and His Men at Gettysburg.* New York: Knopf, 1958.

———. *Lee's Last Campaign: The Story of Lee and His Men against Grant—1864.* Wilmington, NC: Broadfoot, 1988.

Dubbs, Carol Kettenburgh. *Defend This Old Town: Williamsburg during the Civil War.* Baton Rouge: Louisiana State University Press, 2004.

Elmore, Thomas L. "The Florida Brigade at Gettysburg." *Gettysburg,* no. 15 (1996): 45–59.

"Florida under Civil Strife." www.floridahistory.org.

Foner, Eric. *Reconstruction: America's Unfinished Revolution, 1863–1877.* New York: Harper & Row, 1988.

Freeman, Douglas Southall. *Lee's Lieutenants: A Study in Command.* 3 vols. New York: Charles Scribner's Sons, 1970.

———. *R. E. Lee: A Biography.* 4 vols. New York: Charles Scribner's Sons, 1949.

Frye, Dennis E. "Harpers Ferry." In *The Civil War Battlefield Guide,* edited by Frances H. Kennedy, 78–80. Boston: Mariner, 1990.

———. "Stonewall Attacks! The Siege of Harpers Ferry." *Blue and Gray* 5 1 (September 1987): 10–62.

Furgurson, Ernest B. *Not War but Murder: Cold Harbor, 1864.* New York: Knopf, 2000.

Gallagher, Gary W., ed. *The Antietam Campaign.* Chapel Hill: University of North Carolina Press, 1999.

———. *The Confederate War.* Cambridge, MA: Harvard University Press, 1997.

———. "The Fall of 'Prince John' Magruder." *Civil War* 19 (August 1989): 8–15.

———. "Our Hearts Are Full of Hope: The Army of Northern Virginia in the Spring of 1864." In *The Wilderness Campaign,* 36–65. Chapel Hill: University of North Carolina Press, 1997.

———. *The Wilderness Campaign.* Chapel Hill: University of North Carolina Press, 1997.

Gannon, Michael, ed. *The New History of Florida.* Gainesville: University of Florida Press, 1996.

Glatthaar, Joseph T. *General Lee's Army: From Victory to Collapse.* New York: Free Press, 2008.

Gleeson, Ed. *Erin Go Gray! An Irish Trilogy.* Carmel, IN: Guild, 1998.

Goff, Richard D. *Confederate Supply.* Durham, NC: Duke University Press, 1969.

Greene, A. Wilson, and Gary Gallagher. *The National Geographic Guide to the Civil War National Battlefield Parks.* Washington, DC: Random House, 1992.

Haase, Ronald W. *Classic Cracker: Florida Wood-Frame Vernacular Architecture.* Sarasota, FL: Pineapple, 1992.

Hartman, David W., and David J. Coles, eds. *Biographical Roster of Florida's Confederate and Union Soldiers, 1861–1865.* 6 vols. Wilmington, NC: Broadfoot, 1995.

Hawk, Robert. *Florida's Army: Militia/State Troops/National Guard, 1565–1985.* Englewood, FL: Pineapple, 1986.

Hebert, Walter H. *Fighting Joe Hooker.* Indianapolis: Bobbs-Merrill, 1944.

Henderson, William D. *The Road to Bristoe Station: Campaigning with Lee and Meade, August 1–October 20, 1863.* Lynchburg, VA: H. E. Howard, 1982.

Hennessy, John H. *Return to Bull Run: The Campaign and Battle of Second Manassas.* New York: Simon & Schuster, 1993.

———. "Second Manassas." In *The Civil War Battlefield Guide,* edited by Frances H. Kennedy, 74–77. Boston: Mariner, 1990.

Henry, Robert Selph. *The Story of Reconstruction.* New York: Konecky & Konecky, 1999.

Hess, Earl J. *Pickett's Charge—The Last Attack at Gettysburg.* Chapel Hill: University of North Carolina Press, 2000.

Hewitt, Lawrence L. "Edward Aylesworth Perry." In *The Confederate General,* edited by William C. Davis, 5:20–21. Washington, DC: National Historical Society, 1991.

Hillhouse, Don. "From Olustee to Appomattox: The First Florida Special Battalion." *Civil War Regiments* 3, no. 1 (1993): 64–77.

———. *Heavy Artillery and Light Infantry: A History of the 1st Florida Special Battalion and 10th Infantry Regiment, CSA.* Jacksonville, FL: n.p., 1992.

Horn, John. *The Destruction of the Weldon Railroad: Deep Bottom, Globe Tavern, and Reams Station, August 14–25, 1864.* Lynchburg, VA: H. E. Howard, 1991.

Husley, Val. "'Men of Virginia—Men of Kanawha—to Arms!' A History of the Twenty-second Virginia Volunteer Infantry Regiment, CSA." *West Virginia History* 35 (April 1974): 220–36.

"In Memoriam: Francis Phillip Fleming." *Florida Historical Quarterly* 2 (1909): 3–8.

Jackson, Adrian J. "Perry's Brigade of Florida's Fighting Rebels." *Apalachee* 9 (1970): 61–79.

John, John E. *Florida during the Civil War.* Gainesville: University of Florida Press, 1963.

Jones, Frank S. *History of Decatur County, Georgia.* Spartanburg, SC: n.p., 1980.

Jones, Terry L. *Lee's Tigers: The Louisiana Infantry in the Army of Northern Virginia.* Baton Rouge: Louisiana State University Press, 1987.

Kennedy, Frances H., ed. *The Civil War Battlefield Guide.* Boston: Mariner, 1990.

Korn, Jerry. *Pursuit to Appomattox: The Last Battles.* Alexandra, VA: Time-Life, 1987.

Krick, Robert E. L. "Like a Duck on a June Bug: James Longstreet's Flank Attack, May 6, 1864." In *The Wilderness Campaign,* edited by Gary Gallagher, 236–64. Chapel Hill: University of North Carolina Press, 1997.

———. "Robert E. Lee and the Seven Days." *Hallowed Ground* 2 (Spring 1999): 14–19.

———. *Staff Officers in Gray: A Biographical Register of the Staff Officers of the Army of Northern Virginia.* Chapel Hill: University of North Carolina Press, 2003.

Krick, Robert K. "Chancellorsville, 1–3 May 1863." In *The Civil War Battlefield Guide,* edited by Frances H. Kennedy, 108–10. Boston: Mariner, 1990.

———. "It Appeared As Though Mutual Extermination Would Put a Stop to the Awful Carnage: Confederates in Sharpsburg's Bloody Lane." In *The Antietam Campaign,* edited by Gary W. Gallagher, 223–58. Chapel Hill: University of North Carolina Press, 1999.

———. *Lee's Colonels: Biographical Register of the Field Officers of the Army of Northern Virginia.* Dayton, OH: Morningside, 1991.

"Lewis Powell on Trial." www.umkc.edu/faculty/projects/trials/lincolnconspiracy/powell.html.

"Lincoln Plan." www.infoplease.com/c6/history/A0860645.html.

Lindstrom, Andrew Francis. "Perry's Brigade in the Army of Northern Virginia." Master's thesis, University of Florida, 1966.

Loderhose, Gary. *Far, Far from Home: The Ninth Florida Regiment in the Confederate Army.* Carmel, IN: Guild, 1999.

Long, A. L. *Memoirs of Robert E. Lee: His Military and Personal History.* New York: J. M. Stoddart, 1887.

Long, E. B. "The Battle That Almost Was—Manassas Gap." *Civil War Times Illustrated* 11 (December 1972): 20–28.

Lonn, Ella. *Foreigners in the Confederacy.* Chapel Hill: University of North Carolina Press, 2002.

Luvaas, Jay, and Harold W. Nelson, eds. *The U.S. Army War College Guide to the Battles of Chancellorsville and Fredericksburg.* Carlilse, PA: South Mountain, 1988.

Lykes, Genevieve Parkhill. *A Gift of Heritage.* N.p., 1969.

Marvel, William. *Lee's Last Retreat: The Flight to Appomattox.* Chapel Hill: University of North Carolina Press, 2002.

Matter, William D. *If It Takes All Summer: The Battle of Spotsylvania.* Chapel Hill: University of North Carolina Press, 1988.

Miller, J. Michael. "Along the North Anna." *Civil War Times Illustrated* (November 1987): 27–31, 45–49.

"Mrs. Livingston Rowe Schuyler, President General, UDC." *Confederate Veteran* 30 (1930): 4.

Murphree, Boyd R. "Rebel Sovereigns: The Civil War Leadership of Governors John Milton of Florida and Joseph E. Brown of Georgia, 1861–1865." PhD diss., Florida State University, 2007.

Nichols, Richard S. "Florida's Fighting Rebels: A Military History of Florida's Civil War Troops." Master's thesis, Florida State University, 1967.

O'Reilly, Frank A. "'One of the Greatest Feats of the War': Military Milestone at Fredericksburg." *Journal of Fredericksburg History* 2 (1977): 1–24.

———. *Stonewall Jackson at Fredericksburg.* Lynchburg, VA: H. E. Howard, 1993.

Ott, Eloise Robinson. *Ocali Country, Kingdom of the Sun: A History of Marion County, Florida.* Ocala, FL: Greene, 1966.

Peek, Ralph L. "Lawlessness in Florida, 1868–1871." *Florida Historical Quarterly* 40 (1961): 164–85.

Pfanz, Harry W. "Gettysburg." In *The Civil War Battlefield Guide,* edited by Frances H. Kennedy, 117–22. Boston: Mariner, 1990.

———. "The Gettysburg Campaign: After Pickett's Charge." *Gettysburg,* no. 1 (July 1989): 118–24.

———. *Gettysburg: The Second Day.* Chapel Hill: University of North Carolina Press, 1987.

Power, J. Tracy. "From the Wilderness to Appomattox: Life in Lee's Army of Northern Virginia, May 1864-April 1865." PhD diss., University of South Carolina, 1993.

Prince, Sigsbee C. "Edward A. Perry: Yankee General of the Florida Brigade." *Florida Historical Quarterly* 29 (1951): 201–5.

Prior, Leon O. "Lewis Paine: Pawn of John Wilkes Booth." *Florida Historical Quarterly* 43 (1964): 1–20.

Proctor, Samuel, ed. *Florida One Hundred Years Ago.* Coral Gables: Florida Library and Historical Commission, 1960–65.

Quartein, John V. "The Peninsula Campaign: From Hampton Roads to Seven Pines." *Hallowed Ground* 2 (Spring 1999): 8–13.

Rable, George C. *But There Was No Peace: The Role of Violence in the Politics of Reconstruction.* Athens: University of Georgia Press, 1984.

———. *Fredericksburg, Fredericksburg.* Chapel Hill: University of North Carolina Press, 2002.

Reiger, John E. "Deprivation, Disaffection, and Desertion in Confederate Florida." In *Florida's Civil War: Explorations into Conflict, Interpretations and Memory,* edited by Irvin D. S. Winsboro, 61–81. Cocoa: Florida Historical Society Press, 2007.

———. "Florida After Secession: Abandonment by the Confederacy and Its Consequences." *Florida Historical Quarterly* 50 (1971): 128–42.

Rhea, Gordon. *The Battle of the Wilderness, May 5–6, 1864.* Baton Rouge: Louisiana State University Press, 1994.

———. *The Battles for Spotsylvania Court House and the Road to Yellow Tavern, May 7–12, 1864.* Baton Rouge: Louisiana State University Press, 1997.

———. *Cold Harbor: Grant and Lee, May 26–June 3, 1864.* Baton Rouge: Louisiana State University Press, 2002.

———. *To the North Anna River: Grant and Lee, May 13–25, 1864.* Baton Rouge: Louisiana State University Press, 2000.

Robertson, Fred L., ed. *Soldiers of Florida in the Seminole Indian, Civil, and Spanish-American Wars.* Macclenny, FL: Richard J. Ferry, 1983.

Robertson, James I., Jr. *General A. P. Hill: The Story of a Confederate Warrior.* New York: Vintage, 1992.

———. *Soldiers Blue and Gray.* Columbia: University of South Carolina Press, 1998.

Sacher, John M. "'A Very Disagreeable Business:' Confederate Conscription in Louisiana." *Civil War History* 53 (June 2007): 141–69.

Salmon, John S. *The Official Virginia Civil War Battlefield Guide.* Mechanicsburg, PA: Stackpole, 2001.

Schaff, Morris. *The Battle of the Wilderness.* Boston: Houghton Mifflin, 1910.

Scott, Robert Garth. *Into the Wilderness with the Army of the Potomac.* Bloomington: Indiana University Press, 1985.

Sears, Stephen W. "Antietam." In *The Civil War Battlefield Guide,* edited by Frances H. Kennedy, 81–86. Boston: Mariner, 1990.

———. *Chancellorsville.* Boston: Mariner, 1996.

———. *Landscape Turned Red: The Battle of Antietam.* Boston: Ticknor & Fields, 1983.

———. *To the Gates of Richmond: The Peninsula Campaign.* New York: Ticknor & Fields, 1992.

Shepard, John, Jr. "Religion in the Army of Northern Virginia." *North Carolina Historical Review* 25 (1948): 341–76.

Sheppard, Jonathan C. "'By the Noble Daring of Her Sons': The Florida Brigade of the Army of Tennessee." PhD diss., Florida State University, 2008.

Shofner, Jerrell H. *Nor Is It Over Yet: Florida in the Era of Reconstruction, 1863–1877.* Gainesville: University of Florida Press, 1974.

Skoch, George. "Burnside's Geography Class." *Civil War Times Illustrated* 33 (January/February 1995): 34–41.

Sommers, Richard J. "Theodore Washington Brevard." In *The Confederate General,* edited by William C. Davis, 1:128–29. Washington, DC: National Historical Society, 1991.

Stackpole, Edward J. *Chancellorsville: Lee's Greatest Battle.* Harrisburg, PA: Stackpole, 1958.

Starr, Stephen Z. *The Union Cavalry in the Civil War: The War in the East from Gettysburg to Appomattox, 1863–1865.* Vol. 2. Baton Rouge: Louisiana State University Press, 1981.

Stewart, George R. *Pickett's Charge: A Microhistory of the Final Attack at Gettysburg, July 3, 1863.* Boston: Houghton Mifflin, 1987.

Storrick, W. C. *The Battle of Gettysburg.* Harrisburg, PA: McFarlane, 1969.

Studniki, Jim. "Perry's Brigade: The Forgotten Floridians at Gettysburg." www.nps.gov/archive/gett/gettour/sidebar/perry.htm.

Taylor, Paul. *Discovering the Civil War in Florida: A Reader and Guide.* Sarasota, FL: Pineapple, 2001.

Taylor, Robert A. "Rebel Beef: Florida Cattle and the Confederate Army, 1862–1864." *Florida Historical Quarterly* 67 (1988): 15–31.

———. *Rebel Storehouse: Florida in the Confederate Economy.* Tuscaloosa: University of Alabama Press, 1995.

Tebeau, Charlton W., and Ruby Leach Carson. *Florida: From Indian Trail to Space Age—A History.* Delray Beach, FL: Southern Publishing, 1965.

Trimble, Tony. "Paper Collars: Stannard's Brigade at Gettysburg." *Gettysburg* 2 (1990): 75–79.

Trudeau, Noah Andre. *Bloody Roads South: The Wilderness to Cold Harbor, May–June 1864.* Boston: Little, Brown, 1989.

———. "False Start at Franklin's Crossing." *America's Civil War* (July 2001): 32–37, 86–88.

———. *The Last Citadel: Petersburg, Virginia, June 1864–April 1865.* Baton Rouge: Louisiana State University Press, 1991.

———. *Out of the Storm: The End of the Civil War, April–June, 1865.* Boston: Little, Brown, 1994.

U.S. Census for 1860: Population. Washington, DC: Government Printing Office, 1864.

"Village View—'Apple Jack' Raid—Emporia, Virginia." www.waymarking.com.

Warner, Ezra J. *Generals in Blue: Lives of the Union Commanders.* Baton Rouge: Louisiana State University Press, 1995.

Waters, Zack C. "All That Brave Men Could Do: Joseph Finegan's Florida Brigade at Cold Harbor." *Civil War Regiments* 3, no. 4 (1994): 1–23.

———. "Florida's Confederate Guerillas: John W. Pearson and the Oklawaha Rangers." *Florida Historical Quarterly* 70 (1991): 133–49.

———. "Tampa's Forgotten Defenders: The Confederate Commanders at Fort Brooke." *Sunland Tribune* 17 (1991): 3–12.

Wert, Jeffry. *Gettysburg, Day Three.* New York: Simon & Schuster, 2001.

———. "John Echols." In *The Confederate General,* edited by William C. Davis, 2:92–93. Washington, DC: National Historical Society, 1991.

———. "One Great Regret: Cold Harbor." *Civil War Times Illustrated* 17 (February 1979): 23–35.

———. "Roger Atkinson Pryor." In *The Confederate General,* edited by William C. Davis, 5:64–65. Washington, DC: National Historical Society, 1991.

"Who's Who and What to See in Florida." http://susdl.fcla.edu/fh.

Wilkinson, Warren. *Mother, May You Never See the Sights I Have Seen: The Fifty-seventh Massachusetts Veteran Volunteers in the Last Year of the Civil War.* New York: Harper & Row, 1990.

Winsboro, Irvin D. S., ed. *Florida's Civil War: Explorations into Conflict, Interpretations and Memory.* Cocoa: Florida Historical Society Press, 2007.

Winschel, Terrence J. "The Gettysburg Experience of James J. Kirkpatrick." *Gettysburg* 8 (January 1993): 111–19.

Index

Infantry, 69–70; 13th Infantry, 58; 20th Infantry, 45; 57th Infantry, 103
Maxwell, Cpl. David, 16
Mayo, Pvt. George Washington, 167
Mays, Capt. Samuel, 123, 139–140
McAllister, Col. Robert (U.S.), 171
McCaslan, Capt. William E., 78
McClellan, Maj. Gen George B. (U.S.), 13, 16, 19, 21–22; Antietam Campaign, 30, 33, 39; displaced by Burnside, 42, 113
McClellan, Col. James F., 9, 123–124, 139–141
McDowell, Maj. Gen. Irvin (U.S.), 16
McGilvery, Lt. Col. Freeman (U.S.), 76–77
McGowan, Brig. Gen. Samuel, 117
McKenzie, Brig. Gen. Ranald (U.S.), 174
McLaws, Maj. Gen. Lafayette, 43, 50, 67
McLean, Wilmer house, 181
McRae, Col. Duncan, 33
Meade, Maj. Gen. George G. (U.S.), 64
Meagher, Brig. Gen. Thomas F. (U.S.), 33
Melvin, Capt. E. P., 140
Mercer, Pvt. Henry M., 10
Mexican War, 140, 167
Michigan Troops: 7th Infantry, 45; 24th Infantry, 161
Mickler, Capt. Thomas M., 140
Miles, Col. Dixon (U.S.), 31
Miles, Maj. Gen. Nelson (U.S.), 180–181
Mills, Chaplain J. W., 36
Mitchell, Gov. Henry L., 192
Milton, Gov. John, 7, 9, 22–23, 26, 37, 39, 93–95, 122
Minnesota Troops, 1st Infantry, 71
Mississippi Troops: 2nd Battalion, 13–14, 17; 13th Infantry, 43, 46; 16th Infantry, 36; 17th Infantry, 43–44; 18th Infantry, 43; 19th Infantry, 14; 21st Infantry, 43; Posey's (Brig. Gen. Carnot) brigade, 59, 67, 74; Harris's (Brig. Gen. Nathaniel) brigade, 115–117, 178
Mizell, David, 187
Mizell, Judge John, 187
Moore, Col. Walter Raleigh, 4, 9, 34; receives new flag, 47; wounded, 54; leads 2nd Florida at Gettysburg, 67; wounded and captured, 72, 82; postwar, 189–190
Mooty, Capt. A. P., 120
Mosby, Col. John S., 184
Mosely, Capt. Alexander, 22, 72
Mott, Brig. Gen. Gershom (U.S.), 171
"Mud March," 49
Munnerlyn, Maj. Charles J., 154

Nelson Farm, battle of. See Fraiser's Farm
New York Troops, Battery A, First Artillery: 8th Infantry (Heavy Artillery), 130; 42nd Infantry, 45; 50th Infantry, 58; 51st Infantry, 109; 59th Infantry, 45; 72nd Infantry, 72; 89th Infantry, 43; North Anna, battle of, 118–119
North Carolina Troops; 4th Infantry, 36; 14th Infantry, 36

Oates, Maj. William C., 106–108
Ocean Pond (Olustee), battle of, 120, 140, 174
Ochus, Capt. Adolphus A., 123, 139–140
O'Hern, Lt. J. D., 134–135
O'Neil, Capt. John B., 98

Pacetti, Capt. Joseph Anthony, 48
Palmer, Dr. Thomas, 137, 164
Parker, Lt. John T., 18
Parkhill, Capt. George W., 19, 21
Parkhill, Lt. Richard, 21
Patton, Col. George S., 130–132
Pearson, Bird, 191
Pearson, Lt. Col. John W., 126–127; mortal wound, 127, 165
Pearson, Lydia (Mrs. F. P. Fleming), 191
Peeler, Lt. Anderson J., 50, 52, 70, 170
Pegram, Brig. Gen. John, 172
Pender, Maj. Gen. Dorsey, 66
Pendleton, Brig. Gen. William N., 114
Pennsylvania militia, 63
Pennsylvania Troops: 26th Infantry, 69–70, 73; 48th Infantry, 155; 127th Infantry, 45
Perkins, Lt. John Day, 5, 70
Perry, Brig. Gen. Edward A., 10, 12, 16–17, 21, 23, 34, 36; promoted to brigadier general, 39; at the Wilderness, 98–106; wounded, 108; postwar, 188–189, 191, 192
Perry, Gov. Madison Starke, 6, 9, 10
Perry, Sgt. Peter Boyer, 167
Perry, Col. W. F., 102–110
Petersburg: siege of, 23, 26, 129; strategic importance, 142, 143
Pettigrew, Brig. Gen. J. J., 73
Pfanz, Harry W. (historian), 63, 66
Pickett, Maj. Gen. George E., 73–75, 178
Pigman, Lt. William P., 58, 61, 63, 70, 76, 79
Pillans, Capt. William P., 9
Pingree, Lt. Col. Samuel E. (U.S.), 145, 146
Pleasants, Lt. Col. Henry (U.S.), 155–156
Pogue, Pvt. D. M., 78